THE
AVIATORS

STORIES OF U.S. ARMY HELICOPTER COMBAT IN THE VIETNAM WAR, 1971-72

REX GOOCH

**Lighthorse Publishing
Company**

Sioux Falls, SD 57104

Copyright © 2019 by Rex Gooch

ISBN: 9781077296763
Library of Congress Control Number: 2019911098

Edited by David Aretha

Front cover image by Joe Kline Aviation Art
Rear cover photo of Kevin Kelly in AH-1G Cobra courtesy of Jack Hosmer

Dedicated to the
Army Aviators and Crew Members
who served in Vietnam,
most especially, those serving with
Lighthorse Air Cavalry
Vietnam—1971-72.

Welcome Home!

And, to my wife, Karen,
the love of my life,
whose support and assistance
made this book possible.

TABLE OF CONTENTS

FOREWORD

AS I READ REX'S BOOK I was pleasantly surprised at the familiarity of the material. It was like "coming home." As I read of his arrival, I thought of mine. Commercial Air to Bien Hoa, the 90th "Repo Depo," and transit to our new unit. He went in a U-21 twin turbine aircraft and I went to the First Division in the back of a truck full of dirty laundry. The smells, the new culture, the new experiences (rats in the hooches) were common rites of passage for the thousands of Army aviators arriving in Vietnam as "new guys."

We were for the most part young, volunteers, and clueless about what was to come. We were hopeful and ready to ply our new skills with a whopping 210 hours of flight school behind us. So, armed and equipped, we were about to put our lives on the lines for Vietnam, our country, and our brothers.

I flew my first tour with D Troop (Air), 1st Squadron, 4th Cavalry, which was the Air Cavalry troop of the First Division's Armored Cavalry Squadron. Unlike 3rd of the 17th Air Cavalry Squadron, we were a single Air Troop of a larger Armored Cavalry unit of tanks, ACAVS (Armored personnel carriers), and ground fighters. That said, the Table of Organization and Equipment for both my D Troop and Rex's C Troop were identical.

The Air Cavalry Troop in Vietnam was the most flexible, powerful, and multifaceted unit in the theater. We both had organic, reconnaissance (scouts), attack (guns), transport (lift), and ground mobility (aero-rifles). We could find the enemy with scouts, attack, and pound the enemy with guns, transport the aero-rifles with lift, and then recon and (to a limited degree) hold the ground with a rifle platoon put wherever and whenever they were needed. There is no greater joy for a downed jet pilot or helicopter crew than an air cavalry scout circling above him covered by a pair of Cobra gunships and hearing four UH-1 Hueys thundering in with a load of crack infantry on board just to take him home.

I flew my first tour in III Corps in the OH-6 as the scout platoon leader, my second in I Corps as a gun section leader in D Troop, 3-5 Cavalry, attached to the 101st Airborne. We were the remains of C Troop 3-17th after the Laotian Incursion called Operation Lam Son 719. In February 1971, D 3-5 and C 3-17 traded guidons (troop flag) and little else in an organizational name change. C Troop 3-17 became D Troop 3-5 but retained the callsign "Charliehorse," an Army institutional faux pas for a unit beginning with a D. Down South, in IV Corps, D Troop became C Troop 3-17 and retained the callsign "Lighthorse," the troop whose stories are told in this book.

On my third tour I flew Rex's former Area of Operations in C Troop (Air), 16th Air Cavalry, and it was in his retelling of actions of launching at Chi Lang into Cambodia, supporting river convoys to Phnom Penh, and patrolling the Mekong Delta that took me home again. The places were the same, the actions were similar, and only the personalities were different. But they really weren't. Army aviators were pretty much all the same. Gun drivers are known to swagger a bit, to tell lies about their prowess with rockets or flying Cobras upside down with statements like

"Son (he was twenty-three), I invented that maneuver!" They were the "Killers."

Scouts were more brooding and introverted. Quiet, sullen, often contemplating their potential at survival and yet somehow content with their situation but not anxious to draw others in. They were the "hunters."

Lift pilots were more gregarious and family oriented. They flew together as a group, sat around in circles eating C-rations while waiting on the scouts to kick up a fight and for the call to "Scramble the Aero-rifle platoon! Aircraft down!" But when they rolled, they were a sight to behold. In formation, synchronized and focused, door guns blazing, and the epitome of the "Cavalry to the Rescue."

Rex Gooch has told a great story about the life we both lived in Vietnam. I went to war as a 1st lieutenant at the age of twenty and ended Vietnam as a captain at twenty-four. Three tours that collectively were the "best of times and the worst of times." Rex has told the tale of helicopter aerial combat in Vietnam with grace and attention to detail. I only disagreed with Rex on one observation in *The Aviators*...I love powdered eggs!

Hugh L. Mills Jr.
LTC (ret) U.S. Cavalry
Author of *Low Level Hell: A Scout Pilot in the Big Red One*

Rex Gooch

AUTHOR'S NOTE

IN THIS BOOK, I endeavored to present the details as accurately as possible. In addition to describing the firsthand events as remembered, I correlated the dates, people, places, and missions with a pilot's logbook I maintained while serving in Vietnam. Other stories were developed from personal interviews with fellow Vietnam pilots or crew members who served alongside me. If a story presented in this book differs from the recollection of others, it should be kept in mind that many years have passed, memories have faded, and, in some instances, stories have evolved. That said, this book represents my best effort to accurately portray the extraordinary stories of U.S. Army aviators and combat aviation in the Vietnam War, 1971-72.

Rex Gooch

Rex Gooch

PREFACE

IN 1929, ERNEST HEMINGWAY WROTE in his introduction to *A Farewell to Arms*, "...it is the considered belief of the writer of this book that wars are fought by the finest people that there are, or just say people, although, the closer you are to where they are fighting, the finer the people you meet..."[1] Hemingway could have written that about people fighting in any war at any time, but most certainly he describes the helicopter pilots and crew members whom I knew when serving in the Vietnam War in 1971-72.

These young men became aviators not because they were drafted or otherwise forced into their roles. Instead, they chose aviation because they knew they were needed, and they were willing to "go the extra mile" in terms of time and effort to learn the fundamentals of flying. And, they were adventure-seekers, craving the thrill and excitement that can only come from flying in a fast-moving helicopter as it darts and dodges so close to the treetops that the limbs scrape the bottom of the aircraft.

---

[1] Ernest Hemingway, *A Farewell to Arms* (New York: Charles Scribner & Sons), e-book, Author's Introduction

The vast majority of these aviators came from the heartland of America, growing up in small towns or rural areas. Having family members who served in Korea and World War II, these young men shared strong ideals of patriotism and service to their country. Some had college degrees, but most were high school graduates who signed up for the Army's Warrant Officer Rotary Wing Aviator Course. After enduring nine months of intense training and "spit and polish" warrant officer indoctrination, they were transformed into world-class helicopter pilots.

In Vietnam, the new pilots were immediately immersed in the day-to-day chaos and fury of combat aviation where they honed their flying skills, becoming seasoned aviators in a matter of weeks. In combat, they shared a strong sense of camaraderie and would readily put their own life in jeopardy to save a fellow pilot, crew member, or soldier on the ground whether they be American or our ally, the South Vietnamese. Helicopter pilots and crew members, then and always, share a sense of duty to their country and commitment to their fellow soldiers, summed up in the Army Aviation motto, "Above the Best."

This book is a compilation of stories highlighting the incredible people I served with in Lighthorse Air Cavalry, 18th Aviation Company, and the 17th Aviation Group, telling their stories through my experiences—stories of exceptional courage, dedication to duty, and devotion to their fellow aviators. The book also includes lighter moments, humorous events that happened and became a welcomed distraction from the harsh realities of war.

Several stories were conveyed to me by fellow pilots and others by crew chiefs and gunners. All tell personal narratives of combat aviation in Vietnam. There are stories, for example, of surviving a horrific scout helicopter crash, a gallant attempt to rescue POWs held in a jungle prison camp, a covert flight into remote areas of Cambodia, and many more.

Most, but not all, of the stories are aviation related and occurred during my 1971-72 tour of duty in Vietnam—a different war with a new set of rules after President Nixon's 1969 Vietnamization program. This was now a U.S. aviation war supporting the South Vietnamese military—a stark contrast to the earlier war fought by U.S. ground forces.

In this book, I have included stories of not only the aviators (pilots), but also the crew. The crew chiefs and gunners loved flying and played a crucial role in the successful accomplishment of our flying missions. Their contribution to maintaining our aircraft and defending our helicopters against hostile threats cannot be overlooked.

At the end of each chapter is a brief, biographical profile of the main character(s) in the story, describing their life after Vietnam. Despite the sometimes-stereotypical image of a down-and-out, homeless, or drug-addicted Vietnam Veteran, these life histories describe the vast majority who served their country with honor and pride, and later became very successful in their careers and family life.

I am proud to have served with these outstanding "soldiers in the sky" and honored to share their stories with you.

Rex Gooch
Longknife 23

Rex Gooch

x

PART 1

VIETNAM: IN-COUNTRY

C H A P T E R   1

TO NAM

IT IS EARLY NOVEMBER 1971. Dressed in my tropical weight khaki uniform, I am sitting comfortably on an American Airlines Boeing 707 commercial flight with 127 GIs, all bound for Vietnam. Looking around, I see a large number of eighteen-year-old Army enlisted soldiers, mostly privates, with a look of apprehension on their faces. It is clear they have just completed Basic Training and are heading for an uncertain future. Most will likely serve their Vietnam tour in some capacity with Infantry units—ground-pounders or grunts, as I will later hear them called.

Seated in the rows around me are a group of fellow Army helicopter pilots; officers and warrant officers fresh out of flight school. Yes, we are concerned as well, but displaying it differently. Our attitude is rowdy and boisterous, as we pass the time with jokes, laughter, and an occasional outburst of incivility.

It is a long and tedious flight. At some point, my mind wanders, and I reminisce about the previous year. Just ten months earlier, I arrived at Fort Wolters in Mineral Wells, Texas, to attend U.S. Army Aviation School—training to become a helicopter pilot.

I fondly recall the first day of flight school orientation, meeting my sixty-one officer classmates. Having recently completed the highly structured, "by the book" Armor Officer Basic Course at Fort Knox, Kentucky, my initial reaction to this diverse group of young mavericks was, "These guys are crazy; there's not a sane individual in the group."

Later, I realized that the type of person who aspires to fly a helicopter tends to live on the edge, seeking excitement in their every endeavor and savoring the adrenaline rush that comes from pushing the extremes. They are a rambunctious, cocky bunch, playing practical jokes on one another. They are a challenge for most classroom instructors and a party-hard group in their off time. Yet, underneath that unruly exterior, these men are highly competent and motivated to acquire the skills required to fly the complicated helicopter. And, they have a sincere desire to serve their country.

It doesn't take long for me to realize that this describes myself; I am just as rowdy, crazy, and cocky as the rest of the class. And, having grown up in small-town middle America—an Eagle Scout, American Legion Boys State, high school ROTC, and college ROTC—I love my country and feel a strong patriotic duty to serve beside my fellow soldiers in a distant land.

In the nine months of intense aviation training, we endured long days of flight training and classroom instruction. Once we mastered the basic helicopter flying skills, we were taught navigation, formation flying, instrument flight rules, radio procedures, and combat tactics. During that time, we lost six classmates who washed out or were set back a class for failing to meet flying standards, and another student who was severely injured in a helicopter training crash. Six students joined our class from other classes. Upon graduation, all but two of our sixty graduating aviators received orders for Vietnam.

My thoughts return to the present. I am seated next to two of my flight school classmates who happen to be on the same flight. We talk and joke about funny things that happened in flight school and our anticipation of flying helicopters in Vietnam. I tell of chasing a group of six or seven ducks at treetop level across the Texas countryside in a small training helicopter. A buddy tells of getting lost and landing his helicopter alongside a small, isolated gas station to ask directions. This led to his giving the station owner a "free ride" in his helicopter—both highly unauthorized and funny events.

As pilots, we are anxious to start flying with an aviation unit, but at the same time, there is an unspoken trepidation about what lies ahead. Absent from the conversation is any mention of the hazards that we will ultimately face in combat.

The long hours of our flight are a roller coaster of emotions; from elation with aviation to concern about loved ones back home and boredom. One of my classmates brought a book about Vietnam that we both read on the flight. The book, *365 Days* by Ronald Glassner, was written from a medical officer's perspective while serving in an Army evacuation hospital in Japan. Primarily focused on the casualties of war, the book has many references to helicopters being shot down or exploding in midair. Here are excerpts from the chapter titled "Choppers":

> By the time you read this, over 4,000 helicopters will have been shot down, a third of all the chopper pilots who have ever been to Nam will have been killed or medically boarded out of the Army, and the average life span of any Loach pilot, whether in Nam, Laos, or Cambodia will probably be down to somewhere around three months.

Another excerpt from the book:

> My God! One moment the chopper was there, charging
> in protectively across the perimeter, tail up, and the next
> it was gone, torn apart in a monstrous ball of flame. For
> a moment, the sheer unexpected violence of it all held
> them. Stunned, the troopers looking up from the mud,
> watched what was left of the chopper come hurtling
> headless out of the flames, a great torn piece of steel
> plunging blindly on across the paddy.[2] (Note:
> helicopters are made primarily of aluminum, not steel.)

My reaction is, "That's great! Not only am I tasked with
keeping five thousand (sic) moving helicopter parts going the
same direction, I now have to worry about exploding in midair."

In retrospect, this was possibly the worst book a person could
have read on a flight to Vietnam. The author, an Army
pediatrician, gathered his stories from soldiers being treated in
the Zama Army Hospital. As best I can determine, Dr. Glassner
never set foot in Vietnam. Granted, his stories and the pilot
statistics have merit, but his book depicted only the trauma and
tragedy of war. It was unfortunate that we did not have
something more enlightening to read on the long flight.

Despite the raucous laughter and frivolity of my fellow pilots,
the image of a Huey helicopter exploding in midair seemed to
penetrate my subconsciousness during the long flight.
Thankfully, the sordid image faded from my mind after being
immersed in the reality of Vietnam and experiencing the thrill
of flying.

---

[2] Ronald J. Glassner, *365 Days* (New York: Open Road Integrated Media, 1971), e-book, Chapter 13

90TH REPLACEMENT BATTALION

Upon arrival at Bien Hoa Air Base, the doors of the commercial jetliner open and a mobile stairway is positioned alongside the aircraft. We gather our belongings and shuffle to the exit door. Stepping outside, I am hit with a blast of hot, humid air filled with unusual and distinct odors—alternate waves of garlic and spices browning in hot oil, bouquets of flowers, and the stench of garbage, mixed with the smell of jet fuel and diesel common to a military airbase. Welcome to Vietnam.

Walking down the stairway, I am astonished at the bustling activity in every direction. Military Jeeps and trucks of all sizes are crisscrossing the airport's cement apron. Several Army helicopters pass overhead. Various aircraft are taxiing to the runway. The cacophony of mixed noises is nearly deafening after being in the relative quiet of the jetliner. Did I mention it is hot? Yes, it is dang hot. I am already sweating, and I'm still on the stairs.

Reaching the end of the stairway, we are loaded into an olive drab military bus with chicken wire screening on the windows to prevent grenades or other objects being thrown inside. Driving off the airbase, we meander down the local streets lined with Vietnamese vendors on each side. Soon, we arrive at the 90th Replacement Battalion. At some point, the bus stops and the officers are told this is where we get off. Grabbing our duffle bags, we disembark and are escorted to a large GP medium tent. Walking inside, we are told to take a cot among other new arrivals. Here, we are in-processed while awaiting our order assignments. And, as usual for the Army, we wait and wait and wait...

THE CAV

Seated on two cots near the tent doorway, several Army pilots discuss their assignment desires. I take a seat on the end of a cot and listen to the conversation. When it is my opportunity to talk, I say, "I want to fly with the Cav, 1st Cav." My Fort Wolters flight instructor had told me stories about his experiences flying for the "1st Cav," and I, too, wanted to fly for the renowned 1st Cavalry Division, whose troopers wore a big yellow patch in the shape of a Norman shield with a black diagonal stripe and a horse's head profile. I knew it was a tall order, but I hoped my being an Armor officer made me a likely candidate for the Cav.

While awaiting our orders, we attend a multitude of in-processing briefings on Vietnam culture, medical advice, and issuance of fatigue uniforms and supplies. One of the orientations provides extensive instruction on proper brushing of our teeth. Focusing on dental hygiene in a war zone seems a little odd to me, and certainly not a good use of our time when we are anxious to learn our assignments.

Eventually, I am called to the main office and presented with my orders: C Troop, 3rd Squadron, 17th Cavalry, located at Vinh Long, situated on the south bank of the Mekong River, sixty-two miles southwest of Saigon. At first, I am a little disappointed because it isn't the 1st Cavalry. Little do I realize that my momentary sense of disappointment is unfounded. I am about to experience the Air Cavalry in a way I could never have imagined—with Lighthorse!

CHAPTER 2

VINH LONG

THE AFTERNOON AFTER RECEIVING MY orders, I board an Army U-21 (Beechcraft King Air, twin turboprop aircraft holding eight passengers) on a flight to Vinh Long in IV Corp. The plane takes off to the west and turns southward. Looking out the windows, I get the first sighting of my new home for the next year. Stretching to the horizon are never-ending, bright green rice paddies intersected by water canals, narrow tree lines, and dikes creating large grid squares. Then I see long rows of huge, water-filled craters—the results of B-52 bombings, my first glimpse into the reality of war.

> Note: The US military divided Vietnam into four Corp areas from the north, near the DMZ (Demilitarized Zone), to the south. IV Corp was the southernmost Corp area of Vietnam and was also called the "Delta" because this is where the Mekong River spreads out and empties into the ocean.

After landing at Vinh Long Army Airfield, the U-21 taxies to the runway apron, where the turboprop engines come to an idle and we disembark. Carrying my duffle bag with all my belongings, I walk from the airfield to the C Troop, 3-17th Air Cavalry headquarters shack, painted in bright red over white diagonals, similar to the regulation Cavalry flag. Prominently displayed on a large wall near the entry door is the word "Lighthorse," and beneath that is an image of Snoopy wearing a white Cavalry hat next to a Cobra gunship.

Lighthorse HQ

Entering the HQ office, I approach the first sergeant, who greets me and directs me to the commanding officer's (CO) office. Entering the office, I see Captain Robert Goodbary in his Nomex (flame-resistant) flight uniform sitting behind a large desk. Having close-cut dark hair, a disciplined look on his face, and perfect posture, Goodbary is a striking image. With sleeves rolled up precisely above his elbows, his blouse shows he is an Infantry officer. In addition to his aviation and airborne wings, he wears a Combat Infantry Badge, indicative that the captain has the experience acquired from a previous tour of duty in Vietnam.

CO - Captain Robert Goodbary

On the wall behind Goodbary is an impressive painting of an almost life-size stallion with head erect, tail lifted, and forefoot raised high in the air, a perfect image for Lighthorse. Coming to attention in front of the CO's desk, I give a sharp hand salute and announce, "Sir, Lieutenant Gooch reporting for duty," and hand a copy of my orders to the CO. After reviewing the orders, Goodbary looks up at me and says, "Lieutenant, we are short Cobra pilots. You will be flying 'front seat' in Cobra gunships until we receive additional gun pilots." Surely Captain Goodbary recognizes the big grin on my face as I say, "Yes, sir, glad to be in the Cav."

How fortuitous! In flight school, I expressed a desire to fly Cobras, hoping to be selected to attend a gunship transition course after graduation. Instead, I received an OH-58 Kiowa transition—a small, scout helicopter plagued with tail boom separation problems. A big disappointment.

But now, after not being selected for Cobra school, I am going to fly Cobras. Wow! Copilot in a Cobra gunship is better than no Cobra at all. Officially, I am assigned to the lift platoon flying Hueys but will fly front seat in the Cobra until the Gun platoon is fully manned.

GOOCH'S HOOCH AND CRASH

Upon exiting the CO's office, the first sergeant gives me directions to the pilot quarters and tells me someone will meet me there to arrange for a room. Along the way, I meet another new Lighthorse pilot, 1st Lieutenant Chris Rash. Chris is a tall guy with dark hair and a pleasant smile. After a short conversation, we agree to bunk together as hooch mates. We are an unusual pair. Chris is tall and lanky—a sharp contrast to me with my short, small build—but we get along well and make a good team.

Soon, the person in charge of quarters assignments arrives, and Chris and I are escorted to our new home. As we walk down a concrete sidewalk with long buildings extending perpendicular from both sides of the walkway, our guide tells us that Australians constructed the living quarters. We don't know what to expect, but that sounds good, definitely better than tents. The building's perimeter foundation consists of three-foot-high concrete walls topped with wooden slats backed by wire screening for ventilation. With concrete floors, corrugated metal roofs, and entry doors on each end, the buildings are sturdy. Inside, the buildings are divided into four separate living areas measuring about fifteen feet wide and thirty feet long.

Eventually, our guide stops at a building, opens the door, and shows Chris and I our new quarters, an empty room furnished with two folding metal beds and thin mattresses. Welcoming us to the Lighthorse, our guide tells us we have the option of designing and outfitting our hooch (living quarters) however we like.

Chris Rash in our hooch

In our spare time over the following two weeks, Chris and I take great pride in scrounging materials and building our new home. Constructing interior walls, we create a bedroom, closet, and living room. In the living room, we build a bar, complete with a small refrigerator, purchased at the PX (post exchange) and stocked with beer and soft drinks. After painting the walls, we complete our hooch by installing a window air conditioner—a real home away from home. Once we finish, we post two signs on our entry door, "Gooch's Hooch" and "C. Rash." The latter leads to Chris's nickname, "Crash," a name befitting Chris's fate told in a later chapter.

RATS

Not uncommon for swampy terrain, Vietnam is known for its rat population. Returning from the officers' club one evening, Chris and I see a large cat near the door of our hooch. On the other side of the cement walkway is a huge rat about the same size as the cat. Having had a few drinks, we encourage the cat to attack the rat. We must have looked pretty silly, two tipsy Army pilots talking to a cat, with the expectation that the cat would comply with our orders.

Soon the rat ambles slowly across the walkway, seemingly afraid of nothing. The cat sees the huge rat and wisely runs like the wind in the opposite direction. Chris and I get a good laugh—the cat is no fool; he knew he was outmatched. Apparently, that is why there are so many rats in Vietnam. Because of their size, they have few natural enemies.

Chris and I are proud of our hooch, but it still has its deficiencies. Some of the plywood we scrounged does not fit well, leaving gaps along the wall. In the nighttime, rats enter our hooch and chew on almost anything. One early morning I am awakened to gnawing sounds and get up to investigate. Being as quiet as possible, I listen and hear the gnawing is coming from a small, wooden, three-drawer chest next to my bed.

With flashlight in hand, I slowly open the top drawer and peek inside. Two glowing eyes come charging out at me. A rat, slightly larger than my fist, jumps over my left shoulder, scaring the living daylights out of me. Regaining my composure, I peer inside the drawer and see the rat has chewed my electric razor cord into several pieces. Bummer—now I have to get a new razor at the PX.

One night, we are awakened from our sleep by shots fired. *Bam, bam, bam, bam, bam!* Then it is quiet. Grabbing our weapons, we go to the door and find nothing. After several minutes, we return to bed. The following morning, we learn that one of our fellow pilots fired his M-16 rifle at a rat running across the rafters inside his hooch. The pilot missed the rat but made five or six ventilation holes in the corrugated steel roofing. Every time it rains, he is reminded of his rat hunt.

On another night I am awakened from sleep by the familiar sound of a rat gnawing on something. I reach for a flashlight on the wooden chest next to my bed and grab my Smith and Wesson .38-caliber revolver hanging in its holster on the wall above my pillow. With flashlight in one hand and revolver in the other, I slowly search around the room without getting out of bed. There it is, a rat about the size of a squirrel sitting on a ledge about eighteen inches above Chris's head. I whisper, "Chris, Chris, wake up. There's a rat above your head." Chris wakes up, and without moving, looks upward at the rat and says, "Shoot it, Rex. Shoot it." I have my revolver aimed at the rat, but the sight of Chris staring at that unsightly varmint breaks me up—what a hilarious sight. I start laughing so hard that I cannot hold steady aim. Then we both crack up laughing, and the rat runs off. As time progresses, we find and patch the holes in our hooch, and the infiltrating rats become smaller and smaller. Eventually, we have our hooch to ourselves.

LEARNING THE ROPES

Over the coming weeks, Chris and I get settled into our new lifestyle. At the same time, we are immediately immersed in flying, learning the many facets of combat aviation including local area navigation, communications procedures, radio frequencies, artillery clearances, and emergency procedures. It's a steep learning curve—inundated with new policies and procedures at a pace much more rapid than we experienced in flight school.

And, when we aren't flying, we get to know our fellow troopers and become acquainted with the Lighthorse heritage and traditions.

PART 2

LIGHTHORSE

CHAPTER 3

C TROOP, 3-17 CAVALRY

CAVALRY TROOPS OPERATING IN VIETNAM have nicknames, like "Apache," "Centaurs," and "Blue Ghosts." C Troop's nickname is "Lighthorse," a fitting name for a Cavalry troop with a heritage going back to the horse Cavalry of the late 1800s.

Walking through the troop area, I see Lighthorse emblazoned on almost every building and vehicle. And, another name is displayed prominently on various signs and structures: "Bastard Cav."

BASTARD CAV

Lighthorse is also called the "Bastard Cav" because C Troop is a standalone Cavalry troop attached to the 7-1st Cavalry at Vinh Long. Furthermore, C Troop is the only troop of the 3-17th Cavalry Squadron operating in the Delta (IV Corps). Troops A, B, and D of 3-17th Cavalry are based at Dĩ An in III Corps.

The pilots and crew members of Lighthorse readily identify with the Bastard Cav persona—that of being rogues, renegades, and rebels—an appealing image to the troop that stands apart from the other units in the Delta. In combat, C Troopers push the limits of their machines and their flying abilities, and, at times, challenge the rules of engagement when pursuing the enemy. After hours, the troopers party hard and flaunt their Bastard Cav name in friendly banter with their 7-1ˢᵗ Cavalry counterparts. Chris and I promptly get onboard with the Cavalry traditions and eagerly embrace the Bastard Cav image. It's fun and, at the same time, instills personal pride in our troop.

Bastard Cav on Lighthorse TOC entrance

NEWBIES

In Vietnam, new pilots are continually tested and evaluated until they prove themselves worthy of flying the complex helicopter in tactical situations. The more experienced aviators observe the rookie pilot's flying skills, situational awareness, reaction times, and, most importantly, how he responds in combat. Does he remain calm or does he let nervousness or fear overcome his trained responses? During this initiation phase, new pilots are called "Newbies" or "Newb." And, even more crude, they are also referred to as FNGs, meaning F**king New Guy.

As you might expect, the "new guy" handle is overused. Pilots can be heard saying, "Hey, Newb, go to maintenance and get me fifty yards of flight line," or, "That Newbie couldn't find his butt with two hands and a tactical map." This moniker continues until the pilot has proven himself in stressful situations, or until a new group of pilots arrives to carry the title more appropriately.

At some point, the Lighthorse pilots decide it is time for a Cavalry initiation for the new pilots. Gathering in the officers' club, Chris, Warrant Officer Wade Huddleston, and I are three Newbies who are the targets of a great deal of humiliation with the final act being challenged to drink a Green Muthersomething—a gross concoction created from every type of alcohol in the O-club. Yes, it is green from a generous portion of Crème de Menthe. We drink as much as can be tolerated of the nasty, somewhat sweet, yet putrid drink, and that seems to satisfy our tormentors for the time being. The initiation concludes with us three Newbies parading around the O-club, wearing red capes, conveniently acquired from the club's tablecloths, and pronouncing, "We are the caped crusaders!"

Needless to say, we have a terrible hangover the following morning. Relieved that we have endured the initiation, we think this might be the end of the Newbie title but, no, we are still called FNGs, and that label follows us for some time to come.

WHITE CAV HATS AND SCARVES

In addition to being called the Bastard Cav, Lighthorse has another unique distinction—White Cavalry hats. Unlike the black Cav hats worn by other *Cavalry* units, Lighthorse is the only

Cavalry troop to wear white Stetson Cav hats. This tradition dates back to July 1968 when 1st Lieutenant Ace Cozzalio contacted Stetson to place the initial order for "silver belly" color Cavalry hats. (This is described in detail in my first book, *Ace: The Story of Lt. Col. Ace Cozzalio.*)

The white Cavalry hat is a fitting image for Lighthorse since the 5th U.S. Cavalry (C Troop's predecessor unit) fought in the late 1800s Indian campaigns. During those days, the white hat was the working hat of the horse Cavalry while the black hat was worn with the dress uniform. Since Lighthorse is continually in the field, seeking and engaging the enemy, the "working hat" seems most appropriate.

Coinciding with the introduction of the white Cav hats, Ace Cozzalio's grandmother made triangular yellow scarves for every Lighthorse trooper. Worn loosely around the neck, the yellow scarves became a tradition much like the white hats. By the time of my arrival in 1971, only a few yellow scarves remain, worn by several of the longer service troopers.

In December 1971, our troop acquired a large quantity of red and white scarves worn by other 3-17th troops serving in III Corps. From that day forward, the longstanding tradition shifted, and Lighthorse troopers began wearing red and white scarves.

After having proven my flying skills on several missions and surviving the troop initiation, I am honored with the opportunity to order my silver belly Stetson Cavalry hat. After it arrives several weeks later, I roll the brim and attach crossed sabers and my rank to the front of the crown—a proud moment to be a Lighthorse trooper.

Author in Cav hat

RELIVING THE "OLD CAVALRY"

At some point in the early days of my serving with Lighthorse, I pause to reflect upon the outfit I have joined. I am in awe of this bold, unconventional Cavalry unit. These unruly, yet professional, young aviators are reliving the spirit of the Old West horse-mounted Cavalry depicted in the John Ford movies, especially *She Wore a Yellow Ribbon*, starring John Wayne.

Wearing their Cavalry hats, neck scarves, distinctive handlebar mustaches, and sidearms carried in a low-slung holster around their waist, the Lighthorse troopers look the part and embody the spirit of an 1860s Cavalry troop. During the day the Cavalry troopers ride out on their trusty steeds (helicopters) to pursue the hostiles (Viet Cong), and at night they party hard in the saloon (officers' club). Even the log-wall Cavalry fort can be compared, with some imagination, to the Vinh Long Army Airfield protected by a series of soldier-occupied bunkers that surround the compound.

The Lighthorse troopers are deadly serious in the fulfillment of their duties, and they approach their jobs much like the troopers of the olden days, with an air of "Don't mess with the Cav—we are damn good at what we do!" I am honored to be a part of this distinctive Cavalry unit, looking forward to the adventures that lie ahead and earnestly hoping to soon be as skillful a pilot as my fellow Lighthorse troopers.

CHAPTER 4

LIGHTHORSE TROOP

FOR READERS UNFAMILIAR WITH AIR cavalry operations, this chapter gives a brief overview of Lighthorse Air Cavalry and its components. Do not think of it as a must-read and -memorize collection of facts, but as a short summary of this unique Cavalry troop's personnel, organization, and aircraft. You can always refer back to this chapter, if necessary.

CAVALRY TROOP PLATOONS

Lighthorse is composed of three combat aircraft platoons, one aero-rifle platoon, and a maintenance platoon. The combat aircraft platoons are scout, lift, and gunship. Each platoon has a unique nickname that is used as its radio callsign. The scouts are War Wagons, the lift platoon is Longknives, and the gunship platoon is Crusaders.

Military communications procedures dictate that radio calls begin with the person being called, followed by the caller and then the message. A typical radio call between War Wagon 15 and Crusader 33 might sound like this: "Crusader Three-Three, this is War Wagon One-Five. Cover my right flank." In the field, this radio call is shortened to: "Three-Three, One-Five. Cover my right flank." And, when the War Wagon scouts fly low and in harm's way, the radio calls are even more abbreviated: "Three-Three, cover my right flank."

Lighthorse Nicknames and Callsigns				
Platoon	**Aircraft**	**Nickname**	**Callsign**	**Nos.**
Scout	OH-6A LOH	scouts	War Wagon	11–19
Lift	UH-1H Huey	slicks	Longknife	20–29
Gunship	AH-1G Cobra	guns	Crusader	30–39
Aero-rifle			Doughboy	40–49
Maintenance			Scavenger	50–59
Commanding Officer	CO		Lighthorse	6
Executive Officer	XO		Lighthorse	5

WAR WAGON SCOUT PLATOON

The War Wagons fly the OH-6A Light Observation Helicopter, nicknamed "Loach." This small, highly maneuverable aircraft flies at treetop level, or lower, as its crew searches for the enemy. Because of this advance combat reconnaissance role, the OH-6 is also called a "scout," and the men flying them are proud to be called scout pilots. Their mission is not unlike the horse Cavalry scouts of the late 1800s—forward reconnaissance to locate the enemy.

Lightweight and powerful, the Loach is perfect for flying nap-of-the-earth missions, and its twenty-six-foot diameter main rotor allows the nimble aircraft to get into extremely tight areas. It has no hydraulic system, and its electrical setup is used primarily to start the engine—simple even by 1960s standards, which for practical purposes means it is easier to maintain and harder to shoot down than other helicopters.[3]

---

[3] Donald Porter, "In Vietnam, These Helicopter Scouts Saw Combat Up Close," *Air and Space Magazine*, September 2017, https://www.airspacemag.com/military-aviation/snakes-loaches-180964341/

Armed with the XM-134 six-barrel, 7.62-millimeter minigun mounted low on the left side of the Loach, the pilot aims the aircraft at the target and can fire either two thousand or four thousand rounds per minute by pulling a trigger on the backside of the cyclic control between his legs.

War Wagon Loach
Photo courtesy of Mike Galvin

The Loach gunner (also called crew chief or observer; referred in this book as gunner), sitting sideways in the left-side pilot's seat of the cockpit, fires a handheld M-60 machine gun supported by a bungee cord attached to the top of the helicopter's doorframe. Together, the pilot and gunner can throw an awesome amount of firepower at the enemy.

CRUSADER GUNSHIP PLATOON

Flying the AH-1G Cobra helicopter, nicknamed "Snake," the Crusader platoon provides attack and gun cover functions for Lighthorse. The Cobra is the Army's first dedicated attack helicopter. This sleek two-person gunship is fast with a Vne (never exceed) speed of 190 knots (219 mph) and a cruising speed of 150 knots (173 mph). It has stub-wing pylons on each side of the fuselage for attaching an assortment of armament, including 2.75-inch folding-fin rockets and/or wire-guided anti-tank missiles.

Crusader AH-1G Cobra gunship
Photo courtesy of Tom Nutting

Two pilots crew the Cobra. The copilot, sitting in the front seat, controls the steerable nose turret that houses an M-134 six-barrel, 7.62-millimeter minigun, capable of firing two thousand or four thousand rounds per minute, and an M-129 forty-millimeter grenade launcher. The pilot, in the rear seat, aims the aircraft at the target and launches 2.75-inch folding-fin rockets—either high explosive or flechette (2,200 small metal darts). This deadly aircraft is highly effective in attacking both personnel and mechanized vehicles.

LONGKNIFE LIFT PLATOON

The Longknives fly the UH-1 Utility Helicopter, commonly called "Huey." This iconic helicopter is the recognized workhorse of the Vietnam War. The H Model Huey, introduced in January 1969, carries up to eight U.S. soldiers with gear or ten South Vietnamese soldiers. A pilot and copilot fly the Huey, supported by a crew chief and door gunner. Sitting inside open cargo doors, the crew chief on the left side and gunner on the right side man M-60 machine guns.

Longknife UH-1 Huey, aka slick
Photo courtesy of Mike Galvin

Hueys are also called "slicks." This name originated during the time that Charlie Model Hueys, equipped with rockets and forward-facing machine guns, served as gunships, and were nicknamed "guns" or "hogs." Hueys without rockets were called "slicks," referring to their lack of heavy armament. This name stuck with the Hueys even after the introduction of the Cobra gunships.

While the Loach and Cobra helicopters serve as the war machines for the Air Cavalry, the versatile Huey is always there for support, whether it be troop insertion, resupply, medevac, or crash recovery.

OPERATIONS AREA—IV CORPS

Lighthorse Air Cavalry operated in IV Corps, otherwise known as the Mekong Delta. This map displays the city/village locations and staging areas mentioned in the following stories.

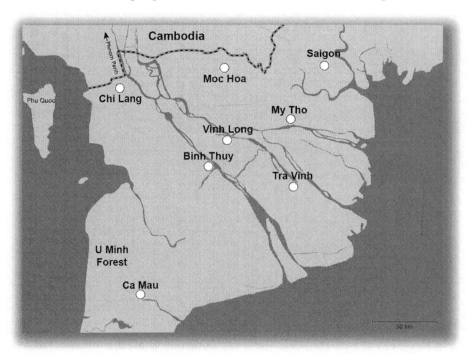

Lighthorse Operations Area: Mekong Delta
Locations in stories

THE TROOPERS

The following chapters tell of incredible events that occurred in the Mekong Delta of South Vietnam in 1971-72. And, most importantly, the stories highlight the duty, courage, and dedication of the pilots and crew members of Lighthorse Air Cavalry.

Most Army helicopter pilots are recent graduates of the U.S. Army Aviation School at Fort Rucker, Alabama. After earning their silver flight wings, they are sent directly to Vietnam to serve as combat aviators.

While I am a twenty-three-year-old officer commissioned through the college ROTC program, many more pilots are talented, nineteen-year-old warrant officers. After graduating from high school, they enlisted in the Warrant Officer Rotary Wing Aviator Course, training to fly and at the same time qualifying to become warrant officers. These young pilots have the skill and expertise to maneuver their aircraft into and out of critical situations, seemingly with ease. Flying their complex helicopters into combat, they handle the heavy responsibility as well as anyone twice their age.

Supporting the pilots are eighteen-year-old crew chiefs and gunners. Like the warrant officers, these young soldiers are high school graduates who recently completed Army training and are now functioning at a high capacity in a war zone. These courageous, thrill-seeking crew members are dedicated to maintaining their aircraft and, while flying, perform as gunners, operating the M-60 machine guns. They too are functioning at a performance level well above their age.

The Lighthorse troopers depend upon one another to get the mission accomplished and share an extraordinary camaraderie. Serving with the Air Cavalry is an exhilarating, life-changing experience. Any Cav trooper will tell you that the most exciting time of their life was "Flying with the Cav!" Enjoy the stories.

**The Wild Bunch – War Wagon door gunners
with pilot on right**

CHAPTER 5

POW RESCUE MISSION

AS A NEW LIGHTHORSE PILOT I am anxious to join the troop on combat missions and chomping at the bit to fly the Cobra. After successfully completing my check ride in a UH-1H Huey, my first three flying assignments are low-profile orientation flights in a Huey to familiarize myself with the local area and to learn the troop's operational procedures. Little do I realize that during this time one of the troop's most daring, dangerous, and secretive missions is being carried out in the notorious U Minh Forest. This chapter describes that mission and is told through the unique and graphic perspective of a Huey crew chief.

HUEY CREW CHIEF

The Huey crew chief is the critical support person who keeps our aircraft in the air. These amazing eighteen-year-old mechanics/gunners are here because the Army trained them for the position or they stepped forward, volunteering to learn the job. Either way, they enjoy flying, take personal pride in their aircraft, and, like the pilots, have personalities that crave the adrenaline-fueled excitement associated with combat aviation.

The Huey crew chief has two primary responsibilities; the first and foremost is to maintain the helicopter and all its systems. They check bearing clearances; replace worn parts; pull oil samples on the engine, transmission, and forty-two/ninety-degree gearboxes (every twenty-five flight hours); and keep the aircraft logbook up to date—a never-ending process! In flight, the crew chief's role is to fire the M-60 machine gun protecting the aircraft and its crew.

This story, told to me by one of the Longknife crew chiefs, Sergeant Ralph Chapman, is about a highly unusual and extraordinary mission to rescue POWs being held in U Minh Forest prison camps. The story is supplemented with information from the pilots who flew the mission.

THE NIGHT BEFORE

At the end of a long day of flying on November 21, 1971, a group of Longknife Huey and Crusader Cobra pilots are summoned to the Lighthorse Tactical Operations Center. Once there, Captain Goodbary, the CO, addresses the group, saying, "Men, because you are among the best and most experienced of the Lighthorse pilots, you have been selected to participate in a highly classified and dangerous mission. It is voluntary, and I recognize that some of you are short-timers, so before I go further, I need to know if any of you would prefer not to take on this responsibility. Your election not to participate will be understood."

Looking at one another, every pilot eagerly voices his decision: "We're in!"

Note: Several of the pilots in the room are within days or weeks of their DEROS date (date of departure from Vietnam) and many of the remaining pilots have less than six weeks remaining in-country, yet none of the pilots hesitate in volunteering for this mission. The call of duty and their dedication to flying exceeds any concern for personal safety.

Goodbary continues, "This highly classified mission has the codename 'Bright Light.' Several days ago, under the cover of darkness, a MACV special operations team (SOG) of three Americans and eleven ARVN (Army of the Republic of Vietnam—our allies) Rangers were inserted by Navy ship off the west coast of Vietnam to infiltrate into the U Minh Forest. Their mission is to locate a POW camp and rescue two American POWs, a sergeant and a lieutenant, and six or seven ARVN prisoners." Reacting enthusiastically, several pilots reply with comments of "All right!" and "Yeah!" and "It's about time."

Note: The Military Assistance Command, Vietnam– Studies and Observations Group (MACV-SOG) was a highly classified, multi-service United States special operations unit that conducted covert unconventional warfare operations before and during the Vietnam War.[4] Their secret missions were not unlike the Navy SEAL operations of today.

The CO continues, "The prisoners are being held in a jungle prison camp and guarded by an unknown number of Viet Cong soldiers. They are frequently relocated from one prison camp to another. Military intelligence has identified a particular camp

---

[4] Wikipedia, "Military Assistance Command, Vietnam–Studies and Observations Group," accessed February 25, 2019, https://en.wikipedia.org/wiki/Military_Assistance_Command,_Vietnam_–_Studies_and_Observations_Group

where the POWs are currently located. This camp is the target location for the special operations team."

Goodbary adds, "Our mission is to pick up and extract the specials ops team after they rescue the POWs. The team is led by a U.S. Marine lieutenant colonel dressed as an NVA (North Vietnamese Army) officer and the rest of the team are dressed as Viet Cong soldiers, in black pajamas, carrying AK-47 rifles."

Someone asks, "How will we know the good guys from the bad guys?" Goodbary answers, "We have been told that the SOG team will carry their AK-47 rifles in their right hand when approaching our aircraft." The pilots look at one another, and you can almost read their minds. *What about the right-handed VC soldier who comes out of the jungle?*

Goodbary closes the meeting, saying, "Our flight of four Hueys and four Cobras will lift off tomorrow morning at 0600 hours. We will stage our operations out of Ca Mau." He pauses. "This mission is confidential. Do not discuss it with anyone."

THE FOLLOWING MORNING

In the early morning hours, Longknife Platoon Sergeant Ralph Chapman is awake and dressed in his Nomex flight uniform before anyone else in the barracks. It is his job to make sure all the Huey flight crews and the day's technical inspector are awake. Walking from cubicle to cubicle, he checks on each crew member and gently wakens a few who are still asleep. Once he confirms that all the Longknife crews are up and moving, he picks up his flight helmet and gloves and walks to the Lighthorse Mess Hall.

Technical Inspector: The role of the inspector is to serve as a technical expert when one of the crew members questions a bearing clearance, fluid seep, flight/combat damage, or other technical matter on the helicopters. The inspector assists in determining whether an aircraft is flyable and has the authority to sign off red X (aircraft unsafe) conditions if the condition is within limits or if the defect was repaired or a component replaced. Each flight platoon has a TI assigned either from the Service Platoon Quality Control Section or a specially trained crew chief.

After going through the mess hall serving line, Chapman carries his tray of food to one of the long tables and takes a seat. As he eats his breakfast, his mind is occupied with thoughts about preparing for today's flight. Ralph knows little about the day's mission, but intuition tells him something big is happening today. With that thought in mind, he hurriedly eats a light breakfast and leaves the mess hall.

Arriving at the troop armory, Chapman checks out his M-16 rifle and .38-caliber pistol. He slides the revolver into the leather holster attached to the wide leather belt strapped around his waist. A strip of leather cartridge loops on the belt holds a row of bullets, much like the gunslingers of the Old West. Slinging his M-16 rifle over his right shoulder, Ralph picks up his flight helmet and walks outside.

One by one, the troopers arrive at the armory, check out their weapons, and assemble outside near a three-quarter ton truck. Once Ralph determines that all crew members and the technical inspector are accounted for, they load into the truck and are driven to the flight line, where each crew is deposited near their aircraft.

HUEY 739

Climbing down out of the truck, Chapman approaches his aircraft. He is filled with pride at the sight of Huey 739 (last three digits of the aircraft's tail number), sitting imposingly between two parallel four-foot-high revetments made of corrugated steel panels with packed dirt inside. Chapman's aircraft stands out from all the other Hueys. Ralph hired a Vietnamese artist to paint the nose cover bright orange with "AMERICA" inscribed above a special message.

Reaching inside the open left-side cargo door, Ralph places his helmet and rifle on his crew seat while the door gunner does the same on the right side. Together, the two crewmen walk to the troop's locked Conex container, where the aircraft machine guns and ammo are stored. Retrieving their two M-60 machine guns, the crewmen return to the revetment to prepare for today's mission.

PREFLIGHT

After checking the Huey's logbook to see if any notations were made since his aircraft was last flown, Ralph starts his preflight inspection. Climbing up onto the roof, he uses his flashlight to inspect the rotor head, pitch change links, and swash plate. Chapman is thorough, yet the entire time he is thinking, *This flashlight makes a good target for VC snipers. I need to be quick with my inspection.*

Meanwhile, the door gunner locks the two M-60 machine guns atop the Huey's M-23 swivel gun mounts located in front of the outward-facing crew seats on each side of the helicopter. The M-23 armament system has a rack welded below each gun designed to hold an ammo can containing 550 rounds of 7.62mm linked ammo. Ralph, who wants more firepower, has installed a large .50-caliber ammo can capable of holding three thousand rounds of 7.62mm linked ammo. After securing the machine guns, the door gunner checks to ensure that both large cans are full of ammo.

Mindful of the time, Ralph realizes the pilots will soon be arriving and his aircraft must be flight ready. He wraps up his inspection and checks with the door gunner, who confirms that he too is finished.

STARTUP

At 0515 hours, the aircraft commander, Warrant Officer Wes Bartley, and his copilot arrive at Huey 739. Gathering together next to the Huey's open cargo door, Wes shares the details of today's mission with Ralph and the door gunner. He concludes by saying they are flying the Chalk 2 position, in a flight of four Hueys.

Note: Helicopter positions in formation flight are called "Chalk" for radio communications; i.e., Chalk 1 (lead), Chalk 2 (mid), and Chalk 3 (trail). The chalk terminology simplifies communications. When the aircraft are loaded and ready for takeoff, the pilots announce on the aircraft radios, "Chalk 1's up," "Chalk 2's up," "Chalk 3's up," signifying that all aircraft are ready to fly.

After performing a quick preflight inspection, the two pilots climb into the cockpit and prepare to start the turbine engine. Ralph unties the rotor blades and calls out, "Clear and untied." Then he walks to the left side of the Huey, taking his position for startup. Standing outside the open cargo door, he puts on his helmet and connects his communication cord while the door gunner does the same on the right side.

After checking gauges and toggling switches, the copilot calls, "Clear," and, after a quick visual inspection of the rotor blades and tail rotor, Chapman and the door gunner call out, "Clear." The turbine engine starts its familiar whining sound, and the rotor blades begin turning slowly. Ralph slides the left-side cargo door forward to allow access to the engine observation door. Peering inside, he makes sure there are no fuel leaks or other problems during startup.

Once the rotor blades are at flight idle rpm, Chapman slides the cargo door rearward and secures the door in the open position with a locking pin. Then he and the door gunner walk forward to the pilot's open doors. There, they slide the pilot seat armor plating forward, lock it in position, and close the doors.

TAKEOFF

After taking their respective positions in the left- and right-side outward-facing seats behind the M-60 door-mounted machine guns, Ralph and the door gunner are ready to fly. Seconds later, Wes takes the helicopter controls and rolls the throttle on. The rotor blades increase rotation until they are spinning at operating rpm. Bartley calls on the intercom, "Coming up to a hover," and Ralph calls, "Clear left," while the door gunner calls, "Clear right." Slowly lifting the collective, Wes brings the Huey to a three-foot hover. He then carefully moves the cyclic forward, and the Huey slowly moves forward out of the revetment. Hovering to the runway apron, he sets the Huey down on the asphalt apron, next to Chalk 1, flown by Chief Warrant Officer 2 Led Symmes.

> Flight Controls: The **cyclic** control is positioned between the pilot's legs with the shaft extending through the floor of the helicopter and is held with the pilot's right hand. Moving the cyclic changes the direction of flight by "tilting" the main rotor disk—left, right, fore, and aft. The **collective** control is operated by the pilot's left hand. It looks like a handbrake in older cars. Lifting up or pushing down makes the helicopter climb or descend. It does this by altering the pitch of the rotor blades and simultaneously increasing or decreasing engine power. Pilots often refer to "pulling in power," or "pulling pitch," meaning they lift the collective to climb, or in combination with forward cyclic, to increase airspeed.

Seconds later, Chalk 3 and Chalk 4 arrive and set down next to Huey 739. With all four aircraft aligned next to the runway,

Led calls the tower saying, "Vinh Long Tower, Longknife flight of four Hueys ready to take off, runway 26." The tower replies, "Longknife flight, you are clear for takeoff, runway 26."

In the darkness of the predawn hours, one by one, each pilot brings his aircraft to a hover, taxies to the center of the runway, does a pedal turn to the left, and takes off to the west, following the navigation lights of the aircraft in front of them.

When Huey 739 passes over the "wire" (outer row of concertina wire encircling Vinh Long Airfield facility), Ralph and the door gunner load a link belt of 7.62mm ammo into their machine guns and chamber a round. They are "locked and loaded" with ammo fed directly from the large can holding three thousand rounds.

Making a sweeping turn to the left, Led Symmes in Chalk 1 takes a compass heading to Ca Mau, 145 klicks (ninety miles) southwest of Vinh Long.

Note: The U.S. military measures distance in kilometers (.62 miles) to facilitate communication with allied forces. This also correlates with military tactical maps (standard 1:50,000 scale) that are laid out in one-kilometer grid squares. The term "klick" is the often-used shorthand/slang for kilometer.

About an hour later, the Longknife flight arrives at Ca Mau airstrip as the sun is just starting to appear above the horizon. The four aircraft land, hover to the refueling pads, and top off their fuel tanks. Then they lift to a three-foot hover and taxi to the gravel-covered apron next to the asphalt runway, where they shut down to remain on standby for today's mission.

THE MISSION

Ralph and the door gunner remain with Huey 739, while Wes and his copilot along with the other Lighthorse pilots attend a mission briefing held by a senior officer from the MACV Studies and Observation Group (SOG). In this meeting, they are given an update on "Bright Light," stating that the SOG team is advancing eastward through the dense jungle toward the POW prison camp and expects to arrive sometime in the next hour. Once they reach the camp and rescue the prisoners, the team will make their way westward to a predetermined pickup zone (a clearing large enough for three Hueys) for extraction.

Because of the covert nature of this mission, unique radio callsigns are issued. The SOG team will use "Little Fauss," and the Longknife slicks, "Big Halsy," both names taken from the 1970 movie starring Robert Redford as a motorcycle racer, titled *Little Fauss and Big Halsy.*

The MACV officer provides the mission details, explaining that one aircraft of the Longknife Hueys will always remain in the air to relay radio communications between the Tactical Operations Command Center (TOCC) located on a Navy destroyer anchored offshore in the Gulf of Thailand and the SOG team on the ground. Using the callsign Halsy 6, the Longknife crew will remain on station two hours until replaced by another Longknife Huey. The pilots are provided radio frequencies, told to launch one aircraft immediately, and instructed to fly a large holding pattern south of the operations area to avoid alerting the enemy of their presence.

The MACV officer finishes his remarks by saying, "In addition to Lighthorse, this mission is supported by naval gunfire from the destroyer and Navy Black Ponies."

ON STANDBY

Aligned next to the Ca Mau runway, the retrieval team of seven Lighthorse helicopters (three Hueys and four Cobras) is ready to launch at a moment's notice—rotor blades untied, and the helicopters' controls preset for a quick start. Remaining close to their aircraft, the pilots and crew members are on high alert, anxious to get into the fray and rescue the POWs.

AMBUSHED

Arriving at the POW camp later that morning, the SOG team discovers it has been recently abandoned. Presuming that their mission has been compromised, they set up a defensive perimeter while maintaining a listening watch. In the midst of a radio call from Little Fauss to Halsy 6, now flown by Led Symmes, the Viet Cong attack, ambushing the small team. AK-47 fire and explosions from grenades and RPGs and can be heard in the background of the radio transmission.

After a brief pause, Little Fauss resumes contact with Halsy 6, who, after providing the grid coordinates, requests Navy gun support from the destroyer.

Led immediately alerts the TOCC on the Navy destroyer, relaying the grid coordinates of the besieged SOG team. Within a minute, the Navy ship responds, saying, "Ready to fire."

The SOG team commander replies with, "Fire!"

After observing the point of impact, Fauss calls Halsy 6, saying, "Adjust one hundred meters east and fifty meters north."

Led relays the message to TOCC and the Navy fires again.

This time the Navy is spot-on target and the SOG commander calls, "You're in the box. Fire for effect."

Led relays the message to TOCC, and the Navy rains high-explosive shells upon the Viet Cong positions. After almost ten minutes of Navy gunship bombardment, the remaining Viet

Cong withdraw, and the SOG team cautiously maneuvers west through the dense, swampy jungle. Their destination: the predetermined PZ located several klicks westward, toward the gulf.

BLACK PONIES

Several hours pass as the SOG team evades the enemy, proceeding slowly and cautiously toward the PZ. During their journey, Navy Black Ponies, flying the OV-10 Bronco, arrive in the area, on call to provide close air support if needed.

Black Ponies OV-10 Bronco
North American Rockwell OV-10A Bronco, June 1969-Mekong Delta. Taken by Chief Photographer's Mate A.R. Hill. Official U.S. Navy Photograph #1139900.

Note: "The OV-10, with its distinctive twin tail boom and forty-foot wingspan, looked somewhat like the World War II P-38 Lightning. Three-quarters the size of the P-38, yet with half the horsepower, the bronco also had three-quarters of the Lightning's performance." This highly maneuverable aircraft was very effective in providing close air support to ground troops or Navy boats patrolling the Mekong River. "The usual weapons load consisted of three pods of four Zuni rockets and one pod of nineteen 2.75-inch rockets underneath, and two Zunis on each wing. The Zuni was a supersonic unguided rocket designed to be fired at ground targets.... The Zuni was fifteen feet long, five inches in diameter, carried a high explosive warhead, and packed an impressive wallop."[5]

In midafternoon, the SOG team is, once again, attacked by the Viet Cong. At this time, Wes Bartley in Huey 739 is performing the Halsy 6 role. Ralph Chapman, crew chief in Huey 739, recalls hearing the radio communications between the Black Ponies and the SOG commander.

After popping a smoke grenade to mark their location, the ground commander tells the Black Ponies, "Hit fifty meters east from the smoke." The Ponies answer, "Roger that, fifty meters east of smoke, inbound with rockets."

With loud explosions in the background, the SOG commander excitedly comes on the radio yelling, "Too close! Too close!" The Black Pony pilot replies, "You wanted fifty meters, you got fifty meters." Evidently, the explosive power of the five-inch Zuni rockets (almost twice the size of the 2.75-inch Cobra rockets) was raining hot shrapnel on the SOG team and too close for their comfort. The commander says, "Make it seventy-five meters." The Pony pilot replies, "Roger that, seventy-

[5] Kit Lavell, *Flying Black Ponies* (Annapolis: Naval Institute Press, 2009), e-book, Chapter 3

five meters, inbound with rockets." After several Pony gun runs, the VC withdraw, and the jungle returns to quiet.

Again, the SOG team makes their way west through the dense, swampy jungle, while evading and occasionally fighting back their enemy pursuers.

Eventually, the team comes upon a small clearing in the jungle. The ground commander decides to forgo the trek to the larger PZ and calls Halsy 6 for extraction.

THE CAV TO THE RESCUE

Halsy 6 calls the Longknife retrieval team of three slicks, sitting patiently alongside the Ca Mau airstrip. He explains that the SOG team has called for extraction, and he concisely describes the mission directives. Instead of the predetermined PZ, the team must now be picked up at a small jungle clearing large enough for one aircraft at a time. The first inbound aircraft will request the SOG team to pop smoke. Finally, Halsy 6 says, "Launch immediately!"

The pilots and crews scramble, and in a couple of minutes, three Longknife Hueys are in the air, heading to the U Minh Forest for the extraction. The flight order and radio callsign designations are:

Halsy 1:	Chief Warrant Officer 2 Led Symmes (AC)
	Chief Warrant Officer 2 Tom Tolar (copilot)
Halsy 2:	Warrant Officer Wes Bartley (AC)
	Copilot unknown
Halsy 3:	Chief Warrant Officer 2 Jack Hosmer (AC)
	1st Lieutenant John Doherty (copilot)

Wes, in Halsy 2, pushes the cyclic control forward and pulls in maximum power as he follows behind Halsy 1 in the lead position. From the back seat, Ralph turns to look at the aircraft instruments and sees the airspeed indicator showing 120 knots (138 mph), maximum airspeed for the Huey. Chapman thinks to himself, *This is awesome—the Cav to the rescue!*

Note: Airspeed indicators on military aircraft are expressed in knots or nautical miles per hour. One nautical mile is equivalent to 1.15 miles. In this book, airspeed is expressed in knots with the equivalent mph shown in parentheses.

On the ground, the SOG commander has half of his team clearing small trees from the pickup zone while the other half holds off the enemy with AK-47 fire and grenades. By removing the taller vegetation, they have created a landing area large enough for one Huey.

HALSY 1

Arriving in the east side of the operations area, Led calls the ground commander. "Little Fauss, this is Halsy 1. We are two mikes out. Pop a smoke." The MACV-SOG commander replies, "Roger that. Smoke's out." Several seconds later, Led sees the smoke and calls, "Fauss, I have red smoke." The commander replies, "Red it is." This confirmation is crucial since the Viet Cong have been known to pop a smoke grenade, setting a diversionary trap for the inbound Hueys.

Led descends to treetop level flying westward toward the smoke while Halsy 2 and 3 fly a holding pattern several klicks to the east. Above Halsy 1, flying at 1,500 feet altitude, are two pairs of Crusader Cobras flying racetrack patterns to provide close air support on each side of Halsy 1 should they take fire.

Flying low and fast, Led closes on the smoke plume and sees the clearing has tall trees on all sides. Pulling back on the cyclic, he flares the Huey nose high and comes to an abrupt, momentary halt above the clearing. Lowering the collective, he settles downward about thirty feet until coming to a hover with the aircraft's skids about a foot above the swampy ground.

Looking to the side, Led sees a group of five soldiers dressed in black Viet Cong clothing and carrying AK-47 rifles in their right hands while running toward his aircraft. Led tells his crew, "Don't shoot! Those are the good guys!" One American and four ARVN Rangers disguised as Viet Cong rush to load into the open cargo doors.

Once the passengers are onboard, Led lifts up on the collective to climb while simultaneously calling on the radio, "Halsy 1 coming out to the west." Upon clearing the trees, Symmes flies low across the treetops to exit the area. Catching the enemy by surprise, Halsy 1 receives no enemy fire either into, or upon exit, from the PZ.

After climbing to altitude, Symmes banks right, setting a course for Navy Binh Thuy.

HALSY 2

Upon hearing Halsy 1 call his exit, Wes Bartley immediately makes a rapid descent to treetop level, flying eighty knots toward the smoke in the distance. Soon, the *pop-pop-pop* of enemy gunfire can be heard, and Ralph sees muzzle flashes in the jungle below. Wes calls, "Taking fire," and pulls in power to increase the Huey's airspeed.

In an instant, Ralph and the door gunner start laying down a continuous stream of protective fire with their M-60 machine guns. From high above, four of the Crusader gunships (one pair on each flank) dive along both sides of the fast-moving Huey, firing rockets into the outskirts of their flight path.

Inside the Huey, the sound is deafening; *rat-tat-tat-tat-tat-tat-tat-tat-tat* coming from both door guns intermixed with *kaboom, kaboom, kaboom, kaboom* from rockets impacting fifty to seventy-five feet off both flanks.

Wes sees the pickup zone ahead. Pulling back on the cyclic and lowering the collective, he stands the Huey on its tail to slow down. Shaking and shuddering, the Huey slows to a near stop above the PZ as Wes simultaneously reduces power to drop down into the jungle opening.

Calling, "Cease Fire," Wes brings the Huey to a momentary hover above the dense vegetation in the jungle clearing and gently lowers the collective, allowing the aircraft to settle into the thick, tangled undergrowth. Looking through the chin bubble, Wes can see the brush pressing against the bottom of the Huey as he continues to lower the aircraft until the skids are resting lightly on the swampy bog. He holds pitch in the rotor blades to keep the skids above the mushy ground and anticipates the passengers loading will tilt the aircraft.

Keeping an eye on his door gun, Ralph sees his M-60 machine gun barrel is cherry-red hot from continuous firing. He thinks, *I sure hope that barrel cools down before I need it again.*

HALSY 2'S EXTRACTION

Looking out at the tree line, Ralph sees a group of soldiers dressed in black VC uniforms running toward his aircraft. In the middle of the group is a guy wearing an NVA uniform. Pointing his M-60 machine gun in their direction, he nervously waits with his right index finger resting lightly on the trigger. Ralph's mind is racing. *Are they carrying their AK-47s in the right hand or left hand? Are they enemy soldiers or the good guys?*

When they get closer, it is evident that these are the friendlies. Ralph sees that a tall American commander, wearing a pith helmet and green NVA uniform and sporting a bushy, brown handlebar mustache, is moving quickly toward his side of the Huey. The commander is escorting a VC prisoner in black "pajamas" with his hands tied behind his back. Arriving at the Huey, the commander lifts the prisoner and shoves him through the open cargo door. Then, the commander and three ARVN team members quickly climb aboard.

Wes calls on the radio, "Halsy 2 is up, lifting off to the west." Climbing up and over the trees, Wes pulls in maximum power to gain airspeed while flying across the treetops. Muzzle flashes are spotted in the trees below the fast-moving helicopter. Ralph and the door gunner open fire with their M-60 machine guns, spraying the wooded areas with a continuous stream of hot lead. Once again, Ralph's gun barrel becomes red-hot.

Soon, Wes calls "Cease fire" on the intercom and climbs to 1,500 feet altitude. Banking the Huey into a wide right turn, he sets a course northeast to Navy Binh Thuy.

Sometime later, Ralph glances right to see the VC prisoner move toward the open cargo door. Ralph knocks the prisoner down and, with assistance from the ARVN team members, ties the prisoner to the cargo rings on the floor of the Huey.

HALSY 3

Still in a holding pattern east of the PZ, Jack Hosmer hears Halsy 2, on the radio, calling his exit from the pickup zone. He descends rapidly to treetop level, flying toward the PZ. By this time, the smoke has dissipated and the only reference point is sighting the spot where Halsy 2 emerged from the jungle. Focusing on that spot, Hosmer flies westward, low and fast across the treetops.

Midway to the PZ, they start taking heavy enemy fire from the trees below and the door gunners return fire with the M-60 machine guns. Closing on their objective, John Doherty, in the right-side pilot's seat, scans the area looking for the opening in the jungle.

Suddenly, in his peripheral vision, John sees a bright streak shooting skyward—a pen flare coming from a small opening in the dense jungle off his left side. In an excited voice, Doherty yells, "There they are, at our nine o'clock!" Having flown past the PZ, Jack makes a tight, left-hand, 180-degree turn, and lands to the east in the small clearing.

Upon settling in the PZ, John looks out the right side to see a Vietnamese man dressed in black, carrying an AK-47 rifle, approaching their Huey. The door gunner, who has his M-60 machine gun pointed at the man, says, "Hey, should I shoot him?" John replies, "No, hold off." The crew nervously awaits as the darkly dressed man continues toward their aircraft. Having received heavy enemy fire on their approach to the PZ, the Huey crew is concerned that the Viet Cong might have overtaken the SOG team.

The armed soldier stops outside John's door, shifts his AK-47, and looks up, saying, "You wait, we come." With a sigh of relief, John glances toward the tree line to see three ARVN soldiers, also dressed in black, and an American escorting a Viet Cong prisoner advance toward the Huey. As they load into the open cargo door, Doherty sees that the VC prisoner is blindfolded, and his hands are tied behind his back.

Once they are loaded, Hosmer pulls in power and lifts out of the PZ. Flying at treetop level to the east, he avoids retracing the same path they traveled on their inbound route. But, the element of surprise is lost. After hearing the noise of three helicopters, the enemy is waiting for them. Concealed in the thick jungle, the Viet Cong soldiers fire upward at the sound of the Huey passing overhead. Calling, "Taking fire," Jack flies low and fast across the treetops as the door gunners return fire with M-60 machine guns and the Crusader Cobras dive to fire rockets along their flanks as they exit the area.

Soon, Hosmer pulls back on the cyclic and climbs rapidly upward to 1,500 feet AGL and flies to Navy Binh Thuy.

SOG TEAM DELIVERY

Arriving at the Navy Binh Thuy airfield, Wes Bartley, in Halsy 2, begins his eastward approach to runway 06. At about 200 feet AGL, the SOG commander in the NVA uniform taps Wes on the shoulder and points to a C-130 cargo plane parked on the apron along the east side of the runway. After coming to a hover over the runway, Wes does a pedal turn to the right and taxies to the waiting aircraft. After setting the Huey's skids on the ground, he rolls the throttle to flight idle. The SOG team disembarks with their prisoner and walks to the open cargo ramp under the tail of the large airplane.

SOG Team Commander in NVA uniform departing Huey 739
Photo courtesy of Ralph Chapman

After dropping off their passengers, the three Longknife Hueys shut down on the runway apron where the pilots and crew members assess their damage. Amazingly, only Halsy 3 has taken a couple "hits" from small arms fire in inconsequential areas of the airframe. After refueling, the three Hueys lift off and return to Vinh Long Airfield where they meet up with the rest of Lighthorse. Mission accomplished.

Lighthorse POW rescue crew
l to r: Jack Hosmer, Ralph Chapman, Led Symmes
Photo courtesy of Jack Hosmer

SUCCESS OR FAILURE?

Since the POWs were never located, the POW rescue mission was unsuccessful. Even so, the MACV-SOG team lost no members, killed or wounded an untold number of Viet Cong on their exit, and captured two VC prisoners for interrogation.

Because of the covert nature of this operation, the Lighthorse Troopers never receive after-action reports on this mission. They are left to wonder about the fate of the POWs, and whether the captured VC prisoners disclosed any useful information on the location of the jungle prison camps.

In the coming days, the POW rescue story becomes a favorite topic over beers at Lighthorse gatherings. The story enlarges and expands to meet the needs of the storyteller. One thing is certain to all: Lighthorse was there and ready to extract the POWs had they been rescued, and they safely extracted the SOG team.

Vietnam Veteran Profile: Ralph Chapman

Ralph Chapman enlisted in the Army with a commitment to attend helicopter maintenance training. After completing basic training, he was sent to Fort Eustis, Virginia, to train as a CH-47 Chinook helicopter mechanic. After four months of extensive training on all aspects of helicopter components, systems, and engines, Ralph was sent to Vietnam and assigned to Lighthorse Air Cavalry.

Since Lighthorse had no Chinook helicopters, Chapman was assigned to the Longknife platoon as a Huey door gunner during the troop's initial incursion into Cambodia. In this position, he learned the role and responsibilities of a crew chief. Weeks later, he became a Huey crew chief and was assigned his first aircraft. Ralph described his Huey that "died an early death of combat lead poisoning." His Huey was deemed "unrepairable at the local level" after taking hits in the fuel cell that leaked into the honeycomb structure of the underbelly. It was then that Ralph took charge of Huey 739 when its crew chief departed Vietnam.

Ralph accumulated over 1,300 combat flight hours in Vietnam, mostly as a Huey crew chief for the Longknife lift platoon. During his time with Lighthorse, he was the recipient of the Air Medal with V device. After serving three years of active duty in the U.S. Army, Chapman served three additional years with the Army Reserves.

After Vietnam, Ralph worked thirty years for the Los Angeles Fire Department before retiring in 2004. Ralph commented on his job, "I was the guy that rode the back of the pumper truck. After arriving at the fire, I hooked the truck hose to the hydrant before taking a hand line hose inside the burning structure to put the wet stuff on the red stuff!"

When asked about his most memorable life accomplishment, Ralph said, "My service in Viet Nam will always top the list. Getting home safely made everything else possible!"

Today, Ralph has a wall in his home proudly dedicated to his Vietnam service. Photos, award certificates, and other memorabilia cover the wall. The centerpiece and most prominent item is a Huey nose cover painted exactly as Huey 739.

Ralph and his wife have three sons and seven grandchildren. Two sons are in law enforcement, and one served twelve years in the U.S. Army as a flight medic for the 160th SOAR (Special Operations Aviation Regiment) and now works as a registered nurse.

**Lighthorse Crew Chief Ralph Chapman
and Huey 739 nose cover**
Photo courtesy of Ralph Chapman

CHAPTER 6

FLYING "GUNS"

AH-1G COBRA GUNSHIP

AFTER MY CHECK RIDE AND orientation flights in Huey 217[6], I am scheduled to fly with the Crusader gunship platoon. Having no gunship training, I am flying "front seat," otherwise known as copilot/gunner in the AH-1G Cobra. The copilot's primary role is to operate and fire the mini-gun and grenade launcher housed in the rotating, flexible turret on the underside nose of the Cobra.

The Cobra is an awesome war machine that has intrigued me since flight school. To say I am excited about the opportunity to fly "guns" is an understatement, even with the understanding that this is a temporary assignment.

At 0400 hours on November 29, 1971, my alarm clock rings, but I am already awake, anxious for my first day flying "guns" with the Cav. After putting on my Nomex flight uniform, I strap on the leather holster carrying my .38-caliber revolver, grab my flight helmet bag, and head out for breakfast. At the troop mess

---

[6] Huey 217 is of special significance to the author. It has the distinction of being the first helicopter he flew in-country, is featured in several chapters of this book, and is destined to reunite with the author thirty-eight years later (as told in the last chapter).

hall, I join a line of pilots and crewmembers standing in the serving line.

After a short wait, I take a meal tray and make my way down the line, choosing bacon, eggs, a small box of cereal, a carton of milk, and a banana. Taking a seat at one of the long tables, I take one bite of the scrambled eggs and immediately react, blurting out, "Yuk! These eggs are terrible." Above the laughter, someone next to me says, "Don't ever eat the eggs. They are powdered." Next, I pick up a piece of bacon, and it disintegrates in my hand, burned to a crisp. Oh well, I have my box of cereal. Tearing open the box, I shake the corn flakes into a bowl and open my carton of milk. Tilting the carton over my cereal, nothing comes out. Looking inside, I can see the milk is frozen solid. So, after eating a minimal breakfast consisting of a single banana, I make a mental note: *Only eat the least-prepared food, like bananas or apples, or, better yet, don't eat at the mess hall.*

After my disappointing breakfast, I am about to exit the dining hall when a fellow pilot points to C-ration boxes stacked near the door, saying, "You need to carry a box of C-Rats for lunch." "Thanks for the tip," I say while selecting a generic-looking brown box and placing it inside my helmet bag.

Once outside the mess hall, I join my friend, Warrant Officer Wade Huddleston, and we walk together to the Lighthorse Tactical Operations Center (TOC) to attend the 0500 hours briefing for today's flight.

Upon entering the TOC, Wade and I are introduced to the lead pilot for today's mission, Warrant Officer Kevin Kelly. I am thinking, *I have heard of Kelly. He is rumored to be one of the troop's most talented Cobra pilots, and I heard he is deadly accurate when firing rockets.* Looking at Kelly, I see a tall, medium-build guy with a natural smile. As Kevin speaks, it is evident that he has an easygoing, pleasant demeanor coupled with impressive knowledge and experience. I can certainly understand why everyone likes and respects him.

Kelly explains that today's mission is in Cambodia. We will fly to Chi Lang, a MACV (Military Assistance Command, Vietnam) command post and ARVN training center situated near the Cambodian border. There, we will refuel and shut down to receive further instructions. The Lighthorse team for this mission is two Crusader Cobra gunships and one Huey serving as Command and Control (C&C). Kelly says that Huddleston will be flying as his front seat and I will do the same for his wingman, Crusader 33, Warrant Officer Larry Coates. Our scheduled liftoff time is 0615 hours.

AH-1G Cobra gunship front profile
Photo courtesy of Tom Nutting

Boarding the troop's three-quarter ton truck, we ride the short distance to the flight line. As we near the Cobra gunship parked between four-foot-high revetment walls, I cannot help but admire this impressive aircraft. Sometimes called "The Snake," the Cobra is long, slender, and sleek. From the front, it is fearsome and intimidating with the rocket pods and mini-guns aimed forward. It is clearly an attack aircraft.

PREFLIGHT

Using a flashlight in the predawn hours, I assist Larry Coates in performing the preflight inspection. Although I know very little about this aircraft, much is similar to the Huey since Bell Helicopter manufactures both aircraft. (More than seventy percent of Cobra parts are interchangeable with the Huey UH-1D Model). Climbing up to stand on the tail stinger, I inspect the tail rotor pitch change links/bearings and the ninety-degree gearbox oil level while Larry inspects the engine and transmission.

Soon, we are ready to board and start the turbine engine. From the left side, I climb into the front cockpit in the nose of the Cobra. Once settled in place with my safety harness fastened, Coates, standing outside the gunship, talks me through the aircraft controls, most of which I am already familiar with.

Then Larry reaches across to dismount the flexible gunsight, mounted on articulating arms, that swings left to center between my knees. Showing me the switches and triggers, he demonstrates how to fire the M-134 six-barrel, 7.62-millimeter minigun and the M-129 forty-millimeter grenade launcher. I ask about aiming, and he points to the clear gunsight prism, telling me not to worry about that because I will figure it out when the time comes. That comment bothers me a bit, but I think, *"OK, he knows better than I do."*

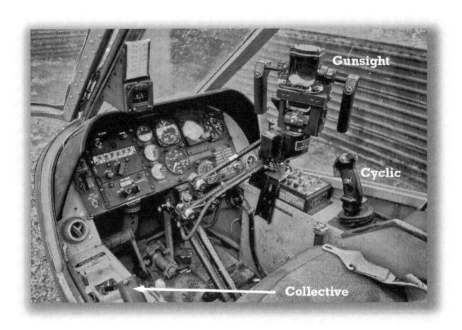

AH-1G Cobra front cockpit and gunsight
Photo courtesy of Lloyd Goldston III

Walking around the nose of the Cobra to the right side of the aircraft, Larry climbs into the rear pilot's seat that is situated higher than the copilot's seat and positioned immediately forward of the aircraft's transmission.

While waiting for Coates to get settled in, I put on my flight helmet, plug in my communication cord, and attempt to familiarize myself with the aircraft flying controls. Unlike the Huey and other helicopters, the cyclic in the front seat is not positioned between the pilot's legs but, instead, mounted on the right armrest so it will not interfere with the flexible gunsight. I am thinking, *This feels really strange*. Then I remind myself that the copilot's job is not to fly the aircraft, but to fire the weapons; flying is secondary. As I further evaluate the cockpit, I am consoled to see that the collective, controlling the engine power and rotor blade pitch, is in its normal position on the left side of the pilot's seat. The flight instruments are similar to what is in the Huey, yet several switches and dials are foreign to me.

THE LIFTOFF

Soon, Coates comes on the aircraft intercom saying, "Are you ready to fly?" I answer, "Roger that." Then Larry calls out, "Clear," and pulls the trigger on the underside of his collective to start the Lycoming 1,400 shaft horsepower engine. The spinning turbine makes a loud whining sound as the rotor blades begin to turn slowly. Then they rotate faster, faster, and faster until there is a blur above us. Seconds later, the rotors are spinning at flight idle rpm (revolutions per minute), and Larry, on the intercom, tells me to close the canopy. Reaching upward with my left hand, I grab the handle and pull the clear canopy downward. Rotating the latch, the canopy is locked in place.

After overcoming the strange, confined feeling of being enclosed in a relatively small cockpit, I realize the visibility is incredible. The curved canopy enables the pilot to see in every direction except the area immediately below the aircraft's slim fuselage.

Seconds later, Coates rolls the throttle on, and the rotor blades increase rotational speed until they are spinning "in the green" on the dual tachometer. We are ready to fly.

In the heat of Vietnam, a fully loaded gunship is too heavy to hover. The pilots must make a running takeoff with the skids sliding across the asphalt runway until the aircraft reaches translational lift (additional lift achieved when forward air passes through the rotor system). It typically takes about fifty to one hundred feet of runway sliding before the skids lift off the ground. Since we are flying into Cambodia and will refuel at Chi

Lang, we carry a full load of rockets, grenades, and mini-gun ammo and a half-full tank of fuel so the Cobra will easily hover.

In the early morning darkness, Kelly calls on the radio asking Coates if he is ready. Coates replies "affirmative" and says he will follow Kelly's lead. Then Coates lifts the collective, bringing the gunship to a three-foot hover, and taxies forward out of the revetments and directly to the runway apron. There, he maneuvers the Cobra to set down alongside Kelly and Huddleston in the lead gunship, facing the runway.

Looking forward, I see two fully loaded Cobra gunships precede us in taking off. Sliding along the asphalt runway, the Cobra's skids are emitting a small shower of bright orange sparks until their aircraft lifts upward in a slow climb. What an impressive sight in the predawn darkness!

Once the Cobras have cleared the runway, Kelly calls the airfield tower to announce our takeoff. Looking to the right, I see Kelly's Cobra lift to a hover, move forward to the runway, do a pedal turn to the left, and take off to the west. Following Kelly's lead, Coates brings the Cobra to a hover and does the same.

TO CHI LANG

Gaining airspeed and altitude, I glance upward and see the navigation lights of both Crusader 34, Kevin Kelly, and ahead of him, the C&C Huey that lifted off earlier. Looking to the right, the rising sun is slowly illuminating the landscape below. I see bright green rice paddies, segmented into large squares by dikes and tree lines—what a beautiful sight! Continuing to climb, we level off at 2,000 feet AGL (above ground level) and follow Kelly to Chi Lang, 105 klicks (sixty-five miles) west of Vinh Long.

After flying about thirty minutes, Larry comes on the intercom telling me to look to our eleven o'clock to see a group of mountains in the distance called the Seven Sisters. Unlike the rest of the Mekong Delta where the elevation varies by only ten to fifteen feet, these prominent terrain features rise high above the rice paddies, the tallest having a height of 2,300 feet. Coates tells me that the mountains serve as excellent navigation features to look for when flying to Chi Lang.

Minutes later, we arrive near the Chi Lang airstrip, which sits along the east side of the tallest mountain, about twelve klicks (7.5 miles) southeast of the Cambodian border. After the air mission commander (AMC) in the C&C Huey makes a broadcast radio call to announce our approach to Chi Lang, our three aircraft land, refuel, and shut down on the apron along the north side of the runway.

MOUNTAIN CAVE

After tying down the rotor blades and securing our aircraft, I join up with Huddleston, Kelly, Coates, and the AMC in a meeting held in the MACV Special Operations Coordination Center (SOCC) headquarters. There, we are told our mission is to hit an ammo cache hidden in a mountain cave northwest of Chi Lang in Cambodia. Toward the end of the meeting, we are reminded that we are not to land in Cambodia.

Note: Flying across the border requires compliance with a unique set of rules that essentially state, "You cannot land, refuel, or get shot down in Cambodia; essentially you cannot be on the ground in Cambodia."

In response to President Nixon's 1970 Cambodia Incursion, Congress passed the Cooper-Church Amendment on January 5, 1971, seeking to limit U.S. expansion of the Vietnam War into neighboring countries. "As a result, all U.S. ground troops and advisors were barred from participating in military actions in Laos or Cambodia, while the air war being conducted in both countries…was ignored.[7] The newly enacted law was silent on U.S. air operations.

The "no ground troops in Cambodia" rule impacts Air Cavalry operations by limiting the use of scouts flying low-level. Evidently, low-level reconnaissance is deemed a component of "ground operations." Thus, today's

Wade Huddleston at SOCC bunker in Chi Lang

---

[7] Wikipedia, "Cambodian Campaign," accessed January 24, 2019, https://en.wikipedia.org/wiki/Cambodian_Campaign

mission has Crusader gunships and no War Wagon scouts.

Returning to our aircraft, I untie the rotor blades while Larry makes a quick pre-flight inspection. Then I walk to the left side, where I climb into the front seat while Coates climbs into his back seat from the right side. Minutes later, the Cobra's turbine engine is running, and the rotor blades are at operating rpm. The C&C Huey hovers to the runway and lifts off in a northwesterly direction. Then Kevin Kelly takes off, and we follow, flying a course to the mountain identified by map grid coordinates.

Arriving thirty minutes later, we circle the mountain searching for the cave opening. Soon, we see switchback trails leading to the open mouth of a large cave about halfway up the northeast side of the mountain. Calling on the radio, the AMC says, "Crusaders, you are clear to engage."

Having already entered a racetrack pattern at 1,500 feet altitude, Kelly initiates the first gun run at the cave, firing a pair of high-explosive rockets that impact near the cave opening. His second pair hit inside the cavern opening. When Kelly breaks off his run to climb away from the mountain, Coates enters a high-angle dive, aiming our aircraft at the cave. Larry comes on the intercom, saying, "Master Arm switch is armed, and your weapons are hot." I reply, "Roger that."

Reaching to my right, I lift the gunsight from its mount and move it to the left, positioning the apparatus between my legs with the sight prism at eye level. Grasping the handles on each side of the gunsight, I align the sighting prism reticle on the cave opening. About that time, Coates punches off two rockets, making a loud "Whoosh" sound. Seated just forward of the rocket pods, I see white smoke in my peripheral vision as two rockets shoot past my side windows, streaking ahead of our Cobra. *Wow! That is awesome!* I say to myself.

After recovering from the excitement of seeing rockets pass by my windows, I return to my gunner duties. Depressing the thumb button on the top of the handgrip, I fire the forty-millimeter grenade launcher, and two rounds make a *dupe, dupe* sound as they exit the barrel. It seems that no matter how quickly you push the button, you fire two rounds.

Five to six seconds later, I see the grenades impact below the cave opening. After making a "Kentucky windage" adjustment with the gunsight reticle, I fire another couple rounds. All the while, we are in a steep dive toward the mountain and rockets continue to streak past my canopy. This time my grenades impact closer to the cave opening. I adjust and fire a third pair about the same time that Coates breaks off the gun run, climbing past the north side of the mountain.

We circle and prepare to do it again. This time, I fire the grenade launcher, and while waiting for the grenades' impact, I use my index finger to pull the trigger on the front of the handgrips, firing the mini-gun. The mini-gun fires at the unbelievable rate of two thousand or four thousand rounds a minute (two-detent trigger switch) and every sixth round is a tracer, so you can follow where the bullets are hitting. It is somewhat like spraying a narrow stream of water out of a high-power water hose.

Once I see where the grenades impact, I fire another pair, each time mentally noting adjustments to make on the gunsight. Eventually, one of the grenades explodes inside the cave opening.

Kelly and Coates are deadly accurate with their rockets. After completing three gun runs, at least half the rockets impact inside the mouth of the cave, yet there are no secondary explosions from the suspected ammo cache. Having expended most of our rockets and ammo, the AMC, circling high above in the C&C Huey, calls on the radio to say our mission is completed. Banking to the east, Kelly sets a course for Chi Lang, and we pull alongside in an echelon right formation.

Kevin Kelly flying Crusader Cobra gunship
Photo courtesy of Jack Hosmer

On the return trip, Larry passes the aircraft controls to me, and I get my first Cobra "stick time." Flying at altitude, I find little difference from the Huey, except that the cyclic control is on the right-side console. Approaching the Chi Lang airstrip, Coates tells me to break right to circle around, allowing Kelly to land first.

As I move the cyclic to my right, the sleek aircraft banks right in a graceful, effortless turn. Completing the circle, I line up with the runway and begin my approach, descending and progressively slowing until I arrive at a three-foot hover above the asphalt runway (the Cobra hovers effortlessly with half our munitions and half our fuel expended). Pushing right pedal, the aircraft nose swings right, and I hover to the refueling area. It is then that I notice a big difference. Because of the Cobra's extended nose, I feel like I am dangling on the end of a long stick. With a little practice, I become accustomed to this and find the Cobra just as fun to fly as the Huey. After refueling, we rearm and shut down on the pad next to the runway.

STANDBY

At this point, we are told to remain on standby, awaiting further orders. It is almost noon when Kevin says, "Hey, guys, let's go to the New Zealand mess hall. They have some of the best chow in the Delta." To me, this is great news since I had no desire to eat the C-rations stored in my helmet bag. Following Kevin, we walk through the compound to the New Zealand mess hall. There, we are seated around a long table covered with a white tablecloth that seats about twenty people. Within ten minutes, we are eating a hot meal, the best meal I have had since arriving in Vietnam (almost three weeks ago).

Note: "In January 1971, the 1st New Zealand Training Team Vietnam (1NZATTV) arrived at the National Training Centre at Chi Lang, in the Mekong Delta near the Cambodian border. The team helped train South Vietnamese platoon commanders in tactics and small-arms techniques."[8] Assigned to the school are forty-nine New Zealand Army officers and one enlisted man, the cook. Having honed his cooking skills in private hotels and restaurants, the cook is an excellent chef and well appreciated by the New Zealanders and their guests.

It should be added, "This was the first war in which New Zealand did not fight alongside its traditional ally, Great Britain. Instead, NZ's participation reflected their country's increasingly strong defense ties with the United States and Australia."[9]

Seated across from Kevin Kelly, I have the opportunity to ask him if he had any close calls while flying Cobras. Kevin welcomes my question and tells me of an air strike against Khmer Rouge (enemy) forces near Phnom Penh. After completing his gun run, firing rockets into the enemy's location, he breaks off his dive to climb upward when a couple of rounds from enemy fire went through the transmission and engine oil cooler. In an animated voice, Kevin tells of barely making it to land at the Phnom Penh airport when his transmission started to grind and tear apart.

WEAPONS/AMMO CACHE

Sometime later, we are summoned to the SOCC and given a new mission—support a Khmer Republic (good guys) ground

---

[8] New Zealand History, "Vietnam War map," Ministry for Culture and Heritage, updated September 15, 2014, https://nzhistory.govt.nz/media/photo/vietnam-war-map

[9] New Zealand History, "The Vietnam War," Ministry for Culture and Heritage, updated December 8, 2016, https://nzhistory.govt.nz/war/vietnam-war

unit in contact with an element of the Khmer Rouge (Communists—very bad guys) on the outskirts of a small village in Cambodia. Riding in the rear jump seat of the C&C Huey, a Khmer Republic officer will serve as "back seat," interpreting the radio communications with the ground forces and coordinating the mission from the air.

Returning to our Cobra gunship, we crank up and lift off, following Kelly to the operations area located forty-nine klicks (thirty miles) northwest of Chi Lang. En route to the village, the "back seat" calls the Khmer Republic ground forces commander who requests that we "take out" three hooches on the outskirts of the village. He reports that a group of Khmer Rouge soldiers are barricaded in fortified structures and his soldiers have reached a stalemate, unable to rout them. The Khmer Republic forces have pulled back, and no "friendlies" are in the immediate area.

Arriving at the village, we find three large structures and several smaller huts situated about two hundred meters west of the road leading into the village. The AMC calls Crusader 34 (Kelly), instructing our Cobra team to attack the three hooches. Kelly replies that he will attack the middle hooch and we are to take the one on the right. Having already established a right-hand racetrack pattern above the three hooches, Kevin enters a diving east-to-west gun run. Looking to the right, I see Kelly's first pair of rockets hit in front of the middle hooch. Then the second pair of rockets hit dead center, and a secondary explosion erupts from the structure with a bright flash and long streams of white smoke.

About the time Kelly breaks from his gun run to climb upward, Coates completes the racetrack orbit and lines up for his attack, aiming our gunship at the right-side hooch. Once again, Larry tells me the Master Arm switch is in the "armed" position.

Using the gunsight prism, I line up the hooch in the reticle and fire a pair of forty-millimeter grenades that exit the turret gun tube with a familiar *dupe, dupe* sound. Then I pull the handgrip trigger, shooting a stream of 7.62mm bullets into the roof of the hooch. While looking for the impact of my grenade, I see Coates's second pair of rockets hit the hooch, and the roof caves inward. As we break to climb, I look back and see fire and smoke, but little remains of the original structure.

Following Crusader 34 in a racetrack orbit, we make two more gun runs that destroy the remaining hooches. We never see enemy personnel, but Kevin hit the jackpot, destroying a Khmer Rouge weapons/ammo cache.

Cobra Gunship firing rockets and mini-gun
Photo courtesy of Ray Wilhite

Remaining on station, we circle overhead while the friendly ground forces sweep the area around the hooches. Soon the "back seat" in the C&C Huey reports that the ground commander is pleased, and our services are no longer required. With this news, the AMC calls to say our mission is accomplished. Turning southeast, we return to Chi Lang to refuel and rearm.

We fly one more mission that afternoon before returning to Vinh Long. Arriving after sunset, we have flown seven hours and thirty minutes. It has been a long and rewarding day. I learned so much, and I'm incredibly pleased to have flown the Cobra gunship.

I fly two more Crusader missions before being replaced by new pilots with formal Cobra training. I move to the Longknife lift platoon and fly Hueys from that point forward. I love the Huey but will forever have fond memories of flying the Cobra gunship.

Years later, Dudley Oatman, Lighthorse maintenance officer, recalls Kevin's emergency landing at Phnom Penh airport. "It was quite the international incident because we were on the 'ground' in Cambodia. Folks from the U.S. State Department (Embassy) made us wear civilian clothes, take no wallets, ID tags or identification of any type and tape over any U.S. markings on our Huey when we went to recover Kevin's Cobra. We had to rent a truck from a local business at the Phnom Penh airport that had a wench boom to change out the Cobra's transmission. We paid a small fortune to rent the truck along with a complete team (maybe 20) of local Cambodians (as 'operators'). The truck turned out to be an old U.S. Army two-and-a-half-ton recovery vehicle complete with U.S. Army markings...so much for our 'stealthy' efforts. The Cambodians did not mention how a U.S. Army wrecker found its way to Phnom Penh, and we did not ask...it worked, so we were happy. Thanks to my superb mechanics and NCOs, who performed a minor miracle, we were in and out in one day. Officially, of course, none of this ever happened."

Vietnam Veteran Profile: Kevin Kelly

Kevin Kelly was one of those incredibly talented pilots whom you meet once in a lifetime. His innate ability to fly enabled him to make his aircraft do things that his fellow pilots could only marvel at and admire. Having grown up in a Navy family, Kevin was destined to have a great military career. After high school, he enlisted under the Army's Warrant Officer Flight Training Program and upon graduation was chosen to attend the Cobra gunship transition course.

In 1971, Kevin arrived in Vietnam and was assigned to Lighthorse Air Cavalry. Flying Cobras for the Crusader gunship platoon, Kevin Kelly logged over one thousand combat flight hours and his aircraft was shot down on two occasions. Kevin commented about flying Cobras, "Our Crusader gunships were armed with seventy-six 2.75-inch folding-fin rockets, three thousand rounds of mini-gun ammo, and 250 rounds of 40mm grenades. I felt invincible. That feeling of invincibility was soon answered with clarity when my gunship was brought down by enemy fire. After surviving a crash landing, I was in the air again. Shaken, my feeling of invincibility had disappeared only to be replaced by a more experienced outlook of a now veteran combat pilot." Combat pilot indeed. Kevin was widely acknowledged to be the "best Cobra pilot" in the troop and was proud to be the first warrant officer one to complete the in-country Cobra Instructor Pilot Course, a notable distinction.

Following his tour of duty in Vietnam, Kevin was assigned to B Company, 7-17th Air Cavalry at Fort Hood, Texas, and became an instructor pilot for AH-1G and OH-58 helicopters. After attending the Warrant Officer Advanced Course, he was assigned to the 2nd Armored Cavalry Regiment in Germany. As one of the early users of night vision goggles (NVG), Kevin logged over six thousand hours of NVG flight time.

Kevin Kelly using night vision goggles
Photo courtesy of Pat Kelly

Kevin's next assignment was Fort Rucker, Alabama, as an instructor pilot. While at Fort Rucker, he attended after-hours college courses and obtained a BS degree in Aeronautics. He then applied for and was promoted from chief warrant officer three to the rank of captain in the Armor branch.

In 1981, Kevin was selected as one of the early members of Task Force 160 "Night Stalkers" (later becoming the 160th SOAR). He served seven years with this highly secretive and elite helicopter special operations unit, initially serving as platoon leader, instructor pilot, and flight lead.

During his time with the Night Stalkers, Kevin flew the MH-6 "Little Bird" (the Army's newest version of the Loach) in the liberation of Grenada (1983). Commenting on that mission,

Kevin said, "I vividly recalled the expressions of fear, then relief, on the faces of the American medical students as they recognized the American flag on the uniforms of the Army Rangers escorting them onto Blackhawk helicopters for their ride to freedom."

In 1987, Kelly, now serving as A Company commander, flew a Little Bird in Operation Earnest Will and was directly involved in three combat attack missions to protect Kuwaiti shipping lanes. Kevin was involved in the attack and scuttling of an Iranian

"Little Birds" 160ᵗʰ SOAR – Night Stalkers
Photo courtesy of Ted Carlson

minelayer, a shoot-out and sinking of three Iranian gunboats, and the demolition of the Iranian Rostam oil platform.

Afterward, Kelly flew fixed-wing aircraft into Panama during the U.S. invasion to overthrow General Noriega and later supported combat operations during the first Gulf War. During his service, he was the recipient of the Legion of Merit, Meritorious Service Medal, Bronze Star, and Air Medal. After serving twenty-one years and seven months, Kevin retired from the military in 1991 with the rank of major.

In his second career, Kevin became a civilian contractor at Fort Campbell, Kentucky, instructing Army pilots to fly Little Birds. He later was employed by a global aviation company, flying both rotary and fixed-wing aircraft internationally. His final retirement came in 2011.

Kevin and his wife, Pat, have two children and five grandchildren. Unfortunately, Kevin Kelly passed away on May 9, 2017, less than two weeks after attending the Lighthorse annual reunion, where he spent time reminiscing with his Air Cavalry buddies.

Author's note: While flying slicks on troop insertion missions with the Longknives, it was comforting to know Kevin Kelly was covering us from above in his Cobra gunship. Kevin's quick reaction time, excellent flying skills, and accuracy when firing rockets was well known and highly appreciated by the Longknife slick pilots. You will read more about Kelly in the following chapters.

Kevin Kelly in AH-1G Cobra cockpit - 1971
Photo courtesy of Pat Kelly

CHAPTER 7

BAPTISM BY FIRE

MOMENTS

WE WHO SERVED IN VIETNAM have our "moments" that are indelibly etched in our minds—events we will remember forever. For me, that event was my "baptism by fire." After being in-country less than three weeks, this was not unexpected, but was nonetheless a shocking event. Yes, it wasn't as consequential or life-threatening as taking hits in your aircraft (another story in this book), but it served as a stunning awakening to the reality of war. And, being a "Newbie," the heat of battle and the professionalism exhibited by my fellow pilots and crewmembers made a significant impression on me. This is my story of that momentous event.

LONGKNIVES

Like my Cobra flying experience, I am immediately placed in the cockpit of the UH-1H Huey helicopter, learning "on the fly," so to speak, during combat missions. Many of the tactics and flying principles I am exposed to are unique to Air Cavalry operations in the Mekong Delta, and highly effective in the war against the Viet Cong. For a new pilot, it is a personal challenge to absorb and learn as much as possible in the midst of the fast-moving action and intensity of combat.

TODAY'S MISSION

At 0500 hours on December 3, 1971, my alarm clock rings and I slowly roll out of bed and put on my Nomex flight uniform. Not being a morning person, this early morning routine is difficult for me, so I decide to forgo breakfast to get a little more sleep. Based on my previous experience with the mess hall's lousy food, I choose to take a different approach.

Strapping on my holstered pistol, I grab my helmet bag and head for the door. Just before exiting, I grab a candy bar and a cold can of soda—breakfast on the way to Lighthorse Tactical Operations Center (TOC) for the 0530 hours meeting to receive our mission instructions.

Having rained during the night, it is hot, humid, and wet as I walk along the concrete sidewalk, enjoying my soda and candy bar. Arriving at the TOC, I join a group of pilots gathered to hear the details of today's operation. Soon, a captain greets us and describes the mission consisting of two Crusader Cobras, two War Wagon Loaches, three Longknife slicks, and the C&C Huey. We are scheduled to lift off at 0630 hours and fly to Ca Mau, where we will receive the mission briefing from a MACV military advisor.

I am assigned to fly copilot for Warrant Officer Wes Bartley in Huey 739. We are Chalk 1 in a flight of three Hueys. In this lead position, Wes has command responsibility for the three aircraft in the Longknife lift platoon.

This is my first mission flying with Wes. I have heard he is one of the best slick pilots in Lighthorse. He certainly looks the part. Tall, with sandy blond hair and a precisely twisted handlebar mustache, he is the iconic image of an aviator. In my mind, I visualize Wes flying Spad biplanes with Eddie Rickenbacker and the 94th Aero Squadron in World War I while wearing a leather aviator skullcap with goggles on his forehead, a long leather jacket, and knee-high leather boots. I digress; back to the story.

Exiting the TOC, we climb into a three-quarter ton truck, waiting to take the pilots to the flight line. Once everyone is aboard, the truck enters the airfield, drives around the runway, and passes along the row of Lighthorse helicopters, dropping aircraft commanders and their copilots at their assigned aircraft.

Arriving at Huey 739, Wes and I grab our helmet bags and climb out of the truck. There we meet our crew chief and door gunner who have the M-60 machine guns mounted, ammo loaded onboard, and are preparing our aircraft for today's mission. After a preflight inspection, Wes climbs up into the left-side pilot seat while I do the same on the right side.

After donning my flight helmet and plugging my commo cord into the receptacle, I begin the engine start procedure. The pilot on the right side usually performs this role because the start trigger is on the collective next to his seat.

In less than a minute the turbine engine is running at flight idle, and the rotor blades have settled into a calm rhythm. After sliding the armor plating forward and closing the pilots' doors, the crew chief and door gunner take their respective positions in outward-facing seats behind the M-60 door guns. Rolling the hand grip on the collective to full throttle, the rotor blades come to operating rpm, referred to as "in the green," and we are ready to fly.

Wes tells me to hover to the runway to stage for takeoff. After calling for clearance from the crew, I slowly lift the collective, bring the Huey to a three-foot hover, and move forward out of the parallel revetments. Upon reaching the south side of the east-west runway, I set the Huey down and wait for the other Longknife slicks to join us.

Shortly after that, all eight Lighthorse aircraft are in the air flying to Ca Mau, 145 klicks (ninety miles) southwest of Vinh Long. Located in the center of the large peninsula that extends southwest of the Mekong River, the Cau Mau airstrip is a common staging area and refueling point for missions into the U Minh Forest.

MISSION BRIEFING

After landing and refueling at Ca Mau, the Lighthorse pilots shut down their aircraft on the gravel-covered apron alongside the asphalt runway. Gathering near the center of the long line of eight helicopters, the Lighthorse pilots attend a mission briefing held by a U.S. Army major, a MACV senior advisor to the ARVNs operating in the Kien Giang Province. I recall the major saying, "Today's mission is to extract a company of South Vietnamese infantry troops that were inserted in the U Minh Forest three days earlier." Looking at my fellow pilots, I see sideways glances that seem to say, *We've been there before, and it's a nasty area.*

Composed of dense jungle and swamps on the western side of the Mekong Delta, the U Minh Forest is a known sanctuary for the Viet Cong. Just the mention of the U Minh increases the tension level for both pilots and crewmembers—ventures into this area typically result in firefights with the enemy.

Note: Under President Nixon's Vietnamization policy introduced in 1969, responsibility for ground war operations transferred to the South Vietnamese Army, with air support provided by the U.S. Army and Air Force. By 1971, the only soldiers we transport into combat are our South Vietnamese allies, otherwise known as ARVNs (Army of the Republic of Vietnam).

Mission Briefing at Ca Mau – l to r: Ralph Winfrey, MACV Advisor, Wes Bartley, Ken Hibl, Chris Rash

TROOP EXTRACTIONS

Under the protective cover of Crusader gunships, the Longknife slicks make three sorties (trips) into a small pickup zone (PZ) in the U Minh Forest. On each sortie, the three Hueys load ARVN soldiers and transport them to a command post (CP) at Chi Mi about twenty klicks (twelve miles) to the south. A group of twenty-five ARVN soldiers remains in the PZ for the fourth and final extraction.

THE LAST RETRIEVAL

After offloading the third group of ARVN soldiers at the CP, the Longknife Hueys lift off in a northerly direction, returning to the U Minh Forest pickup zone. When the three slicks get within two klicks (1.2 miles) of the PZ, Wes calls on the troop radio frequency, "Flight, prepare for approach." This is my cue to keep my hands and feet lightly on the aircraft controls in case Wes is shot or otherwise incapacitated. Flying in stacked trail formation, the Hueys tighten their separation to within one rotor disk and begin their descent. Precise control movements are critical at this point, there is little room for error, and the tension is high as the three aircraft close into a tight formation.

Up ahead, we see the now familiar PZ—a small, triangular-shaped clearing in the middle of a large field of tall elephant grass. The perimeter of the field merges into dense jungle trees extending upward sixty to seventy-five feet high with thick undergrowth below.

Flying at seventy knots (eighty mph), the three slicks continue their approach to the pickup zone. Closing on the PZ, Wes reduces power and pulls back on the cyclic to slow our airspeed. As he flies the lead aircraft, Wes's every control movement is slow and deliberate to ensure the trailing helicopters can react appropriately and remain in formation. About twenty meters from touchdown, Chalk 2 Huey slides left to land at our rear quarter, conforming to the shape of the PZ. Chalk 3, flown by Chief Warrant Officer 2 Tom Tolar, lands directly behind our aircraft.

TAKING FIRE

At the moment the Huey's skids touch the ground, the remaining ARVN soldiers emerge from the perimeter of the eight- to ten-foot-high elephant grass to load onto our aircraft.

About the time the soldiers reach the open cargo doors, we receive enemy fire from both flanks. Initially, I am clueless to what is happening. I hear *pop-pop-pop-pop-pop-pop-pop* and do not realize it is gunfire. It sounds nothing like I had imagined. The helicopter noise and my flight helmet are masking the sounds. Then the radios erupt with, "Taking fire, taking fire, taking HITS."

Flying in the right seat, I turn to look out my door window, expecting to see the Viet Cong firing their AK-47s at our aircraft. Instead, I see nothing but tall elephant grass just beyond the tips of our rotor blades. Then I turn to look out the left-side cargo door and see Staff Sergeant Mullins, door gunner in Chalk 2, leaning outward to the front of his Huey while firing his M-60 machine gun toward the tail. Suddenly, Mullins abruptly bolts forward and slumps over his machine gun. Reality sinks in—we are under attack and taking casualties!

This moment is my "baptism by fire," the quintessential event that I heard described by other pilots and crewmembers. Forty-seven years later, I can see the action playing out in my mind as if it happened yesterday, and it is just as surreal today as it was then. The battle unfolds in a matter of seconds, yet it replays in my mind as if occurring in slow motion.

Explosions, likely mortars and RPGs (rocket-propelled grenades), are hitting around us, and enemy small arms fire continues to *pop-pop-pop-pop-pop*. The Huey crew chiefs and door gunners return fire into the dense grass and undergrowth. The distinctive *rat-tat-tat-tat-tat-tat-tat-tat* of our M-60 machine guns rage from both sides of our aircraft. The smell of gunpowder fills the air and white smoke filters past our helicopter.

Radios blare with pilots yelling, "Get loaded," "Get the hell out of here," and "Our door gunner is hit." On the surface, it appears to be mass confusion, but instead, every pilot and crew member is carrying out their role precisely as they have been taught. Every action has a sequence and it is being played out like a well-rehearsed performance.

Wes, who appears to be perfectly calm, calls on the radio, "Taking fire, 4 o'clock. We'll be lifting off 12 o'clock. Chalk 1 is up." In an instant, I hear radio calls, "Chalk 2's up" and "Chalk 3's up." Wes pulls pitch to take off, and we lift up and over the tall elephant grass to our front. Our door gunners continue firing, *rat-tat-tat-tat-tat-tat-tat-tat*, as we continue to climb and build airspeed, just clearing the tops of tall jungle trees along the perimeter of the field. Wes calls, "Cease fire," and makes a gradual, sweeping turn to the left as we increase altitude over the jungle. At that moment, I hear Tom Tolar in Huey 217 call, "Chalk 3, breaking left."

Safely out of small arms range, I remove my hands from the flight controls and turn to look out the left-side cargo door. I see Tolar's aircraft, flying low over the jungle treetops. About this time, Warrant Officer Kevin Kelly calls on the radio, "Crusader 34, Inbound, Nails." I shift my eyes upward to see Kevin's Cobra gunship diving toward the PZ, firing rockets. What a beautiful sight! In midflight, the rocket projectiles emit red puffs of smoke indicating flechette rounds. At the moment Kevin breaks off his gun run, climbing to altitude, a second gunship, on a similar flight path, dives toward the PZ. Puffs of white smoke can be seen alongside the Cobra when the rockets erupt from the gun tubes.

RETURN TO CHI MI

Our flight of two Hueys, less Chalk 3, turns southward, setting a course to the CP. Arriving at the command post, we land, offload the ARVN soldiers, and shut down our aircraft. Moments later, Tom Tolar in Huey 217 lands to our rear. We were concerned about Tom and his crew, not knowing why they broke from the formation. Later, Tom tells me his Huey took numerous hits in the PZ and continued to take fire as he departed in the Chalk 3 position. By breaking to the left, he placed a line of trees between his aircraft and the enemy fire.

What happened is clear to everyone. The Viet Cong patiently remained in hiding during the first three troop extractions. Then, at the moment the last group of ARVN troops began loading, they ambushed the three slicks—sitting ducks in the small PZ with limited visibility.

After the three Longknife Hueys are "skids down," the pilots and crew members assess the damage. Of the three helicopters, our Huey is the only one to escape unscathed with no hits. Tom Tolar, in Chalk 3, was less fortunate; a bullet passed through the Plexiglas chin bubble of Huey 217, just missing his feet on the pedals. And, his aircraft has two bullet holes in the fuel cell under the cargo floor. Unbeknownst to Tom or his crew, he was leaking fuel on his return flight to Chi Mi. Chalk 2 Huey has several hits, but none in critical locations, and is deemed flyable.

MEDEVAC

Staff Sergeant Mullins, the door gunner on Chalk 2, is shot in the chest. His lung is punctured, and he needs immediate medical attention. Since our aircraft, Huey 739, is the only Huey unscathed from the battle, I am paired with another aircraft commander to medevac Mullins to the 3rd Surgical Hospital at Navy Binh Thuy. Wes Bartley, performing the lead role, stays behind with the Longknife platoon to coordinate the pickup and recovery of the unflyable Huey 217 and oversee follow-up actions.

After receiving field expedient medical treatment to stop the bleeding, Staff Sergeant Mullins is loaded on Huey 739 and tended to by one of the Longknife crew chiefs. Wasting no time, we crank up and lift off, flying northeast 110 klicks (sixty-eight miles) to Navy Binh Thuy. Forty minutes later we arrive and land at the hospital helipad where a group of nurses and a doctor are waiting. The nurses rush to place Mullins on a stretcher and take him into the emergency room. After surgery and several weeks in the hospital, Mullins recovers and returns to Lighthorse.

**Tom Tolar, Chalk 3 aircraft commander
with his fist in chin bubble bullet hole**

NEWBIE NO MORE

Just three weeks earlier, I was a twenty-three-year-old 1st lieutenant, boarding a plane in San Francisco bound for

Vietnam. After a week of in-processing, I began flying with the Crusaders and then Lighthorse, accumulating sixty hours of combat flight time in two weeks. Considering refueling and staging for missions, that is a considerable amount of flight experience in a short time. However, no amount of training or experience prepares you for that first encounter with enemy fire.

Late in the evening, the Lighthorse pilots meet at the officers' club, have a few drinks, and talk about the day's firefight as if it was a commonplace occurrence. That attitude combined with a certain amount of Cavalry bravado about how we kicked ass on the enemy led me to believe I was the only one scared. Later, I realize we all were scared, but everyone handles that fear differently. And, I understand there is an unwritten rule that you never openly admit to the fear of being shot that rides in the background of your consciousness.

For me, today's firefight was an eye-opening experience that, frankly, terrified me. But, now that I have experienced my "baptism by fire," it is also a moment of clarity with the realization that I can face this danger again, do my job, and persevere as a Longknife pilot. And, having experienced the "live fire" of combat, I will no longer be called "Newbie." I hope...

Vietnam Veteran Profile: Wes Bartley

Wes Bartley's desire to be an aviator was formed at the early age of nine when he flew his first flight with his namesake great uncle in a Piper Cub. Later, his decision to enlist in the Army Warrant Officer Flight Program was influenced by his upbringing in a military family—his dad was an Army aviator.

Upon graduation from flight school, Wes completed a CH-47 Chinook transition course before reporting to Southeast Asia. Arriving in Vietnam in July 1971, Wes was assigned to Lighthorse

Air Cavalry flying Hueys for the Longknife lift platoon. After demonstrating his flying skills and his quick grasp of air cavalry combat tactics, Wes made aircraft commander in two months, became senior lead pilot of the Longknife platoon after six months, and was selected to attend the UH-1 Instructor Pilot Course at Vung Tau, South Vietnam. During his Vietnam tour, he was the recipient of the Bronze Star and seventeen Air Medals.

After Vietnam, Wes attended the Aviation Accident Prevention Course en route to Germany, where he flew with D Troop, 3-7th Cavalry as an instrument instructor pilot. Next, after attending Rotary Wing Instrument Flight Examiner Course, he served at Fort Lewis, Washington, as an instructor and instrument flight examiner. While there, Wes had the unique opportunity to fly fifteen hours (U-21 and UH-1H) with his father, a chief warrant officer four whose unit was temporarily assigned to Fort Lewis.

Departing the Army in 1978, Wes worked as a contract flight instructor at Fort Rucker, Alabama, and joined the Alabama Army National Guard. In 1982, he received a full-time civil service (GS) position flying medevac for the 1133rd Medical Company in the UH-IV Huey and later with the 20th Special Forces, flying the C-7 Caribou cargo plane. In 1988, Wes converted to full-time ARNG flying C-12 (Beechcraft) twin-engine turboprop aircraft for HQ STARC (State Area Command). He volunteered for Operation Desert Storm and flew C-23B Sherpa transport aircraft out of Abu Dhabi. In his last position, Wes served as state aviation safety officer and UH-60 Blackhawk pilot/examiner.

While flying for the U.S. Army and Army National Guard, Bartley became qualified on twelve rotary-wing and seven fixed-wing aircraft. After serving twenty-three years and attaining the rank of chief warrant officer five, Wes retired from the military in 2001.

Wes Bartley with UH-60 Blackhawk
Photo courtesy of Wes Bartley

In his second career, Bartley flew the McDonnell Douglas DC-10 and MD-11 heavy jet aircraft internationally for eight years, logging over three thousand flight hours and qualifying as captain in the DC-10. Then he worked for the FAA Flight

Standards Office as aviation safety inspector. His final retirement came in 2014 with his flight logbook showing over 17,000 flight hours, six thousand hours as an instructor, and flying over fifty different aircraft.

Wes and his wife have four children and eleven grandchildren. Two of Wes's children are graduates of the Air Force Academy, and the other two received full scholarships to Auburn and Troy Universities. When asked about his fascinating life, Wes proudly stated, "Needless to say, my children (and now my eleven grandchildren) constitute the greatest contribution I have made to this world!"

Wes Bartley in DC-10 named for his wife
Photo courtesy of Wes Bartley

CHAPTER 8

FIREFLY MEDEVAC

NIGHTTIME SECURITY IS CRITICAL AT U.S. military facilities in Vietnam. This is especially so at Vinh Long since the Viet Cong overran the Army airfield during the Tet Offensive of 1968, killing seven U.S. military personnel and destroying three UH-1 Huey helicopters. The Firefly mission, flown by Hueys or Cobra gunships, is designed to provide early detection of enemy threats during the night.

AIRFIELD SECURITY

The Vinh Long security system consists of a series of fortified bunkers positioned around the perimeter of the Vinh Long airfield facility. Placed at specific intervals, the bunkers provide overlapping fields of fire to fend off an enemy attack. Beyond the bunkers are three rows of concertina (razor) wire, laying in the often-muddy landscape of short grass.

For additional security, a flight-ready helicopter is positioned on the apron near the airfield runway. This mission, called Firefly, requires that the pilots and crewmembers spend the night in or near their helicopter. On call, this crew can launch their aircraft in a matter of seconds to respond to enemy threats.

And, to provide early warning against nighttime attacks, this crew flies two-hour security patrols at random intervals during the night. Flying at one thousand feet altitude, this aircraft circles the airfield, and occasionally descends to fly low-level around the airfield's perimeter. Using the aircraft's forward-focused landing light, they fly at fifty to seventy knots (fifty-seven to eighty mph) and fifteen to thirty feet altitude, searching for any evidence of enemy activity.

When the Longknife platoon is assigned Firefly duty, a cluster of huge searchlights is mounted inside the left-side cargo door of a Huey. Operated by the crew chief, this massive light cluster can be either tightly focused or widened to illuminate a vast area of the perimeter.

NIGHTTIME KILL

On most flights, we never see anything suspicious, and our low-level circling of the airfield perimeter is routine and uneventful. But one night, while flying low-level, we have a startling surprise when the crew chief excitedly yells, "Left side, swing around." Thinking the crew chief has seen a Viet Cong infiltrator or something equally menacing, I make a left banking turn and return to the area we passed. There it is. The searchlights are illuminating the largest rat I have ever seen. It is so big, it looks like a small pig. The crew chief comes on the intercom and asks, "Permission to fire, sir?"

While flying a wide circle around the ominous creature, I call the airfield control tower to advise them that we are about to do a test fire. Then, using the aircraft intercom, I say, "Open fire." The crew chief fires a long burst with his M-60 machine gun, annihilating the rat. Glancing back, I see the crew chief giving the "thumbs up" signal as I level out to continue our perimeter patrol. Cruising along at seventy knots (eighty mph) and twenty feet altitude, we laugh about the monster rat and congratulate our crew chief for getting a kill: a VC rat.

Most pilots look for opportunities to let their crew chiefs and door gunners test fire their weapons. Breaking the monotony of long missions, it is good for morale and reinforces training, and the pilots enjoy it as well. On one particular Firefly mission, we executed a test fire while flying low-level down the Mekong River. This photo, taken during that mission, captures the muzzle blast, rounds ejecting, and bullets hitting the water. Yes, that was fun for the entire crew.

**Door Gunner test fire while flying low-level over
Mekong River**

THE TEXAN

In December 1971, I am flying copilot on a Firefly mission with Chief Warrant Officer 2 Tom Tolar. With jet black hair and bushy mustache, Tom Tolar is a larger-than-life Texan, not only in appearance but in personality. His downhome Texas drawl and rib-splitting funny stories are endearing.

I enjoy spending time with Tom and, of all the Lighthorse pilots to be paired with, he is my favorite. I say this because I recognize that underneath Tom's lighthearted demeanor is a dead serious helicopter pilot. When faced with a precarious or treacherous situation, one of the best pilots to fly with is Tom Tolar. His flying skills and determination to get the job done are beyond reproach. He has the unique ability to evaluate the situation promptly and to react as necessary to get his helicopter, crew, and passengers to safety. This story is about a particular night when Tom's flying skills "save the day."

MEDEVAC

On this night, Tolar and I are scheduled to fly Huey 217. Our aircraft is parked next to the runway, ready to launch at a moment's notice. With rain in the forecast, we decide not to mount the heavy searchlight cluster and instead use our landing light for patrolling.

As we take shelter inside our Huey, heavy rain persists through the evening hours, and low visibility has denied us the opportunity to fly a perimeter patrol.

Around midnight, we receive a radio call from MACV headquarters requesting an emergency medevac of an Army lieutenant experiencing an appendicitis attack. With a sense of urgency, Tom and I climb into Huey 217, fire up the turbine engine, and head for the MACV outpost, about twenty-nine klicks (eighteen miles) northeast of Vinh Long. Arriving about ten minutes later, the rain continues, yet we have decent visibility and can easily see the flashlights directing us to an open area outside the compound.

Wasting no time, Tom flies directly to the illuminated area and brings our Huey to a three-foot hover. Doing a left pedal turn to align our right-side cargo door with the outpost, Tom sets the aircraft on the ground and rolls the throttle to flight idle. Soon, two ARVN soldiers carry the ailing lieutenant to our helicopter and load him into the open cargo door. Experiencing considerable pain, the lieutenant needs immediate medical attention. Rolling the throttle on, Tom brings the rotors to operating rpm and lifts off, heading to the 3rd Surgical Hospital at Navy Binh Thuy, sixty-four klicks (forty miles) southwest. Placing a radio call to the hospital, Tom advises we are inbound with a patient.

IFR FLIGHT

On any other night, this trip would be an easy twenty-five-minute flight; however, the rain and overcast skies make the flight treacherous. Midway to our destination, we encounter heavy storm clouds, and the visibility is practically zero. Flying by instruments in IFR conditions, Tom calls Delta Center asking that they vector (provide course headings) us to the hospital helipad at Navy Binh Thuy, four miles upriver from their location at Can Tho.

Note: Army pilots receive instrument flight training and are "combat rated" for instrument flying, meaning they can fly under IFR (Instrument Flight Rules) conditions in combat or emergencies only.

While Tom flies the Huey and focuses his attention on the instruments, I scan outside the aircraft. Engulfed in clouds and heavy rain, it is pitch dark. With the landing light on, our windshield is illuminated in a bright gray color, unable to penetrate the dense clouds. Looking out my door window, I cannot see anything, up or down. And, the closer we get to our destination, the harder it rains.

Arriving in the vicinity of Binh Thuy, Delta Center advises that we are on course and three klicks (two miles) from the hospital helipad. Since Delta Center radar provides left and right course corrections only, but no vertical guidance, we have to rely on our altimeter. Fortunately for us, most places in the Mekong Delta are ten to fifteen feet above sea level, and the hospital helicopter pad is no different.

Tom begins his descent and slows to fifty knots (fifty-seven mph) while I continue to scan for any glimpse of land below us. Seconds later, Delta Center calls to announce they have lost radar contact with our aircraft, so we have to rely on their last course heading.

Descending through the dense rain clouds, it seems to take forever. I can see nothing but gray clouds to our front and either side of the aircraft. My eyes scan all sides, hoping to see any evidence of land or water. With each passing second, the crewmembers' tension and anxiety level increases. As we continue to descend, it is evident from our altimeter that we are either going to see something or hit something soon.

Suddenly, at fifty feet altitude, we break out of the clouds, and the hospital helipad is directly in front of us. Tom continues his descent and lands on the helipad. Immediately, the hospital doors swing open and two orderlies and an Army nurse appear with a wheeled stretcher to take the ailing lieutenant into the hospital.

With a sigh of relief and return to calmness, I scan the area and see a couple of large concrete pillars on the right side of the helipad and tall radio antennas beyond the hospital. It seems a miracle that Tom made his approach so precisely to miss all the obstacles on our flight path to the helipad. Reflecting on it later, I believe it was not a miracle but, instead, a very skillful pilot with God watching over his shoulder.

The heavy rain continues, so we shut down our aircraft and wait out the storm. An hour later, the weather clears, and we crank up our Huey. Lifting off, we fly back to Vinh Long to continue our Firefly mission.

Vietnam Veteran Profile: Tom Tolar

Tom Tolar developed a love for aviation at an early age while working at the local airport pumping aviation fuel. He used his earnings to pay for flying lessons and obtained his private pilot's license at the age of sixteen. While soaring in a Piper Cub over the north Texas countryside, Tom's delight in flying only increased.

After completing two years of college with the goal of becoming a Navy pilot upon graduation, Tom learned of the Army Warrant Officer Flight Program. He enlisted with a commitment for flight school and the recruiter's promise that he would become a fixed-wing pilot. When the fixed-wing training didn't happen, Tom was initially disappointed, but after learning to fly helicopters, he was hooked. Like most of his warrant officer classmates, Tom received orders for Vietnam immediately after graduation from Army Flight School.

Assigned to Lighthorse Air Cavalry, Tom honed his flying skills and soon became one of the most talented Longknife slick pilots. While flying for Lighthorse, Tom accumulated over 1,100 hours flight time and was the recipient of the Air Medal[10] and Bronze Star medal with V device. When asked about his most significant mission, Tom said, "Operation 'Bright Light' has to top the list since every pilot was handpicked for that mission."

Tom Tolar – armed and ready for action

---

[10] Tom Tolar flew 828 combat and 216 combat support flight hours and should have received thirty-seven Air Medals. In Tom's case, his Air Medal orders were submitted by the troop, but his personnel records (DD-214) show a single Air Medal. This was common in the late phase of the war, as the Air Medal numbers were either missing or inaccurate in the soldier's personnel records. Every Vietnam Veteran profiled in this book earned multiple Air Medals. A notation of a single medal is indicative that the true number is unknown.

After his Vietnam tour, Tom was offered and accepted an early-out program, satisfying his military commitment. He then went to work for a national rail transportation company operating primarily in Texas. After working forty years as a railroad engineer, Tom retired in 2012.

With a love for aviation, Tom flew fixed-wing aircraft in his off time and, on occasion, flew for several corporations. Rated in single-engine aircraft, he flew a variety of airplanes. As Tom says, "Flying is a piece of cake when you are not getting shot at!"

Tom and his wife have two children and four grandchildren, all boys. When asked what he is most proud of, Tom says, "My family, especially our four grandsons." And, after experiencing a nearly fatal heart attack in 2015, Tom said, "I have the heartfelt belief that God has a reason for letting me live. I love being able to serve as a deacon in my church and hope to glorify God with my life for all the days I have left on this Earth."

Rex Gooch

CHAPTER 9

WAR WAGON NEWBIE

IN THE EARLY MORNING HOURS of May 24, 1971, Warrant Officer Keith Harris, otherwise known as War Wagon 15, is pre-flighting his OH-6 observation helicopter in preparation to fly lead scout on today's mission, a visual reconnaissance (VR) mission staging out of Chi Lang.

> Visual Reconnaissance Mission: A team of two scout helicopters seeking the enemy at ground level while covered from above by two Cobra gunships. In this mode of operation, the two scouts fly low and slow, nosing into every nook and cranny as they pursue the elusive Viet Cong and NVA. Upon discovering evidence of enemy activity, the lead scout searches for footprints, clothing, equipment, food, or weapons in an attempt to estimate the enemy's numbers and resources. Meanwhile, the trail scout keeps a cautious lookout while covering and protecting the right flank of his partner.
>
> Should they encounter the enemy, both scouts engage their adversaries in a face-to-face shootout. If the enemy

combatants have the scouts outnumbered or they start receiving heavy enemy fire, the lead gunner drops a smoke grenade and the Loaches rapidly exit, calling on the Crusader gunships to dive from above, firing rockets and mini-guns.

Oftentimes, the VR mission will shift to "search and destroy mode" when the scouts discover fresh evidence of enemy activity.

After completing the pre-flight inspection, Keith checks with his gunner who says he needs to return to the ammo Connex container to get additional smoke grenades. While Keith is waiting his mind drifts back to January. A lot has happened in the past five months.

KEITH'S TRAINING—MID-JANUARY 1971

Having recently arrived in Vietnam and assigned to Lighthorse, Warrant Officer Keith Harris is a Newbie, trying his best to fit in and learn as much as possible, as quickly as possible. He knows that his life depends on his combat knowledge and flight skills when flying the OH-6 scout helicopter in enemy territory.

Today, Keith is flying one of his first flights as pilot-in-command (PIC) in the War Wagon scout platoon. Accompanied by an experienced door gunner, Harris is flying in the trail position for War Wagon 17, Chief Warrant Officer 2 Ray Murphy. Ray is short, of average build, and has an outsized, outrageous sense of humor, often leaving his cohorts in stitches. But when Ray is flying, he is deadly serious. Keith finds it a little intimidating when Ray gives him one basic instruction for today's mission: "Stay at my five o'clock and keep your mouth shut." Harris takes that message to heart, and thinks, *I am absolutely going to stay in the five o'clock position, no matter what.*

After flying a couple of uneventful morning missions, Harris is feeling confident. He has consistently maintained his five o'clock position and has kept his radio calls to a minimum. Now, in the third, and last, mission for the day, the two scouts are, once again, flying in an area of rice paddies that appears to have no enemy activity.

Flying low and fast, the two Loaches pop up and over a row of trees perpendicular to their flight path. On the other side, Ray returns to low-level flight to start his search in a large, open field. In keeping with procedure, Ray slows to twenty knots and enters a wide left-hand turn. Mimicking every move of the lead Loach, Harris follows in the five o'clock position while maintaining a distance of about thirty to forty feet from Murphy's aircraft.

Traveling across the rice paddy, Ray starts turning tighter and tighter. Keith speeds up to stay in position. This continues, and Keith is puzzled by what is happening.

Suddenly, Ray comes to an abrupt halt, hovering motionless over the rice field.

Unable to stop, Keith passes by on the right side and eventually comes to a hover immediately in front of Ray. The two pilots are facing each other, eyeball to eyeball, and Ray has an unmistakable scowl on this face. Keith thinks, *Oh crap, I've really screwed up.*

Abruptly kicking in left pedal, Ray does a sharp left turn and departs while Keith scrambles to return to the five o'clock position off Murphy's right side.

Upon arrival at the staging area, the two Loaches refuel and reposition to set down about thirty meters apart. Harris shuts down his turbine engine, and, with the rotor blades still turning, he looks up to see Murphy walking at a quick pace toward his aircraft. In his right hand, Ray is carrying the twelve-inch broomstick that his gunner keeps onboard in case he has to fly the aircraft. Keith thinks to himself, *Maybe I should keep my helmet on.*

> Note: To accommodate the door gunner sitting in the left seat of the Loach, maintenance removes the cyclic control tube, leaving an open socket below the gunner's seat cushion. This allows the gunner to sit sideways in his seat and swing his machine gun in all directions without hitting the controls. Door gunners carry a twelve-inch piece of mop handle or broomstick that inserts into the open cyclic socket, serving as a "temporary cyclic stick," that allows them to fly from the left seat. War Wagon pilots teach their gunners to fly in case the pilot becomes incapacitated or in those instances when the pilot needs a break.

Approaching the right side, Murphy stops at Keith's door and shouts, "Newbie, I told you to stay at my five o'clock," while repeatedly beating the top of Keith's helmet with the broomstick. Then, Ray leaves as quickly as he arrived, saying nothing more.

Stunned by what has happened, Keith sits there thinking, *Man, this is going to be a long year if this is the way it's going to be.* Trying to make sense of it, Keith concludes that this was just a training experience. *Murphy must have done that to impress upon me the importance of staying in my position.*

Neither Keith nor Ray mentions the incident again, and the next time they fly together all is good. And, that next time comes several days later.

FIRST CRASH

On this day, Harris is once again flying trail for War Wagon 17, Ray Murphy, on a visual reconnaissance mission in the U Minh Forest.

Arriving in the operations area, the two scouts descend rapidly to fly low-level, five feet above the ground, and ten to twenty knots airspeed. Keith maintains the five o'clock position on Murphy's right side as they proceed across an open field with a forested area about one hundred meters off their left side.

After traveling no more than a quarter mile, Keith hears a loud metal grinding noise coming from behind the cockpit. Glancing to his left, Harris has a puzzled look on his face. Realizing this is serious, the gunner says, "We're going down." Keith instantly pulls the commo trigger on the cyclic control, and calls on the troop radio frequency, "I'm going down."

While maintaining the aircraft as level as possible, Harris lowers the collective, taking the pitch out of the rotor blades. The Loach continues traveling forward, slowing to about ten knots before the skids hit the ground and start sliding across the dry field.

Keith vividly recalls what happens next. "I can still see it in my mind as if it occurred in slow motion. We are sliding forward, and suddenly the Loach flips to the left front, and the rotor blades start beating into the ground for what seems like forever. Inside the cockpit, violent vibrations are tearing the aircraft apart and we are being tossed from side to side. Then, the shaking stops, and it is dead quiet." The aircraft fuselage comes to rest on its left side with the gunner low, next to the ground, and Harris still strapped in his seat on the high side.

When Ray hears Keith's "going down" radio call, he repositions alongside Harris's aircraft and follows until he sees the helicopter hit the ground and roll on its side. Then Ray circles to the right and lands his Loach about twenty-five feet from the crash about the same time the ground-thrashing rotor blades come to a halt. Murphy's gunner jumps out, runs to the crash, looks inside, and sees Keith and his gunner still strapped in their seats.

The gunner, not knowing what to do, turns to Murphy and shrugs his shoulders. Ray thinks, *What is going on? Those guys must be dead.* He frictions down his aircraft controls, jumps out of the Loach, and runs to the crash site. When he reaches the upended airframe, he hears talking inside and climbs up to the pilot's door.

Inside the cockpit, Harris hears the noise of someone climbing upon the airframe and looks upward out the door. There in the door frame is Ray Murphy looking down at him.

Ray asks, "Are you guys OK?"

Keith turns his head to look at his gunner and asks, "Are you OK?"

The gunner answers, "Yeah."

Keith turns back to Ray and says, "We're OK."

Ray says, "Well, get the hell out of there. There are VC all over this place."

Both Keith and the door gunner unbuckle their safety harness and climb out of the mangled airframe. The gunner climbs into the back of Ray's Loach and Keith runs to the C&C Huey that landed nearby minutes earlier. The two aircraft depart the area and return to the staging area. Neither Keith nor his gunner suffers any injuries from the crash.

BLOW IT IN PLACE

Later, a Huey arrives to sling load the crashed Loach back to Vinh Long airfield. One of the crew members performing the hook-up later reports seeing several bullet holes in the engine compartment cowling. And, they discover what caused the Loach to roll onto its left side; a pipe, sticking out of the ground, snagged the left-side skid and abruptly stopped the sliding aircraft, flipping it on its side.

Once the crashed Loach is rigged for sling load, the Huey carefully lifts the heavily damaged airframe into the air. As they slowly increase airspeed, they start taking heavy enemy fire and are forced to "punch off" the sling-loaded Loach. The aircraft wreckage smashes into the middle of an open field, rolling several times before coming to a rest.

The "lost Loach" is reported up the chain of command, and the directive comes back to "blow" the Loach in place. All four Crusader Cobras immediately launch as the pilots want to be the first to "take out" a Loach. After destroying the aircraft, the Cobras return to Vinh Long.

That evening in the officers' club, the Cobra pilots laugh and joke about their in-air argument over who would get the first shot at the Loach.

SHOT DOWN AGAIN

The following week, Keith Harris is flying trail for War Wagon 18, Chief Warrant Officer 2 George Schmitz. They are flying a VR mission in an enemy-occupied area of the U Minh Forest where firefights have raged for several days.

Flying in this region of the U Minh Forest is extremely dangerous. In the morning's mission briefing they are told that on the previous day, another Air Cavalry troop working this area lost a Loach crew while attempting to drop a homemade bomb on an enemy .51-caliber anti-aircraft gun position. The OH-6 exploded in midair, killing all aboard.

Upon arriving in the AO, the two War Wagon scouts drop to low-level flight to parallel a tree line about forty meters off their right side. The tree line is known to have two units of ARVN soldiers engaged in skirmishes with the Viet Cong. While traveling about twenty knots airspeed, the two Loaches observe a group of ARVN soldiers in the trees, pass by them, and proceed toward a second group at the end of the forested area where the tree line veers right.

Suddenly, Keith hears *pop-pop-pop-pop-pop* and feels the impact of bullets hitting his aircraft. Looking right, he sees a VC soldier standing in the doorway of a camouflaged hooch in the tree line, aiming an AK-47 directly at him. The VC has a good bead on the slow-moving Loach. His spray of bullets hits the fuel cell under the floor and progresses up the backside of Harris's seat.

Harris calls on the radio, "Taking hits! Taking hits!" as he feels bullets thudding against the armor plating on the backside of his pilot's seat. There is nothing he can do but keep flying to get out of that area.

As the two Loaches approach the end of the tree line, George repositions his aircraft alongside Keith's and says, "You have fuel spewing from your aircraft. Land it—NOW, or the fuel will get sucked into your engine and start a fire." Both pilots know this is a serious danger since they recently refueled at the staging area, and Harris's fuel tank is nearly full.

Keith promptly sets the Loach down in the open field between the ARVNs on the right side and the Viet Cong across the open area on the left side. George lands his aircraft slightly ahead of Keith's Loach, and they immediately start taking hostile fire from across the field. Both door gunners return fire with a constant barrage from their M-60 machine guns.

"WE'RE OUTTA HERE!"

Realizing that George's Loach is heavily loaded and cannot handle the extra weight of Keith and his gunner, Keith begins removing George's mini-gun and ammo box.

In the meantime, Keith's door gunner positions himself between Keith and the VC across the field. With his back to George's Loach, the gunner fires repetitive bursts, covering Harris, who is feverishly working to unload George's aircraft. After dropping the mini-gun in the dirt alongside the skids, Keith turns his attention to the large ammo box behind the pilot's seats.

While Keith is unlatching the ammo box, George looks to the right and sees a U.S. soldier low-crawling toward their aircraft. Making his way to George's door, the MACV advisor stands and frantically yells at Schmitz, "Are you guys nuts?! You have been taking .51-caliber anti-aircraft fire from the moment you dropped out of the sky. They will be waiting for you when you leave." Evidently, the wind was carrying the sound away from the two scouts because they heard nothing. George replies saying, "Thanks, we're outta here—headed the other direction!"

Once Keith drops the ammo box to the ground, he taps his gunner on the shoulder and climbs into the rear compartment of the Loach. Continuing to fire his M-60, the gunner walks backward toward the aircraft. When he nears the door, Keith reaches out to grab hold of the gunner's shirt and pulls him into the Loach.

Keith yells at George, "We're in," and Schmitz pulls in power and pushes forward cyclic to quickly take off, climbing up and away from the hostile fire. Soon they are at a safe altitude and return to the staging area.

Later that afternoon, after several Cobra gun strikes on the enemy positions, a Longknife Huey lands next to the disabled

Loach and retrieves the two mini-guns, ammo, and the aircraft radios. The following day, a Huey sling loads the damaged OH-6 back to Vinh Long for repair. While working on the damage, the maintenance crew finds three smashed bullets inside the aircraft and presents them to Keith as a war trophy.

Newbie Keith Harris gains quite a reputation, having been shot down twice in his first two weeks of flying with the War Wagon scout platoon. In the following weeks, he continues flying trail, gaining valuable combat flying experience. Eventually, Harris is designated as a War Wagon lead pilot.

RETURN TO TODAY—MAY 24, 1971

Keith's attention returns to the present as his gunner arrives with an assortment of colored smoke grenades that he hangs from a wire running inside the aircraft's windshield bubble. Climbing into the right side of the Loach, Harris dons his helmet and connects the commo cord while the gunner unties the rotor blades and enters the left side of the cockpit.

In a matter of minutes, Keith has the turbine engine running and the rotors spinning "in the green" at operating rpm. After lifting to a three-foot hover, he moves to the runway apron where he joins his wingman for the flight to Chi Lang.

Little does Keith know that he is about to embark on a mission that will have dire consequences for his wingman when the two scouts descend into a large component of NVA soldiers. This story continues in the next chapter as told from the unique perspective of the wingman's gunner, Specialist Four Gary Larrow.

Vietnam Veteran Profile: Keith Harris

Growing up in Maryland, Keith Harris admired and respected his two uncles who served as sergeants in World War

II. This influenced Keith's decision, at the age of nineteen, to enlist in the Army and serve as an Infantry soldier. On his way to the Army recruiter's office, he met a friend who had served in the Army who asked Keith if he had considered becoming a warrant officer and flying helicopters. Keith replied that he had never heard of a warrant officer and had never been in an airplane, let alone a helicopter; but he immediately concluded that it sounded much better than being in the Infantry.

Accompanied by his friend, Keith went to the recruiter's office and expressed his desire to become an Army helicopter pilot. The next day he was on his way to Fort Holabird, Maryland, to take an aviation aptitude test and a physical. Passing both, Keith enlisted in the Army Warrant Officer Flight Program.

After graduation from flight school, Keith received an OH-6A (Loach) transition course before reporting to Southeast Asia. Arriving in Vietnam in December 1970, he was assigned to Lighthorse Air Cavalry at Vinh Long. Several months later, he completed the OH-6 instructor course at Vung Tau and became the troop's Loach instructor pilot and War Wagon lead scout.

After flying 965 combat hours in Vietnam, Keith Harris returned stateside and joined the Maryland Army National Guard, serving in various aviation assignments to include instructor pilot, safety officer, electronic warfare officer, and maintenance test pilot flying the OH-6, OH-58, UH-1, AH-1G, and UH-60 helicopters.

During his military career, he was the recipient of twenty-nine Air Medals (one with V device), Bronze Star, Meritorious Service Medal, Legion of Merit, and State of Maryland Distinguished Service Cross.

Retiring in 2010 after thirty-six years of military service, Keith attained the rank of chief warrant officer five, and his last position was command chief warrant officer for the Maryland

Army National Guard. In 2018, Keith was inducted in the Maryland Army National Guard Warrant Officer Hall of Fame.

When asked what he is most proud of Keith replied, "I loved flying helicopters and believed the warrant officer rank to be the best rank in the Army. I flew helicopters in forty-six of the fifty states—what a beautiful country! God bless America."

Keith and his wife have a combined family of three children and six grandsons.

Keith Harris's last flight in a UH-60 Blackhawk - 2006
Photo courtesy of Keith Harris

Vietnam Veteran Profile: Ray Murphy

While serving in the Special Forces at Fort Bragg, North Carolina, Ray Murphy was participating in a multiday winter survival exercise in the swamps. Cold and shivering, with ice forming on his fatigues, Ray looked up to see a helicopter flying overhead. He thought to himself, *I bet the pilots are warm.* When he returned to his company area, he immediately volunteered for the Army Warrant Officer Flight Program.

Like Keith Harris, Ray received an OH-6A (Loach) transition course after graduation from flight school. He then reported to Vietnam and was assigned to Lighthorse Air Cavalry, where he became one of the War Wagon's most respected scout pilots.

Upon his departure from Vietnam, Ray Murphy was assigned to D Troop, 2nd Squadron, 4th Cavalry Regiment, 1st Armored Division in Germany. Departing the Army in 1972, Murphy served five years and was the recipient of the Air Medal with V device and two Bronze Star Medals.

After graduating from the University of North Carolina with a degree in Economics, Ray worked fifteen years with a computer software company specializing in developing optimal network strategies for major petroleum companies worldwide.

Later, Ray became an economics professor at Northeastern State University in Tulsa, Oklahoma. In 2019, he retired after teaching seventeen years.

Forever a motorcycle enthusiast, Ray took great pride in building motorcycles and owned a motorcycle dealership.

Ray and his wife have two daughters and five grandchildren

When asked about his greatest achievement, Ray jokingly says, "Everyone still likes me."

Vietnam Veteran Profile: George Schmitz

After Vietnam, George Schmitz was assigned to D Troop, 2-4th Cavalry, which was later re-designated to D Troop, 1-1st Cavalry in Katterbach, Germany. He returned to the United States in 1978 and served with the 210th Air Cavalry at Fort Ord, California. After receiving his degree in Professional Aeronautics and an associate degree in Aircraft Maintenance from Embry Riddle, George returned to Germany and served with the 8th Combat Aviation Battalion at Mainz-Finthen Army Airfield. In 1984 he was assigned to Fort Eustis, Virginia, where he served as the OH-58 maintenance test pilot track chief.

Schmitz retired from the Army in 1988 after serving twenty years and was the recipient of the Silver Star Medal, Distinguished Flying Cross with oak leaf cluster, Bronze Star Medal with two oak leaf clusters, and fifty-four Air Medals, two with "V" device.

After the Army, George worked the next twenty-six years as a field manager on the civilian helicopter maintenance contract at Fort Rucker, Alabama.

In 2006, George was one of the founding members of the Friends of Army Aviation, Ozark. This nonprofit organization located in Ozark, Alabama, is dedicated to presenting the Army Aviation story to the American people through static displays of legacy Army aircraft and a helicopter ride program with their airworthy UH-1H Huey (Lighthorse Huey 123). He serves as board member and director of maintenance, rotary wing.

When asked about his most memorable accomplishments, George said, "I have two, my participation in the Katterbach Test to develop an air-to-ground laser system for anti-armor helicopters that led to the TOW Cobra and future attack helicopters and, more recently, the last twenty years volunteering my time to restore Vietnam era aircraft."

George and his wife have a son who is an Army Aviator and a UH-60M (Blackhawk) maintenance test pilot and a granddaughter.

**George Schmitz and Author with FOAA-Ozark
Lighthorse Huey 123**

CHAPTER 10

WAR WAGON GUNNER

THE WAR WAGON GUNNERS PERFORM a crucial role for Lighthorse Air Cavalry. They are the eyes on the ground, searching for telltale signs of enemy activity whether it be footprints, trails, bent grass, campfire remains, clothing, bunkers, or anything suggesting the enemy's presence. Simply put, the gunner's job, working in close coordination with his pilot, is to seek out and find the enemy—often by attracting enemy fire.

True to their "Bastard Cav" image, the War Wagon scouts' tactics differ from scouts in most other Cavalry units. Instead of positioning the gunner in the rear seat or having two door gunners, the War Wagons put the single gunner in the front left-side seat, next to the pilot. Hence, they design their maneuvers around left-hand turns, giving the gunner maximum visibility and field of fire. It is the pilot's responsibility to maneuver the aircraft into the optimal tactical position to enable the gunner to have maximum visibility while looking for signs of the enemy and, if necessary, to defend the aircraft against hostile forces.

Over time, this relationship of working together and depending upon each other develops into a tight bond. This partnership is so close that they often anticipate each other's actions and react without speaking. The level of trust between the two troopers is exceptionally high, and, as one gunner said, "We were closer than brothers."

The gunner's role as a scout, seeking the enemy, quickly shifts to a counter-attack role when fired upon by hostile forces. Hanging out the left-side door, firing the M-60 machine gun, the gunner defends the aircraft while the pilot maneuvers out of harm's way, allowing the heavily armed Cobra gunships to dive from above, attacking the enemy combatants. In other situations, when the scout team surprises the enemy, the gunner becomes the aggressor, initiating the attack, striking the first blow before the pilot moves the aircraft out of the way as the gunships strafe from above.

The gunners confront every day knowing they are likely to be targeted, possibly shot, wounded, or seriously injured. They accept that danger with steadfast determination, confident that when face-to-face with the enemy in combat, they will fight to win.

The following story is told by a War Wagon gunner, Specialist Four Gary Larrow. On this day, he is flying with Warrant Officer Frank Jones (assumed name; the pilot is deceased, and his family requested his name be withheld).

TAKE OFF

On May 24, 1971, Gary Larrow is awakened from a deep sleep by his good friend, Sonny Palazzo, saying, "Hey, buddy, it's time to go. Get up and get moving; you're gonna be late." Gary rolls out of bed, looks around his room in the crew hooch, and thinks to himself, *This early morning stuff sucks.* He purposely slept in, choosing to skip breakfast and get a little more shuteye before today's flight. Now, he needs to hustle because it's time to be on the flight line.

After quickly dressing in his Nomex flight uniform, Larrow picks up his flight helmet and walks outside. Sonny, who is one of the troop armorers, is waiting in a Jeep and says, "Hop in—I will give you a ride." Gary climbs into the right seat, and Sonny speeds off to the airfield.

Arriving at the flight line, Sonny drives between two rows of Lighthorse aircraft parked on the asphalt apron near the runway. Passing by several War Wagon revetments, Sonny stops in front of Gary's Loach, tail number 289, where Larrow jumps out and thanks Sonny for the ride.

Walking toward his aircraft, Gary pauses briefly to admire his Loach. The OH-6 is a fierce fighting machine with its menacing six-barrel mini-gun mounted low on its left side. Yet, the small aircraft appears diminutive and out of place when parked between the widely spaced, four-foot-high revetment walls designed to accommodate the larger Huey or Cobra helicopters.

Frank Jones, who is pre-flighting the scout helicopter, looks up to see Gary approaching and says, "Let's go get our guns." Together, Frank and Gary walk to the War Wagon Conex container to retrieve their weapons. After opening the large doors, Gary reaches for his M-60 machine gun, and Frank picks up their M-79 grenade launcher along with the "frag bag" (grenade bag) loaded with smoke grenades and M-79 ammo. Then, they return to the Loach where Frank continues his pre-flight inspection. At the same time, Gary connects his M-60 machine gun to the end of a bungee cord attached to the top of the left-side door frame and places the frag bag on the floor in front of the gunner's seat.

Note: Most War Wagon gunners carry an assortment of grenades in their frag bag, a mix of fragmentation, CS (tear gas), incendiary, and smoke. And, some of the more creative gunners make homemade bombs by inserting a concussion grenade inside a cola can and filling the void with strips of C-4 plastic explosives. Unlike the other War Wagon scout teams, Jones and Larrow prefer to carry the M-79 grenade launcher instead of bombs because they feel it is more accurate when blowing bunkers and other structures. Their frag bag is heavily loaded with at least a dozen M-79 rounds of high explosive, CS, and buckshot. In addition to the frag bag, Gary carries a variety of colored smoke and CS hand grenades strung on a wire stretched along the inside of the windshield bubble, well below eye level, and within his immediate reach. It gives Larrow a variety of options when marking a target or blowing a structure.

Next, Gary checks the large mini-gun ammo bin in the rear compartment floor to be sure it is fully loaded with two thousand rounds of 7.62mm linked ammo, feeding into the mini-gun mounted on the left side of the Loach. He also makes sure that he has two smaller ammo cans holding a total of 1,500 rounds of linked ammo for his M-60 machine gun. This ammo is routed up and over Gary's seat back to feed his bungee-mounted gun.

When Frank's pre-flight inspection is complete, Gary unties the rotor blades, climbs into the left-side pilot's seat, puts on his helmet, and plugs in his commo cord. Frank, already in the right-side pilot's seat, calls out, "Clear." Gary looks left and calls out, "Clear." Then Frank depresses the starter button on the end of the collective, and the turbine engine starts whining as the rotor blades begin slowly turning.

In less than a minute, Jones has the engine and rotor blades spinning at operating rpm. He lifts the collective, bringing the Loach to a three-foot hover, and taxies forward, out of the revetment. Frank joins War Wagon 15, Warrant Officer Keith Harris, and the two Loaches hover to the runway. After calling the tower for clearance, they take off and are followed by two Crusader Cobras and the C&C Huey flying northwest to Chi Lang, the staging location for today's mission.

CHI LANG

After landing and refueling at Chi Lang, the Lighthorse Cav Pack of five helicopters shut down alongside the runway. The aircraft commanders gather together and walk to the MACV SOCC bunker for a mission briefing.

In the meantime, Gary and several crew members walk to the New Zealand Training Team mess hall. There, they eat a hearty, delicious breakfast, a vast improvement over the Cav mess hall at Vinh Long. The hot meals served in the New Zealand mess hall are not to be overlooked when staging out of Chi Lang.

In the mission briefing, the Lighthorse pilots are told that today's operation is a visual reconnaissance, seeking enemy forces in "The Tram," southeast of Chi Lang. This expansive area of flat and seasonally marshy land has, at times, proven to be a hot spot for enemy activity. This is confirmed when they learn that ARVN units have been in firefights with the NVA for the previous two days. At the close of the meeting, the AMC, Captain Dale Johnson, is provided grid coordinates for the area of operations.

BAD GUY, COUNTRY

Returning to their aircraft, the pilots and crew members start their helicopters and align next to the runway for takeoff. With the C&C Huey in the lead, the five aircraft take off to the southeast.

Lighthorse Cav Pac
Photo courtesy of Mike Galvin

Arriving at the operations area twenty minutes later, Johnson (AMC) calls War Wagon 15, Keith Harris, telling the scouts to check out the east side of a north/south tree line.

With Harris in the lead, the two scouts descend rapidly. Nearing the ground, Harris levels out at five feet above the ground and slows to twenty knots to begin their search in a northerly direction with the tree line on their left side.

Jones slides his Loach to the right, taking the five o'clock position off Harris's right flank. With his machine gun pointed out the door, Larrow scans out the left side of the aircraft, keeping a watchful eye on the tree line.

Within seconds, Harris flies directly over evidence of recent enemy activity: cooking pots, clothing, and the smoldering remains of extinguished campfires. Clearly, they have discovered a large enemy unit, and they must still be nearby.

Looking into the tree line, Gary sees an NVA soldier wearing a pith helmet and a dark blue shirt attempting to hide behind a tree. The left-handed soldier raises his AK-47, aiming at their moving helicopter. For a split second, Gary thinks, *This is odd. I have never seen a left-handed guy shooting at me.* But that thought is instantly replaced by instinct and training as Gary opens up, firing a long burst with his M-60 machine gun. Glancing to the left, Frank sees Gary's bullets hitting the tree and center mass on the soldier aiming at their Loach. Later, Frank recalls Gary's shot, and doesn't hesitate to say, "I was very impressed! You got that guy before he got us."

"I'M HIT"

At the moment Gary starts firing, all hell breaks loose with an onslaught of enemy fire coming from seemingly every direction. Leaning out the door, Larrow is shooting at enemy soldiers who suddenly appear out of nowhere as they emerge from their hiding places.

Harris, in the lead Loach, loudly calls, "Taking Fire," while simultaneously pushing the cyclic forward and increasing power to exit the area rapidly. Following Harris's lead, Jones attempts to do the same. But, before he can react on the aircraft controls, Frank sees Keith's Loach fly to the left of an NVA soldier lying in the grass holding an AK-47 across his chest. Shocked, he watches the enemy soldier swing his rifle to aim at his aircraft. Frank realizes that his gunner is about to be broadsided by the hidden soldier.

Pushing left pedal, Frank swings the aircraft's nose to the left in an attempt to fire the mini-gun, but he is too late. The NVA soldier shoots at point-blank range, the bullets ripping into the bottom of the Loach as it passes overhead.

The bullets explode the chin bubble, hitting the bottom of Frank's left foot and his right leg above the ankle. Frank yells on the radio, "I'm hit! I'm hit!"

In his peripheral vision, Gary sees Frank's left leg recoil upward toward his chest. Realizing his pilot is hit, Gary hurls his M-60 out the door and turns to take the controls. (Note: Gary always kept his short broomstick mounted in the cyclic socket for such an emergency.) With his right hand almost touching the cyclic broomstick, the M-60 comes rebounding back into the cockpit, smacking Larrow on the side of his helmet. Gary thinks, *Boy, I didn't see that coming.*

In those brief seconds, Frank is able to overcome the shock and pain of his injury and reaches left, tapping Gary's arm and telling him, "I've got it." Gary immediately turns back to grab his still free-swinging M-60 and continues covering the left side while Frank flies the Loach, wincing in extreme pain.

CRASH LANDING

After Frank's distress call, Keith reduces his airspeed to allow the trail helicopter to close the gap between them. Quickly evaluating their situation, he calls to Frank, saying, "Give the aircraft controls to your gunner and follow me." Taking the lead, Harris flies about a mile to an open area in tall grass and calls to Frank, saying, "Put it down here." Then Keith slows and moves to the side to watch the landing. Not knowing the seriousness of Frank's injuries or the condition of the aircraft, he is concerned about his wingman and stands ready to react.

Unknown to Keith, Frank never relinquishes the controls, instead continuing to fly while enduring severe pain from his badly wounded feet. Approaching the grassy area, Frank lowers the collective, and the aircraft comes down hard. Just before impact, Gary looks forward, seeing the fast-approaching ground, and thinks, *This is going to hurt.*

The Loach impacts the ground so hard that the skids spread and bury into the soil. The aircraft comes to an abrupt halt with the fuselage lurching forward, tail high. The rotor blades chop the tail boom in half and violently beat into the dirt in front of the nose-down airframe. The noise of the thrashing rotor blades and straining turbine engine is deafening.

Gary immediately unbuckles his safety harness, jumps out of his left-side door, and ducks low under the still-beating rotor blades to reach Frank's door. There, he finds Frank, who has unbuckled his safety harness, leaning out of the door, struggling to pull himself up and out of the cockpit that now sits low to the ground. Gary reaches down, putting his arms under Frank's, and pulls him from the crashed airframe and onto the ground.

Frank attempts to stand and immediately falls to his knees. Bending down, Gary grabs Frank's left arm and wraps it around his neck to lift him upward, transferring Frank's weight to Gary's right shoulder. With Larrow carrying most of Jones's weight, the two limp through the knee-high grass toward the waiting C&C Huey, which moments earlier landed near the crash site.

By this time, the turbine engine has quit running and two rotor blades are stuck in the dirt in front of the crashed airframe. Crusader Cobra gunships dive to fire rockets in the adjacent tree lines protecting the aircrews on the ground.

Dale Johnson, flying the C&C Huey, looks out to see Gary half-carrying Frank toward his helicopter and thinks, *What a classic image of the Air Cavalry, a gunner carrying his injured pilot to safety.*

MEDEVAC

Arriving at the door of the Huey, the crew chief helps Gary lift Frank and place him on the cargo bay floor. Gary climbs in, taking a seat near his wounded pilot. Frank, in a lot of pain, looks over at Gary and asks, "Are you OK?" Gary, who is moved by Frank's selflessness, replies, "Yeah, I'm fine, but I'm concerned about you."

Johnson lifts the collective to bring the Huey to a hover and takes off to the east. Once they are in the air, the Huey crew chief turns his attention to Frank, bandaging his left foot and right leg to stop the bleeding.

Johnson, whose aircraft is low on fuel, calls Lighthorse operations requesting another Huey to transport Frank and Gary to the hospital. Twenty minutes later, the two Hueys meet midway to Vinh Long and land at an ARVN outpost along the Mekong River. Frank and Gary are transferred to the other Huey, and they take off, flying to the 24th Evacuation Hospital at Long Binh, near Saigon.

Upon their arrival at the hospital, they are admitted for treatment and observation. Frank's left foot wound is bandaged, and his right leg is repaired and placed in a cast up to his knee. He returns to Lighthorse several days later and spends the next five weeks recuperating while walking with crutches. After that, he is cleared to fly and has a distinguished flying record with the War Wagons.

Gary has superficial cuts and lacerations. He is bandaged and returns to Vinh Long the following day to continue flying gunner for the War Wagon scouts.

The crashed Loach, tail number 68-17289, was retrieved by sling load and returned to Vinh Long. In the photo, Gary Larrow is inspecting the airframe as maintenance prepares the aircraft for salvage (doors have been installed). Note the chin bubble is blown out on both sides of the aircraft as well as the Plexiglass "greenhouse" on the roof where the bullets exited the top of the airframe. The tail boom is severed, and the pilot's left pedal is missing, removed by maintenance because of combat damage.

Gary Larrow and the crashed Loach
Photo courtesy of Gary Larrow

The wrecked airframe was shipped stateside and rebuilt at the Lexington Army Depot in Avon, Kentucky. It returned to Vietnam in August 1972 and was assigned to The Blue Ghosts, F Troop, 8th Cavalry, stationed at Da Nang in I Corps. On September 30, 1972, while flying trail scout on a VR mission near Chu Lia, the Loach received many hits from small arms fire and suffered an engine failure while exiting the area. With rotor rpm dropping, the pilot autorotated from three hundred feet AGL.

Nearing the ground, he flared nose-high to slow forward airspeed, and the tail hit a rice paddy dike, ripping the tail boom off. With a huge splash, the aircraft impacted in the water-soaked rice field and came to rest in an upright position. The pilot and gunner escaped with minor injuries and were rescued by the lead Loach. The crashed airframe could not be recovered because of heavy enemy activity in the area and was blown in place by Cobra gunships.

Vietnam Veteran Profile: Gary Larrow

After basic training, Gary completed the Airborne Training Course at Fort Benning, Georgia, earning the Parachutist's Badge. During his tour of duty in Vietnam, Larrow was the recipient of the Purple Heart and the Air Medal with V device. After serving three years on active duty, he joined the Connecticut National Guard. Following that, he was a member of the Rhode Island National Guard, proudly serving in an Air Cavalry troop for a combined eight years in the Guard.

In his civilian career, Gary drove tractor-trailer trucks for forty-seven years, primarily on the eastern coast of the United States and Canada. As a driver, he was a part of a major working group providing critical services contributing to our nation's strong economic growth. He is a third generation Teamster, which is the nation's largest and most diverse labor union.

When asked about his most memorable event, Gary says, "Without a doubt, it was my time serving with Lighthorse. Today, I look forward to attending the troop reunions, spending time with my Cavalry buddies, and reminiscing about our younger days when we felt we were fearless and invincible."

Gary has three children and three grandchildren.

CHAPTER 11

TAKING FIRE, OR NOT?

HELICOPTER PILOTS HAVE A REPUTATION for being mischievous practical jokers, taking advantage of every opportunity to lighten the mood or stir up trouble. This story is about one practical joke that plays out during a combat mission and backfires or, stated more precisely, fires back.

OUR MISSION

On January 20, 1972, three Longknife slicks, accompanied by Crusader gunships and War Wagon scouts, lift off from Vinh Long Army Airfield, flying southeast sixty-two klicks (thirty-nine miles) to an ARVN command post in the Tra Vinh Province. After arriving at the CP, they shut down their aircraft and await further instructions for today's mission.

Sometime later, the Lighthorse aircraft commanders are called together for a mission briefing with the commanding officer (CO). He discusses the details of a troop insertion in an area of rice paddies and then mentions that a *Life* magazine photographer will be accompanying the Longknife platoon to take photos of the mission. In closing, the CO says, "This area has reported enemy activity. You have suppression inbound."

The meeting concludes, and the aircraft commanders return to their helicopters.

> Note: The first troop insertion sortie (trip) is cleared for "suppression," which authorizes the door gunners to fire their M-60 machine guns on final approach to the LZ to keep the enemy at bay. And, diving from high above, two Cobra gunships alternate high-angle gun runs, firing rockets and 40mm grenades in the area adjacent to the inbound slicks. Subsequent sorties are without suppression fire since friendly forces are on the ground.

Assembling near the Hueys, the three Longknife aircraft commanders meet with the copilots, crew chiefs, and door gunners to inform them of the details of their mission. As the meeting comes to a close, the aircraft commander of the lead slick says, "Let's show this photographer what it's really like in the Cav. When we lift out of the LZ, I'll call 'taking fire,' and everyone will let rip with the door guns like we are being attacked." The pilots and crewmembers eagerly agree, anxious to have some fun with the *Life* photographer. The group breaks up and returns to their respective aircraft.

LIFT OFF

Today, I am flying copilot for Chief Warrant Officer 2 Robbie Young. Having flown together on several missions, I respect Robbie's flying skills and proficiency as an aircraft commander. Tall and slender with jet black hair, Robbie has a positive attitude and a delightful sense of humor. I enjoy the time spent flying with him.

Stepping on the toe of Huey 217's skid, I climb up and into the right seat. After buckling my safety harness, putting on my flight helmet, and connecting the commo cord, I turn my attention to the overhead console to initiate the engine start procedure. In the left seat, Robbie is tuning radio frequencies and preparing for takeoff. Outside, the crew chief and door gunner connect the communication cords to their helmets and take their respective positions on each side of the aircraft, with the crew chief monitoring the engine compartment during startup.

After toggling numerous switches and checking circuit breakers, I call out, "Clear." The crew chief and gunner both respond in unison, "Clear." Pulling the start trigger on the underside of the collective, the starter motor groans as the turbine engine starts to rotate. A familiar clicking sound is heard from the engine compartment when the fuel igniters begin sparking and lighting the JP4 jet fuel as it's sprayed into the combustion chamber. The engine surges to life and a thick cloud of black, sooty smoke emits from the large exhaust pipe of the Lycoming T-53 engine, and the air fills with the heavy smell of burning jet fuel. The Huey rocks from side to side as the rotor blades turn slowly at first, then faster and faster. After I release the start trigger at forty percent N_1 speed (first compressor fan in the turbine engine), the engine is running on its own.

After the exhaust temperature stabilizes, I twist the throttle all the way to full. Soon, the vibrations calm down to a smooth rhythm, and the rotors are spinning at operating rpm. It's time to fly.

After sliding the armor plating forward and closing the pilot's door, the crew chief turns and motions to a group of ARVN soldiers in the distance, waving them over to our Huey. Carrying their weapons and equipment, the soldiers approach and load into the open cargo doors on each side of the aircraft. Flying in Chalk 2 position, the *Life* photographer chooses to board our helicopter, presuming that it will be the best vantage point to photograph the lead Huey to our front and both sides of our aircraft. He positions himself behind the radio console between the pilot seats and sits on the floor of the cargo bay.

When all three Hueys are loaded, Longknife lead calls, "Chalk 1's Up." Then Robbie takes the aircraft controls and calls, "Chalk 2's Up," and that is followed by, "Chalk 3's Up."

> Because of the importance of the first insertion and the added complexity of suppression fire, the first sortie is typically flown by the aircraft commander, who then alternates with the copilot on subsequent sorties.

Chalk 1 calls on the troop radio frequency, "Longknife flight lifting off to the north." Coming to a three-foot hover, Chalk 1 does a pedal turn to the right and lifts off. Following in sequence, Chalk 2 and 3 do the same. Once at altitude, we assemble in loose trail formation, flying northeast toward the operations area.

TROOP INSERTION

When we get near the landing zone, Chalk 1 calls, "Flight, prepare for the approach." Robbie tightens our separation to within one rotor disk of the lead Huey. Holding this formation, we begin our descent to the LZ.

Flying copilot, I place my hands and feet lightly on the Huey's controls to be instantly ready to back up Robbie, whose eyes are intently focused on the lead aircraft. Robbie does the same backup for me when I am flying.

When the three slicks are about 150 meters from the LZ, Chalk 1 calls, "Flight go hot." At his command, our door gunners commence firing out both sides of the Huey: *Rat-tat-tat-tat-tat-tat-tat. Rat-tat-tat-tat-tat-tat-tat.* Diving from above, two Crusader Cobra gunships alternate firing high-explosive rockets into the rice paddies off the right flank of our flight path. Loud *kaboom, kaboom* explosions drown out the roar of the machine guns.

Coming to a hover above the water in the rice paddies, Robbie gives the command, "Cease fire! Cease fire!" The crew chief and door gunner immediately stop firing and the ARVN soldiers exit both side cargo doors, momentarily standing on the skids before jumping into the muddy rice paddy.

On the radio, I hear, "Chalk 1's up, Chalk 2's up (Robbie), Chalk 3's up." Then Chalk 1 calls: "Flight coming out to the north." Simultaneously, the three Hueys lift their tails, tilt forward, and take off, flying ten feet above the ground.

TAKING FIRE

Once we attain an airspeed of about fifty knots and an altitude of around twenty feet, Chalk 1 announces on the radio, "Taking fire! Taking fire!" Immediately the door gunners on all three Hueys start shooting their M-60 machine guns, acting out their roles in this staged performance. *Rat-tat-tat-tat-tat-tat-tat. Rat-tat-tat-tat-tat-tat-tat.* I steal a glance to my left and see the photographer in a kneeling posture snapping pictures as fast as he can advance the film in his camera.

This scenario plays out for several seconds. Then, suddenly, and unexpectedly, we hear Chalk 1 frantically yell into his radio, "No sh*t, we are *really taking fire, taking fire,* TAKING HITS! Damn it!" Our contrived performance instantaneously changes to a serious and intense response. Upping the intensity of their firing, our door gunners spray the area with hot lead, hoping to hit the unseen adversary below.

Upon attaining eighty knots airspeed, Chalk 1 pulls back on his cyclic control to climb and, following his lead, all three helicopters quickly lift up and away from the danger. It all happens so quickly that we are past the peril before we can effectively locate and engage the enemy.

Concealed and lying in wait beyond the end of the landing zone, the Viet Cong patiently held their fire until the three slicks were low and slow-moving targets exiting the LZ. The lead Huey took several hits in the tail boom but suffered no serious damage.

Climbing to altitude, the pilots and crew on all three Hueys are laughing hysterically—fueled by the adrenaline from taking fire and the absurdity of the failed prank. Even with the laughter, I doubt the photographer realized what happened. Surely, he was able to take some dramatic combat photos, but we never saw them, nor did we hear of a *Life* magazine story about our "performance" that day. Our "five minutes of fame" was short-lived, and our practical joke on the photographer turned out to be a joke on us.

My adventures while flying with Robbie continue in the next chapter.

CHAPTER 12

STINKING, SINKING HUEY

ON JANUARY 22, 1972, I am flying copilot for Robbie Young, and it has been a busy morning. While staging our operation out of the airstrip at Ca Mau, our flight of three Longknife Hueys has already made four insertions of ARVN soldiers into an LZ in the U Minh Forest. After the last insertion, our three slicks return to the Ca Mau airstrip to refuel. Then, we lift off, flying to an ARVN command post where we will shut down and remain "on standby," awaiting orders to retrieve the South Vietnamese soldiers or perform other duties as necessary.

BODY BAGS

During the flight to the ARVN command post, Longknife Lead receives a radio call from the air mission commander requesting a helicopter to pick up and transport two deceased ARVN soldiers. Robbie offers to take the mission. Lead confirms, and we bank to the right, away from the formation.

Using a tactical map and grid coordinates, I navigate while Robbie flies our aircraft to the location where another ARVN infantry unit is actively engaged in battle with the Viet Cong. Once we are near the area, I call the ground commander and ask that they "pop a smoke" to mark their location. Seconds later, we see the smoke rising upward from a rice paddy in the distance. I call to identify yellow smoke, and the ARVN commander confirms the color.

To avoid enemy small arms fire, Robbie makes a rapid descent to fly low-level, ten feet above the ground and eighty knots (ninety-two mph) airspeed. Closing on the smoke, he flares the Huey nose high and settles to a hover above the rice paddy. Soon, several ARVN soldiers, carrying two black plastic body bags, slog through ankle-deep, muddy water and load the long black bags into the left-side cargo door.

When the soldiers have moved to a safe distance away from our Huey, Robbie does a 180-degree pedal turn to the right and exits, tail high, flying low above the flooded rice paddies. Flying at ten to fifteen feet above the ground, he steadily increases airspeed until attaining eighty knots. Then, he pulls back on the cyclic control and does a "cyclic climb." At eighty knots, the Huey screams rapidly upward. *What a great maneuver!* I think to myself. After attaining one thousand feet altitude, Robbie pushes the cyclic forward to resume normal flight and passes the aircraft controls to me. Then, he turns his attention to the radio console, dialing a frequency to make a call.

About that time, our crew chief comes on the intercom announcing, "Boy, do these guys stink!" He is right; the smell is terrible. I have never smelled anything so offensive. It is evident that the bodies inside the plastic bags have been baking in the hot Vietnam sun. To minimize the odor, I fly out of trim (pushing right pedal) to keep the air flowing through the Huey's cargo doors.

Robbie calls the air mission commander to inquire about our destination. We are told to return to the ARVN command post and shut down to await further instructions. This delay, and indecision, about our destination is highly unusual. We assume the bodies in the bags are not the average South Vietnamese soldier, but of individuals entitled to special handling. I make a slight turn to the right and take a compass heading to the CP.

YIKES! MY SKIDS ARE MISSING

As we near the ARVN command post, I see the Lighthorse aircraft parked in a row. Not wasting any time, I lower the collective control to descend and make my approach directly to an open area on the right side of the Hueys. As soon as the skids touch down, Robbie says, "Lieutenant, shut down the aircraft; I am getting out of this stinking machine." He immediately bolts out of the helicopter with the crew chief and door gunner right on his heels. Rolling off the throttle, I rapidly begin the Huey shutdown procedure. At one point, I look up to see a group of my fellow Cav troopers standing in front of the Huey, laughing at the lieutenant, who is stuck inside the cockpit with the overpowering stench of death.

While waiting for the turbine engine to wind down, I look up from observing the instruments to see two pilots in front of the aircraft, just beyond the still spinning rotor blades, waving their arms to get my attention and pointing to the Huey's undercarriage. I turn to the right, look out my window, and see the helicopter's right skid has disappeared in the wet, soggy ground. All that is visible is the footrest atop the skid's upward-curved toe. The helicopter increasingly lists to the right as I roll the throttle on and anxiously wait the few seconds for the rotors to come up to operating rpm. By now, the Huey has a noticeable tilt to the right side.

Lifting upward on the collective with my left hand and keeping the cyclic centered, I slowly increase pitch in the rotor blades to lift the skids out of the mud. I am careful not to apply too much power, or the Huey will launch skyward when the skids break free from the thick muck.

Seconds pass, and the Huey slowly begins to right itself. Soon, the skids slip free from the mud, and I bring the Huey to a three-foot hover. Sliding sideways to the left, I see what appears to be firmer ground and slowly lower the collective until the Huey's skids gently touch down. Once I am confident that the Huey is not sinking, I shut the engine down as fast as possible and exit the helicopter.

Upon rejoining my Lighthorse buddies, everyone has a good laugh at my expense. I try my best to smile, but the stench is still lingering on my Nomex flight uniform.

A short time later, Warrant Officer Kevin Kelley approaches and says, "Good job, Gooch. You kept your cool and pulled that Huey out of the mud before the situation got worse." "Thank you," I reply. "I was a little nervous moving the Huey by myself." Kevin smiles and says, "Well, you did good."

I am tremendously honored by Kelley's comments. Kevin is one of the most respected pilots in Lighthorse. And, it was Kelly who covered us when we took fire in the U Minh Forest, diving from above, firing rockets on our exit from the hot PZ.

Kelly's compliment made my day. Gaining the respect of the senior pilots meant a great deal to me. And, in my opinion, warrant officers were the best of the best.

FINAL DELIVERY

After a short lunch break, we receive instructions to transport the bodies to Ca Mau where an ambulance will await our arrival. After boarding, I rapidly crank up our Huey and lift off to the southeast. Once again, we endure that dreadful smell for the flight to Ca Mau. About ten minutes pass before I see the airstrip, aligned west to east. After calling to announce our landing, I enter the base leg and bank left to align with the runway.

On final approach to the airstrip, I glance out to the right and see an olive drab Jeep ambulance with a red cross emblazed on its side, parked near the runway. Descending to a three-foot hover over the middle of the runway, I do a ninety-degree right pedal turn and taxi to the staging area adjacent to the airstrip, where I slowly lower the collective control until the skids come to rest on the ground.

The ambulance drives to our aircraft and parks just beyond the rotor blades as I roll the aircraft throttle to flight idle. Four ARVN soldiers emerge from the rear doors of the ambulance, carrying two canvas stretchers. In solemn silence, they remove the bodies from our aircraft and place the heavy black plastic bags on stretchers. Then, with one soldier on each end, they lift the stretchers and carry the bodies to the ambulance. After loading the two bodies, they close the doors and drive off.

We hover to the refueling pads, top off our fuel, and take off to the northwest, returning to the ARVN command post to join the other Longknife Hueys on standby. On the return flight, we talk about what happened, expressing our curiosity about the deceased soldiers. Why did their remains receive special handling? Who were they, and how did they die? We never know and ultimately write off the experience as another strange incident of this war.

Later that afternoon, the Lighthorse aircraft crank up and return to Vinh Long. At day's end, we have flown six hours and fifteen minutes and transported thirty-four soldiers, two bodies, and three hundred pounds of supplies. It was a typical day of flying with the Longknives.

In the next chapter, I fly another mission with Robbie that has a funny twist and another boost to my confidence as an Army aviator.

Author at the end of a long day
flying Slicks with the Longknives

CHAPTER 13

THE "THUMPER"

ON FEBRUARY 1, 1972, I am, once again, flying copilot for Chief Warrant Officer 2 Robbie Young. Arriving at our aircraft before dawn, we preflight the Huey and prepare for today's mission. Finishing the inspection early, we have about thirty minutes to spare before our scheduled takeoff. Like usual, it is a hot, humid day, so I am not surprised when Robbie suggests we remove the pilot doors to allow additional ventilation through the cockpit. The crew chief and I agree so we set about removing the doors. I soon discover that Young has an ulterior motive for his suggestion.

Robbie walks away while I assist the crew chief and gunner in removing the pilot door hinge pins, lifting the doors off and carrying them to a nearby Conex storage container. About the time we are finished, Robbie returns carrying an M79 grenade launcher (nicknamed the "thumper" because of the sound it makes when fired) and two bandoliers of grenades. As he lays the shoulder-fired weapon and ammo near his pilot's seat, he looks at me with a big grin and says, "I have always wanted to fire the thumper from a helicopter." I don't know what he has in mind but, knowing Robbie, it is bound to be interesting.

M79 grenade launcher
US DOD photo

"The M79 grenade launcher is a single-shot, shoulder-fired, break-action grenade launcher that fires a 40×46mm grenade, which uses what the US Army calls the High-Low Propulsion System to keep recoil forces low, and first appeared during the Vietnam War. Because of its distinctive report, it has earned the nicknames of 'Thumper,' 'Thump-Gun,' 'Bloop Tube,' 'Big Ed,' and 'Blooper' among American soldiers."[11]

Robbie and I climb into our pilot's seats and begin the engine start procedure. A short time later, with rotor blades spinning at operating rpm, I lift the Huey to a hover and move to the runway. At 0730 hours, we are among eight Lighthorse helicopters departing Vinh Long and flying southwest to the Ca Mau airstrip.

---

[11] Wikipedia, "M79 Grenade Launcher," accessed February 25, 2019, https://en.wikipedia.org/wiki/M79_grenade_launcher

MISSION BRIEFING

After landing at Ca Mau, the Lighthorse helicopters refuel and shut down alongside the asphalt runway. Then the pilots walk to the parked C&C Huey to attend a mission briefing. There, we are told that today's operation is a troop insertion of an ARVN infantry company into a large rice paddy on the eastern side of the U Minh Forest. The ARVN soldiers have orders to sweep an area in the dense jungle, seeking a reported unit of Viet Cong.

Returning to our Huey, Robbie explains the mission to the crew chief and gunner, saying, "We are flying to a command post where we will load ARVN soldiers and carry them to an LZ near the U Minh Forest. When we come to hover in the LZ, you guys need to hustle the ARVNs off our aircraft." Turning to me, he smiles and says, "Gooch, you will fly the first insertion. Since we have suppression fire, I'm gonna fire the thumper." I'm thinking, *All right, it's my first time to fly an insertion with suppression fire. That's awesome!* And, I am honored to know that Robbie has confidence in my flying skills. At the same time, I cannot help but wonder what he is planning to do with the thumper.

RECON THE LZ

Minutes later, the C&C Huey, two Crusader Cobra gunships, and two War Wagon OH-6 scouts take off to the northwest, flying thirty-five klicks (twenty-two miles) to the area of operations (AO).

Arriving at the AO, the Loaches descend to five feet above ground level to conduct a low-level reconnaissance of the landing zone. Meanwhile, two Cobra gunships fly a racetrack pattern at eight hundred feet altitude, keeping a watchful eye on the scouts below. Flying above the gunships, the air mission commander in the C&C Huey oversees and directs the air operation.

PICK UP THE ARVNS

Back at Ca Mau, the Longknife pilots and crew members go through the startup procedure, and soon all three Longknife Hueys are loaded and ready to fly. Longknife Lead comes on the radio asking, "Are the Longknives ready?" I pull the radio trigger on my cyclic and say, "Chalk 2 is up." Then immediately following, I hear, "Chalk 3 is up."

Looking right, I watch as Longknife Lead comes to hover and moves forward. I lift the Huey to a three-foot hover and follow the Lead Huey to the runway. Aligned in trail formation with our Huey in the mid position, the three aircraft tuck their noses, lift their tails, and take off to the west. Making a sweeping right turn, I maintain our position behind Chalk 1, flying in loose trail formation (two rotor disks separation) to the north.

Located midway between Ca Mau and the operations area, we soon have the ARVN command post in sight. After closing our intervals to a tight trail formation, we land at the CP and promptly load the ARVN troops, weapons, and supplies. In less than a minute, we lift off, flying north to join the Lighthorse Cav Pack at the AO.

TROOP INSERTION

Upon our nearing the operations area, Longknife Lead (26) calls the air mission commander to announce our arrival. The AMC, in turn, calls War Wagon Lead (18), who is still flying low level, scouting the landing zone, and tells him to "pop a smoke." The lead scout's gunner drops a colored smoke grenade at the far end of the landing zone and two War Wagon Loaches exit to the east, climbing to altitude.

Seconds later, a spiraling column of smoke emerges from the distant rice paddy. Longknife Lead calls to confirm the smoke color by saying, "Longknife 26 has purple smoke." In response, War Wagon 18 replies, "26, this is 18. Roger that—purple it is." Then Longknife Lead announces, "Flight prepare for approach."

That is my cue. I slowly move our aircraft forward to tighten our separation to one rotor disk from the lead Huey. At this distance, I am peering over Chalk 1's tail rotor, which is so close I can seemingly reach out and touch it. Mimicking every move of the lead Huey, I maintain this position as we begin our descent to the LZ. Keeping my eyes focused on the lead aircraft, I carefully make very small, precise changes to the flight controls. Reaction time is critical, and my anxiety level is extremely high!

When the lead aircraft is about 150 meters from the LZ, Chalk 1 calls: "Flight Go Hot." At his command, our door gunners commence firing out both sides of the Huey. *Rat-tat-tat-tat-tat-tat-tat. Rat-tat-tat-tat-tat-tat-tat.*

Glancing left, I see Robbie crack open the grenade launcher (akin to opening an old double-barrel shotgun), load a large 40mm shell into the breech, fold it shut, and aim out the left-side pilot's door opening. I hear a *thump* sound, followed by a loud explosion off our left flank. Robbie yells out, "Wahoo!" and then loads another round and fires again. Laughing and shouting after every round, Robbie is clearly having far more fun than the rest of us. I cannot help but smile as I intently hold my position behind the lead aircraft.

Suddenly, loud *kaboom! kaboom!* explosions can be heard above the roar of the M-60 machine guns and Robbie's "thumping." Diving from above, a Crusader Cobra gunship fires high-explosive rockets into the rice paddies about twenty-five meters (eighty-two feet) off our right flank, between our aircraft and a tree line. In my peripheral vision, I see thirty- to forty-foot eruptions of water and white smoke as the rockets impact along our right side. *Wow, that's awesome! Keep 'em coming,* I think to myself.

When we near the ground, I see the lead Huey's tail drop as he flares, nose high, to slow down. In a split second, I pull back on the cyclic and lower the collective to likewise flare and come to a hover above the water in the rice paddy.

I call, "Cease fire! Cease fire!" on the aircraft intercom. The crew chief and door gunner immediately stop firing their machine guns and turn their attention to ushering the ARVNs out the side cargo doors. Standing on the Huey's skids, the soldiers jump into knee-deep water and slog away from the helicopter. I hold the aircraft steady as the Huey rocks from side to side, the load shifting each time a soldier jumps off. Robbie stows the grenade launcher and turns his attention to our task of offloading the troops

About the time the last ARVN soldier jumps from our Huey, I hear on the radio, "Chalk 1's up." I immediately reply, "Chalk 2's up," and then hear, "Chalk 3's up." In an instant, Chalk 1 calls, "Flight lifting off zero-one-zero (compass heading)." The instant I see the lead Huey's tail lift upward, I move the cyclic forward and pull in power with the collective. Chalk 3 does the same, and, in unison, the three Hueys lift their tails and tilt forward to take off. Again, I am careful to mimic every movement of the lead aircraft and maintain our spacing of one rotor disk apart.

Looking out our windshield, I see that the lead slick is tail high directly in front of us. Rice paddies blur rapidly below the Huey's nose as we increase our airspeed while flying about ten feet off the ground. Upon reaching eighty knots, Longknife lead calls, "Coming to altitude," and pulls back on the cyclic doing a rapid cyclic climb. I follow his lead, doing the same, and feel the "rush" as the Huey climbs rapidly to altitude. After leveling off at 1,500 feet, we assemble in loose trail formation and return to the CP for another load of ARVNs.

ANOTHER DAY IN THE LIFE OF A SLICK PILOT

At the end of the day, our flight of three Hueys made four troop insertions and logged five hours and forty-five minutes of flight time.

I smile and laugh quietly to myself when I recall this day of flying with Lighthorse. Robbie's firing the M79 grenade launcher from the pilot's seat was highly unorthodox and funny. In the midst of combat, it broke the tension and gave everyone a good laugh. And, like other events that exceed the boundaries of propriety, the oft-used saying applies: "What are they going to do, send me to Vietnam?"

And, this day is a personal landmark for me. Robbie's trust in my flying skills has boosted my confidence, and I am one step closer to qualifying as an aircraft commander.

Vietnam Veteran Profile: Robbie Young

Upon his return from Vietnam, Robbie Young was assigned to Fort Hood, Texas, serving as an instructor pilot for the UH-1 Huey and AH-1G Cobra helicopters. After attending the Rotary Wing Instrument Flight Examiners Course in 1977, Robbie served in Germany as an instrument flight instructor for UH-1 Huey, AH-1S Cobra, and OH-58 helicopters. Returning to Fort Hood in 1979, Robbie served as instrument flight examiner and UH-1H/AH-1F standardization instructor pilot.

While serving at Fort Hood with D Troop, 2nd Squadron, 1st Cavalry, 2nd Armored Division in 1981, Robbie was acknowledged as "Army Aviator of the Year" for the Fort Hood Chapter of the Army Aviation Association of America (AAAA).

Robbie Young flying a UH-1H Huey
Photo courtesy of Lenny Young

In 1982, Robbie completed the Fixed Wing-Multi-Engine Qualification Course and transitioned to the U-21A (Beechcraft King Air) airplane. Afterward, he was, again, assigned to Germany, flying the RU-21H, and served as maintenance officer for the 330th Electronic Warfare (EW) Aviation Company.

In 1985, Robbie was assigned to 1st Attack Helicopter Battalion, 24th Aviation at Hunter Army Airfield in Savannah,

Georgia, serving as instrument flight examiner and standardization officer for the AH-1 SIP Cobra.

Young retired from the Army in 1990 as a chief warrant officer four after serving twenty years. During his military career, he was the recipient of the Meritorious Service Medal and twenty Air Medals.

After the military, Robbie became a pilot for the Georgia Forestry Service, flying the Cessna 182 fixed-wing aircraft.

Robbie and his wife have one son, two daughters, and six grandchildren.

Robbie passed away on May 23, 2000, at the age of forty-nine. He is missed by all who knew and loved him.

When asked about his father, Robbie's son, Lenny, said, "I remember the funny things about Dad. He loved telling the story about flying a Cobra helicopter out of Hunter Army Airfield in Savannah, Georgia and 'visiting' the nearby family farm in Fitzgerald, Georgia. Hovering over a combine working late one afternoon, Dad scared the 'living daylights' out of Uncle Tommy."

CHAPTER 14

BILL'S LUCKY DAY

ONE STORY IS TOLD AND retold among Vietnam gunship pilots—the story of a Cobra crew losing an engine door in flight and living to tell about it. This story is about Bill Wiscombe, a Crusader Cobra pilot who gained a certain amount of notoriety for surviving the "Engine Door Incident" described in this chapter.

MOC HOA

In late 1971, a Lighthorse Cav Pack of two Cobra gunships, two Loaches, and the C&C Huey are shut down next to the runway at Moc Hoa, fifty-six klicks (thirty-five miles) north of Vinh Long. Today's mission is a VR (visual reconnaissance) of an area located in the infamous Plain of Reeds.

> Note: The Plain of Reeds is an enormous marshy area, stretching from Tan An in the east to the Cambodian border in the northwest, a distance of about 110 klicks (sixty-eight miles) in length, and sixty klicks (thirty-seven miles) at its widest. Its name is derived from the vast open areas of tall reeds and elephant grass growing out of waist-deep, leech-infested water. In earlier times,

U.S. Infantry soldiers called this area the "Sea of Reeds" because the grasses looked like waves as they undulated in the wind when looking down from the open door of a Huey. Widely recognized as a sanctuary for the Viet Cong, the Plain of Reeds with its wood-lined canals and thick vegetation gives "Charlie" plenty of places to hide.

After being briefed on today's mission, the Lighthorse pilots and crewmembers walk to their respective aircraft to preflight their machines and prepare for takeoff. Flying lead gunship is Crusader 35, Warrant Officer Charlie Brown with Warrant Officer Larry Coates flying his front seat. Flying in the wingman position is Crusader 38, Warrant Officer Bill Wiscombe with Captain Jerry Williams flying his front seat.

This is Bill's first mission as aircraft commander using the 38 callsign. He is somewhat concerned about flying into the Plain of Reeds, knowing this area is a haven for the bad guys and the potential for a firefight is high. Aiming a heavily armed gunship at an enemy shooting at you is not to be taken lightly. It is a huge responsibility, and that thought weighs heavily on his mind.

Not wanting any surprises once they get in the air, Bill is very cautious and precise with his pre-flight inspection, double-checking everything to ensure his aircraft is in top condition. Before climbing into the cockpit, he stops to make one last check of the ammo doors to ensure they are properly latched.

TAKEOFF
Once Bill is settled in the rear pilot's seats, he puts on his flight helmet, plugs in the commo cord, checks circuit breakers, and flips a number of switches. With the canopy doors open, Bill calls, "Clear," and pulls the start trigger on the underside of the collective. In seconds, the rotor blades are turning at flight idle.

After Bill and his copilot close and latch their canopy doors, Wiscombe rolls the throttle on and brings the rotor blades to operating rpm. He is ready to fly.

After placing a radio call announcing their departure, Crusader 35 hovers to the runway and takes off to the west. Following 35's lead, Bill comes to a hover, moves to the runway, and does a pedal turn to the left. After a quick check of his instruments, he pushes the cyclic slightly forward and pulls up on the collective. The Cobra lifts its tail and moves down the runway. After traveling about fifty feet, the aircraft passes through translational lift and starts climbing upward, following behind Crusader 35.

THE ENGINE DOOR

Passing through four hundred feet altitude, Bill experiences harsh feedback through the aircraft's pedals, making the Cobra's tail swing left and right about four feet—and then it stops. Alarmed, Bill has never felt anything similar to this. He immediately thinks, *It must be the SCAS since the feedback was through the pedals.*

> SCAS: Stability Control Augmentation System is used to improve the helicopter's stability and handling qualities in lieu of the Bell-developed crossbar installed in other rotor systems. The SCAS cancels undesired motion of the helicopter during flight, especially in rough air, to make it a highly stabilized weapons platform. This is accomplished by inducing an electrical input into the flight control system to augment the pilot's mechanical input. This is very much like the shock absorbers on a car or truck, smoothing out the rough spots in the road to give a more stable ride.

Neither Bill nor his copilot have any idea what happened, and they are both shocked by the experience.

Just then, Wiscombe receives a radio transmission from one of the Lighthorse troopers on the ground at Moc Hoa, saying, "Hey, 38, your door's open." Bill replies, "Roger that," and thinks, *This is crazy. I know I closed all my doors.*

Charlie Brown calls on the radio, "Come up on my left side and let me look you over." Increasing power, Bill moves up beside Crusader 35's left side. After looking closely, Brown says, "Looks good to me. Move over to my right side."

Slowing his airspeed, Bill drops back and crosses behind the lead Cobra. Moving forward, Bill comes alongside Brown's gunship. The front seat, Larry Coates, looks over, does a double-take, and excitedly points toward Bill's aircraft.

Charlie Brown turns to look out the right side and starts laughing as he comes on the radio, saying, "Hey, William, how's your engine running?"

Bill answers, "Just fine. Everything is in the green."

Brown says, "You better take it back."

Bill says, "Why? It is running pretty good."

Brown replies, "You are missing your left engine door. Let me get a closer look." After a pause of several seconds, Brown says, "Naw, take it back—we are going back now."

AH-1G Cobra with engine doors open – Note size of rear door
Photo courtesy of Ray Wilhite

SOMEONE WAS LOOKING AFTER US

Bill makes a sweeping turn to the right, and Crusader 35 follows as the two Cobras return to the Moc Hoa airstrip. As Bill makes his final approach to land, he sees the commanding officer, Captain Robert Goodbary, and the maintenance officer, Captain Dudley Oatman, watching the new aircraft commander return with his crippled gunship. Bill thinks, *This is great! Everyone is watching me to see if I screw up.*

Upon landing and shutting down the turbine engine, the rotor blades are still slowly turning when Captain Oatman walks around the front of the Cobra and comes to the pilot's open canopy. Placing one foot on the skid and the other on the footrest, Oatman looks into the cockpit and says, "Can I touch you?" Bill says, "What are you talking about?" Dudley replies,

"Hey, man, you got somebody looking over your shoulder. You are missing the entire left-side engine door, armor plate, the whole nine yards." He continues, "Bill, it went up through your tail rotor. This is how serious it is. I have heard of this happening to three aircraft, and you are the only two guys to have survived it." Bill thinks, *Now you have my attention, and I am scared sh**less.*

Climbing out of the cockpit, Bill and Dudley walk to the left side and see that the nearly four-foot square engine door had opened in flight, ripped off its hinges, and hit the tail rotor driveshaft cover, right above the #3 (midway along the tail boom) hanger bearing. The impact smashed the cover and deeply dented the hangar bearing mount but miraculously did not damage the bearing itself or the driveshaft. The door then likely flipped over and hit the forty-two-degree gearbox before it slid up the right side of the vertical fin and off into the wild blue yonder—never touching the tail rotor blades mounted on the left side of the vertical fin. *Wow! Were we lucky!*

Captain Goodbary walks up to Bill and says, "Are you all right?" Bill answers, "Yeah, I'm fine," even though his voice is wavering as he thinks about his close call. Goodbary says, "Bill, I think you better ride home with me in the Huey." Bill agrees. "Yeah, it might be safer," he replies.

Years later, Bill commented, "I have thought about this incident so many times. My only explanation is that when the door assembly passed by the tail rotor it must have created a differential in rotor thrust. The feedback I felt in the controls must have been the SCAS system trying to accommodate for that change in thrust. This, in turn, caused the abrupt movement in the aircraft. Whatever it was, we were extremely fortunate."

Cobra tail boom hit locations
Photo courtesy of Ray Wilhite

Vietnam Veteran Profile: Bill Wiscombe

Following his return from Vietnam, Bill Wiscombe attended the Army Aircraft Armament Supervisors course at Aberdeen Proving Grounds, Maryland, and afterward was assigned to serve with the 334th Attack Helicopter Company at Fort Knox, Kentucky, when the company moved to Germany.

After a subsequent assignment in Savannah, Georgia, Bill attended the Instructors Pilots course at Fort Rucker, Alabama. He next served three and a half years as the instructor pilot for B Company, 3rd Aviation Battalion in Giebelstadt, Germany.

Returning to Fort Rucker, Bill became an instructor at Cobra Hall, and later a section leader. Upon promotion to chief warrant officer four, he attended the AH-64 Apache Course and instructed night vision systems. Then he became project pilot on the AH-64 with the US Army Test and Development Activity at Cairns Army Airfield at Fort Rucker.

When he retired from the Army in 1991, Wiscombe had served twenty-one years. He was the recipient of twenty-seven Air Medals and the Bronze Star.

Following his military service, Bill began a second career with the Maricopa County Sheriff's Office, lasting twenty-three years. He retired in 2012.

Wiscombe said, "I am most proud of my career dedicated to public service, especially my military service, but my most important contribution to this world is my children."

Bill and his wife have a combined family of three children, three grandchildren, and three great-grandchildren.

Vietnam Veteran Profile: Dudley Oatman

Dudley Oatman served his first Vietnam tour in 1968, flying both Huey and Cobra gunships with Company D (Smiling Tigers), 229th Aviation Battalion, 1st Cavalry Division. Wounded in action while flying gunship support for Dustoff (medevac) helicopters near Utah Beach, Dudley was medically evacuated stateside where he spent six months recuperating before returning to active duty. In 1971, he returned to Vietnam and was assigned to Lighthorse as the Scavenger (maintenance) platoon leader.

After Vietnam, Dudley was assigned as a research and development pilot at Laguna Army Airfield, Yuma Proving Ground, Arizona. He was involved in the development of the AH-1Q, R, and S model Cobras, TOW missile system, GPS navigation, aircraft Missile Detection System, flat plate canopy, aircraft laser designator, and initial Nap of the Earth (NOE) flight profiles. Yuma was followed by command assignments at

Fort Eustis, Virginia, and Fort Hood, Texas, numerous schools, a tour of duty in Korea, and a number of staff positions.

When he retired from the Army in 1986, Dudley had served twenty years and had flown ten different rotary and fixed-wing aircraft. He was the recipient of the Distinguished Flying Cross, Bronze Star, Purple Heart, three Meritorious Service Medals, four Air Medals, and the Master Aviator Badge.

Following his military service, Dudley flew ten years with Atlantic Southeast Airlines as captain, Training Department flight instructor, and check airman on the E-110 and ATR-72 aircraft.

Then Dudley served sixteen years with the Federal Aviation Administration (FAA) as an Aviation safety inspector and Boeing 727/737 Aircrew Program manager, providing oversight for Continental and American Eagle Airlines. He retired from the FAA in 2013.

When asked about his military service, Dudley said, "I am most proud of the Scavenger platoon's officers, NCOs, and maintenance crews who provided the best maintained, safest, and combat-ready aircraft to some of the best and bravest pilots and crews I have ever known."

In retirement, Dudley volunteers with the San Diego Air and Space Museum. His personal Vietnam memorabilia, including his Lighthorse Cav hat and scarf, are displayed in the Vietnam War exhibit.

Dudley and his wife have two children and two grandchildren.

Scavenger 56, Dudley Oatman, in his hooch
Photo courtesy of Dudley Oatman

CHAPTER 15

CHRIS RASH CRASHED

ON FEBRUARY 4, 1972, MY hooch mate, Chris Rash, is assigned to replace another scout pilot on a "last light" mission. The purpose of this mission is to expose any threats to Vinh Long Airfield that might develop in the local area. This has been a daily ritual since the Viet Cong overran the airfield during Tet of 1968. And, since Tet is three days from now, the mission receives additional emphasis.

Based on intelligence reports of recent enemy activity, the area of operation will be on the north side of the Mekong River, directly across from Vinh Long Airfield. Directing a heavy team of two Loaches and four Cobra gunships, Captain Walt Gale, Lighthorse executive officer, is serving as air mission commander in the C&C Huey.

There are two unusual occurrences on this mission. Warrant Officer Wade Huddleston, a slick pilot, replaces Chris's door gunner. Because he aspires to fly scouts, this mission is an orientation/training role for Huddleston. Furthermore, a Catholic chaplain is riding as a passenger in the C&C Huey. The chaplain voiced a desire to join the troop on a mission, and Chris arranged for him to fly this evening.

LAST LIGHT

Departing first, the C&C Huey flies a short distance to pick up a U.S. Army captain MACV advisor and an ARVN major to function as "back seat," meaning they are consulted for permission-to-fire clearances and communications with friendly ground forces. Upon his return to the Vinh Long area, Captain Gale calls for the heavy team to launch.

Taking off from Vinh Long Airfield, two scouts and four Cobras join up with the C&C Huey on the north side of the Mekong River. With Cobras high at 1,500 feet altitude and C&C beneath the gunships, the two Loaches descend to begin their low-level reconnaissance. Captain Gale provides course corrections from above as the two scouts are guided to the area of interest. This frees the scout pilots to concentrate on seeking the enemy and not be concerned with their location.

Flying in the trail position, Chris maintains a distance of about ten to fifteen meters (thirty to fifty feet) behind and to the right side of the lead scout. It is his job to cover lead's unprotected right flank, always ready to engage the enemy if the lead aircraft receives hostile fire. Mimicking every move of the lead Loach, Chris keeps a watchful eye out the front while Huddleston, in the left seat, scans the left side and operates the M-60 machine gun hanging from a bungee cord in the open-door frame.

Entering the operations area, Captain Gale gives the command, "Cleared to go hot." Flying slow left-hand circling patterns at three to five feet above the ground, the Loach door gunners begin firing short bursts with the M-60 machine guns, hoping to flush out any VC in the area. After about fifteen minutes, Huddleston's M-60 jams. Following established procedure, Chris notifies C&C, and the two scouts exit the area and climb several hundred feet altitude while Wade clears the jam.

TAKING FIRE

With the M-60 cleared, Captain Gale directs the scouts back into the area, only this time he vectors the scouts to enter the operations area at a point different from where they exited. Flying about seventy knots (eighty mph), the two Loaches pop up and over a line of nipa palm trees bordering a small canal and dive downward on the other side. Leveling off at five feet above the ground, they slow to begin their recon.

Seconds later, they start receiving heavy small arms fire. Calling, "Taking fire," the lead Loach breaks left, and Chris breaks right to vacate the area (per procedure). Crusader 35 (Captain Loran "Bear" Bryant), circling overhead, immediately calls, "Coming hot" and dives his Cobra gunship toward the Loaches.

Banking to the left, several "hits" disintegrate the Plexiglas windshield and knock out the radio on the lead Loach, yet the pilot continues to fly and safely exits the area. With radio dead, the pilot knows nothing of the plight of his wingman. Unable to communicate, he flies to a nearby ARVN outpost, lands, and shuts down the damaged Loach.

On the right flank, Chris pulls in maximum engine torque and noses his Loach over to gain airspeed while Wade fires his M-60 machine gun out the left-side door, making a loud, continuous *Rat-tat-tat-tat-tat-tat-tat-tat-tat-tat-tat*. Tracer rounds are coming from all directions, and rice paddies pass beneath the nose of the Loach in a fast-moving blur. Glancing at his instruments Chris sees the needle on the airspeed indicator pass through one hundred knots (115 mph).

THE CRASH

Suddenly, Chris feels an impact to the backside of his head that he later described as like "getting hit in the head with a baseball bat." A small arms round, likely from an AK-47 rifle, hits him in the backside of his neck. The force of the impact throws Chris forward into the aircraft controls. The Loach noses into the rice paddies and starts rolling. Chris recalls seeing pieces of the aircraft flying in all directions as they roll over and over.

Captain Gale, observing from the C&C Huey, later remarks, "I saw Chris's Loach, tail high, racing across the rice paddies at maximum speed. In my mind's eye, I can picture Chris with the collective pulled up under his armpit. Then, in an instant, the Loach plunged nose first into the wet ground. I saw the rotor blades fly off, then the tail boom, then the skids. Nothing remained except the egg-shaped airframe that continued to roll at least four and, possibly, five times."

Eventually, the mangled orb of twisted aluminum comes to rest in the water-filled rice paddies, lying on its right side with Chris still strapped into his pilot's seat, unconscious. What Chris remembers next is remarkable. He tells of an "out of body experience" in which he is standing outside the crashed aircraft, looking in to see himself in the pilot's seat. Then, while experiencing a "peaceful feeling," he slowly floats off, farther and farther from the crash site, moving toward a bright light. Suddenly, he sees a vision of his wife, and hears her say, "It's not time for you to leave. Come back."

Chris regains consciousness and discovers his face partially submerged in the muddy rice paddy water. Lifting his head out of the water, he struggles to get his safety harness unfastened, but cannot release the buckle. Looking upward, Chris sees Wade above him still strapped in his seat and also struggling to release his safety harness.

Eventually, Huddleston manages to release the buckle, drops onto Chris, and scrambles out the front of the aircraft. Realizing they are taking enemy fire from the nearby tree line, Wade turns to reach for the M-60 machine gun still attached to the bungee cord and dangling above Chris's head. It is then that he discovers his left arm is limp and useless, shattered in the crash. Desperate to fend off the enemy, Wade pulls his .45-caliber automatic pistol from its holster but cannot chamber a round with only one hand. He turns his attention to Chris but cannot extract him from the wreckage.

GUN COVER

When Bear Bryant initiates his gun run, he sees a fortified bunker about one hundred meters from the crashed Loach—likely the gun that shot Chris. Lining up his Cobra, Bear fires two seventeen-pound rockets that impact in the bunker gun ports. Continuing downward, he sees a group of sampans hidden in tall grass about fifty meters right of the bunker. Shifting his aircraft's nose toward the long, narrow boats, Bryant fires his second set of rockets into the sampans. Breaking off, he climbs upward as his wingman dives to fire rockets into the bunker. Fearing for the fate of the downed Loach crew, Bear swings his Cobra to the right and returns to the crash site.

Hearing a helicopter nearby, Chris peers out through the crumpled airframe to see a Cobra gunship pass overhead, about fifteen feet above the ground. The Cobra circles the crash, like a protective mother hen. After making several circuits around the downed aircraft, the C&C Huey approaches from the north, and the Cobra departs to the south, climbing to higher altitude.

This is aggressive flying on the part of the Cobra pilot because the gunships usually remain at high altitude and seldom maneuver near the ground. Chris later learns that the Cobra pilot is none other than Bear Bryant, boldly protecting the downed aircrew.

THE RESCUE

Seeing the Loach hit and roll, Captain Gale, flying the C&C Huey, descends to make a low pass over the mangled remains of the aircraft, expecting to see that no one has survived such a horrific crash. Flying about fifteen feet above the ground and seventy knots (eighty mph) airspeed, Gale approaches the crash site and sees Huddleston waving with his one good arm. Pulling back on the cyclic control, Gale stands the Huey on its tail in an attempt to slow down; however, the fast-approaching Huey has too much airspeed. Passing by the crash site, the chaplain jumps from the now slow-moving aircraft, hitting with a splash and rolling in the flooded rice field. Jumping to his feet, the chaplain runs to assist Chris and Wade.

Struggling to free himself, Chris looks up to see the chaplain looking down at him, saying, "Don't worry, Chris, we will get you out of here." Extending his arms into the water, the chaplain unbuckles the safety harness and pulls Chris out of the crumpled airframe. With assistance from the aircrew, Chris is loaded in the open cargo door of the Huey. Using the aircraft's first aid kit, the chaplain bandages Chris's neck in an attempt to stop the bleeding. With both Chris and Wade onboard, Gale lifts the Huey to a hover, does a pedal turn to the right, and takes off toward Vinh Long Airfield.

Once the Huey has departed the area, the three Crusader Cobras make repeated gun runs into the area adjacent to the crash site, firing HE rocket, nails, 40mm grenades, and mini-guns until their ammo is nearly depleted. Satisfied that the enemy is no longer a threat, they return to Vinh Long.

MEDEVAC

Realizing that Chris's injuries are serious and beyond the capabilities of the Vinh Long Infirmary, Gale decides to take Chris to the 3rd Surgical Hospital at Navy Binh Thuy. Having never visited Binh Thuy, Captain Gale is not familiar with the hospital's location. Calling on the troop radio frequency, Gale asks for directions.

Sitting on the refueling pad at Vinh Long Airfield, Chief Warrant Officer 2 Tom Tolar is preparing to refuel his Huey. Tom answers the call, volunteering to lead Gale to the hospital. Lifting off immediately, Tom meets the C&C aircraft in the air. With Tolar in the lead, he sets a course to Navy Binh Thuy, thirty-two klicks (twenty miles) southwest. Midway, Tom calls the hospital saying, "Astro 3, this is Longknife 20. We have a Huey with two critical injuries onboard, ETA ten mikes (minutes)." The hospital replies, saying they will have medical personnel waiting on the helipad.

When Captain Gale has the hospital helipad in sight, Tolar breaks left and calls for clearance to land directly at the Can Tho Airfield refueling pads, seven klicks (four miles) east. Having illuminated fifteen minutes ago, Tom's twenty-minute low fuel warning light reveals he is dangerously low on fuel. Cleared to ignore the airfield flight pattern, Tom flies directly over buildings and parked aircraft to land on one of the refueling pads. With a sigh of relief, he thinks, *That was close. I must have been running on vapors.*

Back at Binh Thuy, Gale flares the C&C Huey to land at the 3rd Surgical Hospital helipad where four Army nurses and two doctors are waiting with two wheeled stretchers to take Chris and Wade into the emergency room for triage. Once inside, the doctors discover the bullet entered the back right side of Chris's neck, destroying his lower right jaw and exiting his right-side lower lip. They stabilize Chris and load him on a Dustoff helicopter bound for the 24th Evacuation Hospital at Long Binh, near Saigon.

CHRIS'S RECOVERY

In the following three weeks, Chris has three surgeries to repair internal and external facial injuries before he is evacuated stateside to Walter Reed Army Hospital. Over the next eighteen months, Chris has multiple surgeries to repair his jaw, which must be reconstructed with bone removed from his hip.

Chris and I correspond by letters throughout the remainder of my Vietnam tour. He keeps me advised on his recovery and I keep him up to date on the action in Vietnam. Over the years, we lose touch with one another, but thirty-six years later, we reunite in Denver, Colorado, to reminisce and celebrate our having survived the war.

Author and Chris Rash - 2007

WADE'S RECOVERY

Remaining at Navy Binh Thuy hospital, Huddleston has his left arm surgically stabilized with a pin, and his arm/upper torso are placed in a body cast. Several days later, Wade is flown to Saigon and then to Zama hospital in Japan. Eventually, he is flown stateside and recovers in the Fort Lewis, Washington, hospital. Proud to be a Lighthorse trooper, Wade wears his silver belly Cav hat the entire trip.

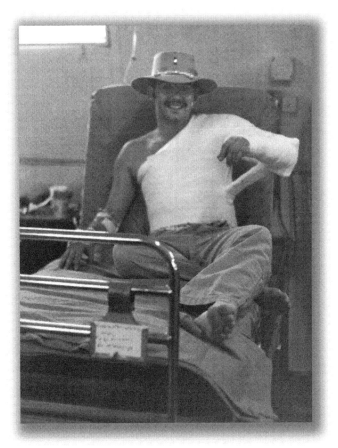

Wade Huddleston in Binh Thuy Navy Hospital
Photo courtesy of John Elliott

Vietnam Veteran Profile: Chris Rash

After recovering from his injuries, Chris continued flying helicopters and was assigned as aviation section leader with 1st Squadron, 3rd Armored Cavalry Regiment at Fort Bliss, Texas. Then, he served in Germany in Air Defense Artillery command positions. Returning stateside, Chris was scout platoon leader and XO, B Company, 229th Attack Helicopter Battalion and S-4 101st Aviation Regiment at Fort Campbell, Kentucky.

While serving with the 229th at Fort Campbell, Chris was one of two officer pilots with OH-6 combat experience chosen to organize and develop a highly secretive unit with a special mission focused on night operations. Through recruitment of the most experienced aviators, especially those with OH-6 qualifications, and intense night operations training, this unit developed into the Army's premier aviation night fighters. This special operations unit later became the renowned 160th SOAR (Special Operations Aviation Regiment (Airborne)), nicknamed "Night Stalkers."

Later, Chris served as weapon system manager for Air Defense Artillery and Aviation at Rock Island Army Arsenal and then chief of supply and maintenance for the National Guard Bureau at the Pentagon.

After a distinguished twenty-two-year career in the United States Army, Chris retired in 1992 at the rank of lieutenant colonel. When asked what he is most proud of, Chris replied, "I am very proud of my Vietnam service and my role in the initial establishment of the 160th SOAR."

After the Army, Chris worked for a logistics company in northern Virginia, supplying humidity-controlled storage facilities to locations in forty-three states and ten foreign nations. As senior vice president, he retired in 2014.

Chris and his wife have two children and seven grandchildren. In 2003, Chris and his family created WestRash Charities in 2003, raising funds to support the fight against childhood cancer.

Side note: In Chris's shortened Vietnam tour he was the recipient of three Air Medals, but never received his Purple Heart. Although he proudly wore the Purple Heart ribbon on his uniform, it was never officially awarded. Eighteen years later, while working at the Pentagon, the oversight was corrected, and Chris was officially awarded his Purple Heart.

Vietnam Veteran Profile: Wade Huddleston

Upon his recovery and release from the Fort Lewis hospital, Wade was assigned as a scout pilot flying for 3rd squadron, 4th Cavalry at Schofield Barracks, Hawaii. He departed the Army after serving five and a half years and is the recipient of five Air Medals.

After the military, Wade had an impressive forty-eight-year career flying helicopters for aviation corporations. His first five years of employment were flying BV-107 helicopters in the Pacific Northwest for the logging industry. Then, he flew the next twenty-two years for an air ambulance helicopter company as regional manager and instructor pilot.

After that, Wade flew twenty-one years as a pilot and instructor pilot for several international helicopter companies flying Puma and Super Puma helicopters in the Persian Gulf, Yemen, Afghanistan, Guam, and Abu Dhabi. Some assignments were Navy "VERTREP" contracts transporting cargo from ship to ship by sling load. He is rated in an incredible number of helicopters, including the MD-900/902, Hughes 500, Bell 412, Eurocopter Twin Star, A-Stars, and Super Puma. Wade retired in 2018 with over 16,000 hours flight time.

Huddleston says, "Other than the time spent with my wife, my happiest moments have been while flying, especially in the mountains." Wade and his wife have a combined family of four sons, one daughter, ten grandchildren, and three great-grandchildren.

Wade Huddleston and Super Puma helicopter in Afghanistan, 2011
Photo courtesy of Wade Huddleston

CHAPTER 16

TANK HUNT IN CAMBODIA

IN EARLY 1972, TENSIONS ARE building, and intelligence reports reveal the North Vietnamese are accumulating resources for a major attack. Rumors are circulating that involve the enemy's use of armored vehicles; i.e., tanks. Many suspect an attack to occur during Tet, the Vietnamese New Year, but Tet passes with no significant military engagements.

Note: The concerns and rumors are legitimate but slightly premature. Following this story, on March 30, 1972, the Easter Offensive began when NVA troops and Soviet tanks advanced across the DMZ (Demilitarized Zone) in I Corps, the Laos border in II Corps, and the Cambodia border in III Corps. "The attacking force included 14 infantry divisions and 26 separate regiments, with more than 120,000 troops and approximately 1,200 tanks and other armored vehicles. The main North Vietnamese objectives were Quang Tri in the north, Kontum in the Central Highlands, and An Loc farther to the south."[12]

GEORGE ANDERSON

On February 26, 1972, a Cav team of two Crusader Cobras and a C&C Huey are shut down on the apron alongside the east/west runway at Chi Lang, near the Cambodian border. The pilots and crew members are on standby, expecting to be called at a moment's notice to perform a search and destroy mission in Cambodia.

The air mission commander, flying the Huey, is Captain George Anderson, Crusader gun platoon leader. George is considered the "old man" in the troop, which is composed mostly of nineteen-year-old warrant officers. At twenty-seven years old, this is Anderson's second tour of duty in Vietnam. He previously served as an infantry officer in the 101st Airborne Division, where he was awarded the Silver Star for gallantry in combat.

George is an outstanding platoon leader—he leads from the front and is cool under pressure, and his laconic Arkansas accent rarely reflects any sense of stress when he talks on the radio. The Crusader pilots admire and respect George's leadership and dedication to mission completion. And, they appreciate his downhome, "country boy" sense of humor. Bill Wiscombe, Crusader 38, recalls, "George would come around in the morning to make sure we were awake and ready to roll. He would 'half-knock, half-pound' on the hooch door, enter, then start

---

[12] History.com Editors, "U.S. forces respond to North Vietnamese offensive," accessed March 22, 2019, https://www.history.com/this-day-in-history/u-s-forces-respond-to-north-vietnamese-offensive

singing the Kellogg's 'Good Morning' jingle. It always made me laugh and put me in a good frame of mind."

FIND THE TANK

Around 1100 hours, the Cav team gets scrambled to fly into Cambodia seeking a North Vietnamese tank that was sighted by a VNAF (South Vietnamese Air Force) FAC (Forward Air Controller). Having heard rumors that Russian PT-76 tanks are operating in Cambodia, the Cav troopers are psyched; it's not every day that you are asked to take out a tank.

Hunting a tank will require low-level reconnaissance, searching wooded areas where armored vehicles might seek cover and concealment. As mentioned in an earlier chapter, scout helicopters (Loaches) are prohibited from operating in Cambodia. And, the high-speed Cobras gunships are not optimal for low-level search operations. So, in an unusual departure from standard operating procedures, George Anderson, flying the C&C Huey, will perform the low-level reconnaissance for today's tank hunting mission.

Returning to the airstrip, the flight crews run to their respective aircraft and "kick the tires and light the fires" (aviation jargon meaning rapid startup). Soon, the rotor blades are "in the green," and ready to fly. Taking off first, George lifts his Huey to a hover, makes a right-hand pedal turn, and takes off on a compass heading to the map grid coordinates, fifty-three klicks (thirty-two miles) to the west. Seconds later, Crusader lead gunship lifts off, closely followed by the trail gunship. Meeting at 1,500 feet altitude, they fly toward the area where the tank was reported.

THE SEARCH

Upon arriving several klicks from the operations area, George makes a rapid descent, leveling off about twenty feet above the ground while flying eighty knots airspeed. The two gunships maintain 1,500 feet altitude while the lead gunship copilot (front seat) follows the Huey's path on the map and provides course corrections to Anderson, vectoring him to the area where the tank was sighted.

The terrain is flat, a floodplain dotted with tall, slender trunk palm trees. In some areas, the land is slightly elevated, covered with thick undergrowth, bushes, and shorter trees in addition to the palm trees, creating more of a small forested appearance.

After flying low-level for several minutes, Crusader Lead calls George telling him he is closing on the tank's location. To minimize the Huey's exposure as a tank target, George starts jinking (abrupt turns) left and right and alternating his airspeed between thirty knots and sixty knots. Overhead at 1,500 feet altitude, the Cobra gunships are flying a racetrack pattern, with the inner-orbit gunship ready to dive and cover the Huey at a moment's notice should they take fire.

WE'RE HIT

Suddenly, George calls on the radio, shouting, "We just took a hit! I don't know what it was, but it busted out the chin bubble!" When scouts pilots call, "Taking fire," it is standard procedure for the Cobra pilots to declare, "Coming hot," and dive inbound, firing rockets. However, this call seems strange. Seeing no signs of enemy activity and no flash or smoke from weapons fire, Crusader Lead delays his response.

The Huey continues flying low to the ground, and after a few seconds, George keys his microphone and excitedly says, "There's blood all over the place!"

In response, Crusader Lead asks, "Who's hit?"

A brief silence follows, then George answers, "We had a bird strike—blood and feathers are all over the place, and our chin bubble has a big hole in it." Then, with a chuckle, George calls, "Maybe we should report an Enemy B-one-R-D KIA (killed in action)."

THE "TANK"

Coming to altitude, George and Crusader Lead discuss their options: either abort the mission or continue the search. George is adamant; he wants to continue the mission. Crusader Lead agrees, and George descends to low-level flight and continues jinking toward the area identified by the map grid coordinates.

Minutes later, George comes upon a set of wide tracks cutting northeast into a group of palm trees amongst bushy undergrowth. Making a sweeping left turn, George calls to say he will follow the tracks and asks the guns to cover him. Crusader Lead replies, "Roger that. Got you covered."

Completing his turn, George lines up on the "tank trail" and while still jinking, follows the tracks to the point they disappear in the trees. After a couple of minutes, George calls on the radio, saying, "I found the tank." He pauses. "It's a big green tractor!"

The "tank," parked amid the bushy undergrowth, is a large, green John Deere tractor with oversize, wide rear wheels. There are no people in the area and no evidence of how the tractor got there. It is a highly unusual sight, in either Cambodia or South Vietnam.

Reporting their find to the MACV Special Operations Coordination Center, they are instructed to return to Chi Lang.

Climbing to 1,500 feet altitude, George joins the two Crusader Cobras, and they set a return course to the east. For George and his crew, it is a breezy trip with the wind blowing through the large hole in the chin bubble.

That evening in the officers' club, the pilots laugh and joke about today's mission. One of the Cobra pilots comments, "We should have taken out the tractor. Then we could have reported two Communist KIAs—a B-one-RD and a JD-1 tractor."

Vietnam Veteran Profile: George Anderson

During his second tour in Vietnam, George served as Crusader gun platoon leader and accumulated over 1,700 helicopter flight hours. Following his Vietnam tour, Anderson was assigned to 1st of the 4th Cavalry Regiment at Fort Riley, Kansas. After subsequent assignments in Hawaii and Oklahoma, he attended Command and General Staff College at Fort Leavenworth, Kansas.

George's next assignment was at Fort Rucker, Alabama, as Commander, Flight Standards Division DES (responsible for worldwide standardization of flight procedures for instructor pilots). He next served at Fort Campbell, Kentucky, as operations officer S-3 and then deputy commander for the 160th Special Operations Aviation Regiment (Airborne), the Night Stalkers.

Returning to Fort Leavenworth, Kansas, George became an instructor at the Command and General Staff College.

George retired from the military in 1988 with the rank of lieutenant colonel after serving twenty-two years. During his service, he was the recipient of the Silver Star, Purple Heart with oak leaf cluster, Bronze Star with V device and two oak leaf clusters, and twenty-five Air Medals.

After retirement, George became a civilian mission instructor for the 160th Special Operations Aviation Regiment for two years. He then flew emergency medical helicopters for seventeen years and, following that, was employed by a global aviation company, flying both rotary and fixed-wing aircraft internationally for eleven years. His final retirement came in 2018.

When asked about his most memorable career experience, George said, "It was my time as deputy commander of the 160th SOAR, and, later, as a pilot flying high-level security missions internationally."

George and his wife have one daughter.

George Anderson flying Russian MI-17 helicopter in Afghanistan – 2015

Photo courtesy of George Anderson

CHAPTER 17

LIGHTHORSE STANDS DOWN

UNFORTUNATELY, ALL GOOD THINGS MUST come to an end. President Nixon's Vietnamization Program eventually catches up with Lighthorse, and in late February 1972, C Troop receives stand-down orders. Over the next three weeks, all aircraft and equipment are turned in for redistribution to other U.S. units, transferred to the South Vietnamese Army, or returned stateside by ship. As the aviation duties come to a close, the Lighthorse troopers await their reassignment orders.

Troopers with at least six months of Vietnam service are reassigned to C Troop, 3rd of the 4th Cavalry, stationed at Schofield Barracks, Hawaii. Since I have five months with the troop, I do not join my Cav buddies in Hawaii—drat! Instead, I am transferred to 18th Corps Aviation Company in Can Tho, thirty klicks (nineteen miles) southwest of Vinh Long.

In late March, C Troop, 3rd of the 17th Cavalry, folds its colors. The troop guidon (troop flag) is sent to squadron headquarters at Dĩ An to rejoin the other 3-17th troops as they, likewise, stand down and depart Vietnam. The Lighthorse legacy has come to a close, leaving many troopers with fond memories of their time with the "Bastard Cav."

PART 3

GREEN DELTA

CHAPTER 18

18TH AVIATION COMPANY

THE 18TH CORPS AVIATION COMPANY (18th CAC) was created as an outcome of the drawdown of U.S. Army aviation assets in South Vietnam. When aviation units deactivated, portions of their equipment and personnel were transferred to the 18th CAC, whose mission is to provide ongoing aviation support to ARVN military units and regional militia operating in IV Corps (the Mekong Delta).

Note: By 1972, most, if not all, U.S. military ground forces have departed Vietnam, transferring their combat responsibilities to the ARVN forces. This is especially true in the Delta where no U.S. ground forces remain.

Headquartered at Can Tho Army Airfield, the 18th CAC has four helicopter platoons: two platoons of UH-1H Iroquois ("Huey") helicopters using the radio callsign "Green Delta," one platoon of CH-47 Chinook heavy lift helicopters with the callsign "Hillclimber," and one platoon of OH-58 Kiowa helicopters with the callsign "Bartender."

Flying the majority of the 18th CAC operations, the Green Delta Hueys fly unescorted, single-ship missions across the Mekong Delta, supporting the South Vietnamese ground units and their American advisors. Their objective of supporting the ground forces is basically the same as it has been throughout the war, but the pilots are keenly aware of the differences with this new scenario of no-fly zones, no-fire zones, and the communications challenges that come with supporting a non-English-speaking military.

Unlike the Air Cavalry, Green Delta has no scout or gunship support. The reality of knowing that should they get shot down, it could take hours before friendly forces come to their rescue weighs heavy in the minds of the pilots and crewmembers. Nevertheless, these talented aviation crews perform their jobs and, at times, take on extraordinary tasks, always dedicated to completing their mission and returning to home base safely.

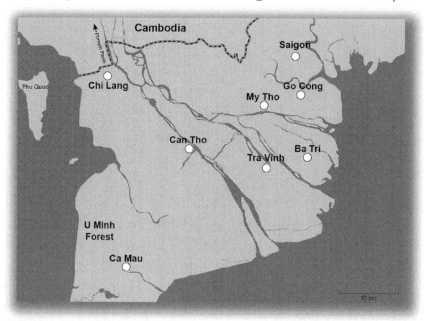

Green Delta Operations Area: Mekong Delta
Towns and villages in stories

CHAPTER 19

CAN THO

IT IS LATE MARCH 1972. I am in my room at Vinh Long packing my duffle bag for the short trip to my new assignment at Can Tho. Glancing around the hooch I see the bedroom, closet, bar, and living area created by the walls Chris Rash and I constructed from scrounged lumber. We were proud of our home. Now, five months later, it will be abandoned, and I am struck by a momentary sense of sadness. But that is quickly replaced by a sense of loneliness, realizing that my good friend, Chris, is no longer here. I pray he is doing well in stateside recovery at Walter Reed Hospital.

Taking one last look inside my hooch, I walk outside, shutting the door behind me for the final time before removing the "Gooch's Hooch" sign attached to the door. Carrying my overstuffed duffle bag, I walk along the paved sidewalks toward the flight line. Passing by row after row of empty officer hooches, I realize the Lighthorse Troop area is now a ghost town. Not a soul can be seen: no pilots, no crew members, not even the Vietnamese hooch maids who typically are busily going about their cleaning chores. I think to myself, *This is downright spooky, and, at the same time, sad.*

Eventually, I reach the flight line and walk to a Huey helicopter setting on the runway apron, waiting to transport a group of the last remaining Army soldiers to Can Tho. I climb aboard and take a seat looking outward. The Huey lifts to a hover and takes off to the south. Climbing to altitude, I look back at Vinh Long with mixed emotions and countless memories, wondering what lies ahead at Can Tho.

FRIENDS REUNITED

Arriving at Can Tho, I am greeted by a Green Delta pilot who welcomes me to the unit and walks me to the company area. After dropping off my duffle bag, I am given a quick tour of the pilot quarters, mess hall, and officers' club. Along the way, I am introduced to several pilots. Suddenly, I see a familiar face: It is Donny O'Connor, a good friend from my flight school class. Donny tells me he is bunking with Tim Halstrom, another flight class member, and invites me to join them in their hooch. I eagerly agree.

After settling in, I tell Donny and Tim about the valuable goods left behind at Vinh Long. There are tools, furniture, supplies, and, best of all, the refrigerator and air conditioner from my hooch, all for the taking. After some discussion, we decide to take advantage of this opportunity. Since none of us are scheduled to fly the following day, we decide to drive to Vinh Long. And, since Donny's duty assignment is motor pool officer, he arranges our transportation.

OFF TO VINH LONG

The following morning, we three lieutenants, dressed in our fatigue uniforms, wearing our holstered sidearms, and carrying two M-16 rifles, climb into an Army "deuce and a half" (two and a half ton) truck—compliments of Donny. Driving out of the compound gate, Donny turns right onto the road into Can Tho. After traveling about a mile, he turns left for a short distance and positions the large, heavy truck at the rear of a long line of Vietnamese carts, small trucks, and motorcycles waiting to board the ferry across the Mekong River. Forty-five minutes later, we are across the mighty Mekong, traveling north along Highway 4, on our way to Vinh Long, approximately eighteen miles ahead.

Along the way, we pass mile after mile of fertile rice paddies, intersected by dikes, creating huge green squares. Beyond the rice paddies, tree lines in the distance form a lush backdrop. It is a beautiful day and a pleasant drive.

Arriving at Vinh Long Army Airfield, Donny drives through the gate and onto the airfield roads that are so familiar to me. I provide driving directions, and soon we arrive at the abandoned Lighthorse pilot quarters. We spend the day finding anything of value and loading it onto the truck. We gather refrigerators, air conditioners, tools, furniture, and all sorts of other, smaller items. After that, we stop by the now deserted officers' club and pick up bar stools, glasses, and bar equipment. Then we stumble upon our treasure—a nickel slot machine.

Realizing it is getting late in the day, we load the slot machine in the truck, close the tailgate, and depart. Driving along Highway 4, the sun has set, and dusk is slowly setting upon us. It is then that we know we have a dilemma. Our heavily loaded truck with three lightly armed lieutenants would make an ideal target for the Viet Cong. Scanning the countryside on both sides of the truck, the once beautiful landscape now looks ominous, and the once-distant tree line now seems much closer than before.

Arriving at the ferry after dark, we encounter a long line of Vietnamese vehicles in a queue to board the ferry. Nervously, we await our turn as Vietnamese trucks, motorcycles, and carts load ahead of us. We are the only Americans amid a sea of South Vietnamese.

The ferry loads, crosses, and returns two times before it is finally our turn to board. As the ferry slowly traverses the broad river, we collectively say with a sigh of relief, "Almost home." Arriving at Can Tho Airfield, it is nearly midnight when we park the truck at the motor pool and make our way back to the hooch. Walking along, we mutually agree that what we did today was stupid, but now that we have returned safely to Can Tho, we are also happy about our procurements.

The following morning, we unload our goods, delivering the refrigerator, bar stools, and air conditioner to our hooch. The remaining items are either given to fellow pilots or used to barter.

RALPH

After examining our prize possession, the slot machine, we discover it is loaded with nickel slugs, which we remove and place in an empty coffee can. And, we realize it is missing its base. So, we mount the one-armed bandit atop a three-foot-high wooden chest of drawers. Cutting a hole in the top of the chest allows the winnings to dump into the first drawer, making a *clunk, clunk, clunk* sound that is vaguely familiar to the *clink, clink, clink* sound of a casino slot machine.

After playing the slot machine for a while, we find it has a pretty good payoff ratio, so we name him Ralph because he "ralphs" coins. Soon Ralph becomes a big hit with other pilots who come to our hooch to "pull his arm." This often becomes an annoyance, and we have to politely ask those "addicted to Ralph" to leave so we can sleep.

Tim Halstrom, Donny O'Connor, and Author

CHAPTER 20

MY PERFECT HIGH OVERHEAD APPROACH

GREEN DELTA

AFTER A CHECK RIDE WITH the company's instructor pilot, I am cleared to fly Hueys with the 18th Aviation Company. Flying with Green Delta is much different than flying with the Air Cavalry. The typical mission is a single Huey flying U.S. military advisors, ground commanders, VIPs, or supplies to locations throughout the Mekong Delta. There is no gunship support and no backup if you find yourself in trouble. Instead, you are on your own, flying a solo helicopter across the vast expanse of the delta without another aircraft in sight. Compared to the Cavalry, the flights can be tedious and mind-numbing. Yet, in the midst of the boredom is the always present trepidation of knowing the risks when flying in the absence of backup.

My time with Lighthorse prepared me well for flying with Green Delta. In addition to having many flight hours in the Huey, I am familiar with the towns, villages, fuel locations, and military outposts throughout the Mekong Delta. This combined with the knowledge of navigation procedures and artillery clearances enabled me to promptly assume flying duties with my new unit.

However, my transfer to Green Delta comes with one considerable drawback—I have to restart my aircraft commander qualification by accumulating flight time with a new unit. And, since I have a high number of flight hours with the Air Cavalry, I am assigned to fly copilot with second tour captains who are getting their "flight legs" back. They are good pilots, but their recollection of flying in Vietnam years before when supporting U.S. ground troops bears little similarity to the flying environment in 1972 supporting ARVNs. At times, I find myself explaining the reality of the "new war" flying environment to these seasoned aviators, especially the importance of avoiding unnecessary risks when flying a single aircraft far from friendly forces.

THE CAVALRY TAUGHT ME WELL

In addition to improving my flying skills while flying with Lighthorse, I learned several combat critical maneuvers not taught in flight school, nor acknowledged by aviation standards. The most memorable is the *High Overhead Approach.* This story tells how I used that maneuver while flying with Green Delta, but first I need to step back in time to describe how I acquired this unique skill.

Some of my most memorable experiences with the Air Cavalry were while flying with Captain Ken Hibl, Longknife lift platoon leader. Ken was an extraordinary pilot. He sat low in the Huey's pilot seat with his right forearm resting on his thigh to steady his right hand, lightly holding the cyclic control between his legs. Ken had an effortless, fluid control touch that made the Huey dance through the air—and then glide smoothly on its approach path to land gently on the exact spot he intended.

I flew many missions as copilot for Captain Hibl, and he taught me many things, but the most memorable is the *High*

Overhead Approach. This combat-developed technique is used to get the helicopter quickly to the ground while avoiding exposure to enemy ground fire. This maneuver is not for the faint of heart and should only be attempted by accomplished pilots. To be perfectly honest, the *High Overhead Approach* is an adrenaline rush—more thrilling than the most extreme roller coaster ride.

In the *High Overhead Approach*, the pilot, in the right seat, flies directly over the landing zone at an altitude of one thousand to 1,500 feet. Then he slows to forty to fifty knots airspeed and, with his left hand, bottoms the collective, taking the pitch out of the rotor blades. At the same time, with his right hand, he slides the cyclic control between his legs abruptly to the right, rolling the aircraft into a downward, spiraling ninety-degree turn. This is the exciting part—it feels like the bottom drops out as the aircraft enters a tight spin, circling rapidly toward the ground below. With a rate of descent of eight hundred to one thousand feet per minute, it literally feels as if the helicopter is falling out of the sky.

The pilot focuses intently out his right-side window, looking directly at the landing zone that seemingly rotates below the rapidly descending aircraft. He carefully times his recovery from the spin to initiate his final approach at approximately one hundred feet above the ground. At the precise time, he eases the cyclic to the left, rolling out of the turn, and simultaneously lifts the collective to slow the descent. Then he pulls back on the cyclic, transitioning the aircraft to a nose-high attitude. At this point, the Huey shakes and rattles as it strains to slow down. If timed correctly, the pilot drops the nose, and the aircraft comes to a hover directly above the intended target. I can still remember that exhilarating maneuver as if it was yesterday— What a thrill!

Returning to my story....

MY PERFECT DAY

While serving with Green Delta, I am especially proud of one particular *High Overhead Approach*. On this day, I am flying with Captain Cranky (fictitious name). Cranky is one of those officers who seems to enjoy "pulling rank" and takes pleasure in making life miserable for the lower ranking officers in the company.

Even though Cranky is a second tour captain, it is apparent he has not experienced combat aviation to the extent I have while serving with the Air Cavalry. He recognizes this and seems determined to validate his rank by overriding my decisions while flying. I make every effort not to show my frustration, but find it challenging.

It is mid-April 1972, and our mission takes us to an ARVN command post (CP) in the Mekong Delta that is known to have Viet Cong combatants in the surrounding area. As we near the CP, I call to announce our arrival. The ARVN commander responds, saying they are receiving small arms fire and advises that we take the necessary precautions. I consider my landing alternatives. A normal approach is out of the question because we would be low and slow, right over the enemy.

Relying on my Air Cavalry experience, I know exactly what to do. Flying in the right seat, I turn left to look at Captain Cranky and tell him I am about to make a *High Overhead Approach*. It is evident from the blank look on his face that he has no idea what I am talking about. Shifting my vision further left, I see my crew chief, in the left side gunner's seat, grinning from ear to ear. He knows what is about to happen.

Maneuvering the Huey directly over the outpost, I slow my airspeed, drop the collective, and bank hard right until I am looking out my side window, straight down at the landing pad.

The Huey drops precipitously, entering a steep downward spin. I hear Captain Cranky yell on the intercom, "What in the hell are you doing?" I calmly reply, "I'm making my approach." As we continue spiraling downward, I glance left to see Captain Cranky desperately grasping the handhold on the doorframe with one hand and the instrument panel with the other, yelling and cursing all the way down. I pull out of the tight spiral descent at about one hundred feet altitude and gradually lift the collective to slow our descent. Easing back on the cyclic control between my legs, I flare the Huey nose high to decelerate. The Huey's airframe begins to strain and groan as it slows and settles downward. My timing is perfect. As our forward airspeed slows to a near stop, I drop the nose and set the Huey down softly on the CP landing pad. It is, without a doubt, my best *High Overhead Approach.*

Rolling the throttle off, I initiate the Huey shutdown procedure, and the turbine engine begins to whine down. As the rotor blades progressively slow to a stop, I remove my flight helmet and turn to look at Captain Cranky, who is still cursing. At that point, he feels he has my complete attention and proceeds to "read me the riot act." I vividly recall him yelling, "Lieutenant, don't you ever do that again!" As he continues his shakedown interlaced with a variety of colorful curse words, I turn to look at my crew chief, standing outside the open left-side cargo door. He has a big grin on his face and is giving me the "thumbs up" sign with his flight-gloved right hand. Try as I might, I cannot suppress the smile on my face as the captain continues his rant. My crew chief's approval overrides the captain's criticism and makes my day.

That *High Overhead Approach* was special, and I will remember it forever. Scaring the hell out of Captain Cranky was the highlight of my flying with Green Delta. And, it brought back sweet memories of flying with "The Cav."

Vietnam Veteran Profile: Ken Hibl

Captain Hibl and I flew many missions, with Ken as the air mission commander and me at the controls of the C&C Huey. In response to my comment about the heavy responsibilities of the air mission commander, Ken said, "It is incredible to think that a young captain flying C&C had access to all that firepower: off-shore Navy guns, couple flights of fast-movers (Air Force jets) above, and our own Cav gunships. All available with the click of a mic button. Pretty awesome!"

After Vietnam, Ken was assigned to 4th Battalion, 63rd Armor Regiment, 1st Infantry Division at Fort Riley, Kansas. He then had various aviation assignments in Europe, Saudi Arabia, and Europe again. After that, he served as Defense & Army Attaché for six African countries with the U.S. Defense Intelligence Agency, and, following that, as inspector general for the Puerto Rico National Guard in San Juan.

Discussing his role as attaché Ken said, "We saw a lot of Africa because, at that time, we had the only DOD aircraft based on the continent, and the C-12 was ideally suited for landing on unimproved runways yet had the speed and the endurance to quickly crisscross the vast expanse of Africa."

U.S. Army Beechcraft C-12 Huron
Photo courtesy of Martyn Wraight

Ken served thirty-one years active duty, including two tours in Vietnam, and was the recipient of sixty-one Air Medals, three Bronze Star Medals, the Soldier's Medal, and three Distinguished Flying Crosses. He retired in 1997 at the rank of colonel.

Ken Hibl, Colonel (Ret)
U.S. Army
Photo courtesy of Ken Hibl

After his military retirement, Ken's career shifted to the private sector, where he has been a city manager in Michigan for the past twenty-one years, a role he continues to enjoy today.

Ken and his wife have a combined family of four children and eleven grandchildren. Ken's oldest granddaughter is serving in the U.S. Air Force.

C H A P T E R 2 1

LOST MY CHERRY

CHERRY

IF NEWBIE ISN'T ENOUGH, THERE is another label conferred upon aviators, and that is "Cherry." A Cherry pilot is one who hasn't experienced his aircraft taking hits from enemy fire. In the bravado of pilot chatter, it is common to hear someone speak of another pilot as "He's still cherry." This distinction continues until the day the aviator's helicopter is hit. From that day forward, he is referred to as having "lost his cherry." Taking hits is not a distinction everyone looks forward to, yet once a pilot survives this event, he wears the moniker with a certain amount of pride. This story is about the day I "lost my cherry."

ASH AND TRASH

On April 24, 1972, I am flying Huey 827 on a late afternoon "ash and trash" mission from Can Tho Army Airfield to Dong Tam with Chief Warrant Officer 2 Jim Addington. Jim is a second tour aviator, having flown with the 101st Airborne Division and the 48th Aviation Company on his first tour. After flying several missions with Jim, I have great respect for his flying skills and proficiency as an aircraft commander. He was one of the most talented warrant officers in Green Delta. Like me, Jim is short with a medium build and sports a mustache. We are not only physically similar but when flying together we make a good team.

> Note: In Vietnam, not all flight missions are related to combat or combat support operations. Those nonessential missions were called "Ash and Trash," a term derived from earlier days when soldiers were given a duty assignment to pick up the ash (cigarette butts) and trash (litter) in the company area. For helicopter operations, ash and trash missions could range from carrying food/supplies to delivering the mail, transporting VIPs, or hauling a live pig. Yes, we transported a live pig to an ARVN outpost. Kicking and squealing the entire trip, the porker didn't enjoy the ride in our Huey. Perhaps he knew he was destined to be the main event at a Vietnamese barbecue. Enough of the pig; on with the story.

MEDEVAC MISSION

After landing and offloading our cargo, we lift off from Dong Tam and climb to two thousand feet altitude for the return trip to Can Tho. About midway along our route Jim answers a radio call from Green Delta Operations asking that we take a medevac mission to transport several wounded ARVN soldiers from an outpost to a hospital at My Tho. The outpost is north of Ba Tri village in the Vinh Binh Province about fifty-three kilometers (thirty-three miles) to the southeast. Jim questions the nature of the injuries and is told the soldiers have leg and arm wounds.

Before accepting the mission, we discuss the facts. With the sun setting below the horizon, it will be dark by the time we arrive at the outpost. Having a reputation for requesting unnecessary medevac missions, the ARVN request is suspicious, yet we realize it could be serious. And, we are the only option since the ARVN Air Force at Soc Trang refuses to fly their Hueys at night.

After some discussion, we agree to take the mission. Jim calls Green Delta Operations, asking for the location of the outpost and its radio frequency. Provided with map grid coordinates, Jim plots a course to our destination, and I swing left to a compass heading of 110 degrees.

About twenty minutes later, we arrive in the vicinity of the outpost. It is dark with a clear sky and a three-quarter moon providing partial illumination on the landscape below. As we fly at two thousand feet altitude, it is difficult to recognize anything except the lights emitting from small villages scattered across the flat Mekong Delta terrain.

According to our estimates, we are within three kilometers (two miles) of our destination. Jim places a radio call to the ARVN outpost while I turn off the aircraft clearance lights and begin our descent, hoping to see distinguishable terrain features at a lower altitude. Leveling off at six hundred feet, I see what appears to be never-ending rice paddies streaming below us. Based on the tactical map, we know the outpost is located amid a forested area bordering a canal running north to south, but there are no other distinguishing terrain features.

A short time later, I see the rice paddies ahead of us merge with a long line of trees perpendicular to our eastward flight path. About that time, the ARVN radio contact calls to say he hears our helicopter and will guide us in with a flashlight. Homing in on the ARVN radio frequency, Jim advises me to make a course correction ten degrees left. Turning left, I descend to three hundred feet and slow our airspeed to sixty knots (sixty-nine mph).

When our aircraft passes over the perimeter of the tree line, the ground contact calls again saying he hears our Huey, and we are very close. Once again, using the radio call for homing, Jim tells me to turn slightly to the right. Slowing our airspeed to fifty knots (fifty-eight mph), I descend further to around two hundred feet. Shifting my vision from left to right, I still see nothing but tall trees passing underneath us. Then, all of a sudden, I see the flashlight directly below. It is too late to react— I am too fast to land. The outpost is in an open area about sixty meters (two hundred feet) wide surrounded by forty- to fifty-foot trees that make a normal approach angle impossible.

I continue flying east past the outpost and cross over a canal. Banking to the left, I circle around and make another slower approach on a similar easterly path. Soon, I see the light and come to a high hover above the trees. Then, I lower the collective and slowly settle down into the clearing, touching down in front of an ARVN soldier holding a flashlight.

After the Huey's skids settle onto the ground, seven wounded ARVN soldiers are assisted into the left-side cargo door of our Huey. They appear to have superficial leg and arm wounds. Alert and talking, the wounded soldiers seem to be less than critical and likely could have waited until the following day for extraction.

I pass the controls to Jim so he can fly the return leg of our mission. Lifting the collective, he brings the Huey to a hover and continues climbing straight up and over the top of the tall trees. This high hover is dangerous, but our only option. The small clearing and high trees prohibit a normal takeoff using the rotor blade's ground effect. And, the additional load of seven passengers requires even more engine power to climb above the trees.

Note: When a helicopter hovers, part of its lift is provided by the cushion of downward air hitting the ground. This is called ground effect. As the helicopter hovers higher, the ground effect is lost, and additional power is required. Pilots are taught to avoid the high hover because the helicopter is too low and slow to autorotate in case of engine failure.

TAKING FIRE!

Once over the treetops, Jim carefully moves the cyclic forward while monitoring the engine torque gauge. The combination of our load and the high hover is consuming all available engine power. The Huey's nose drops slightly and starts moving gradually across the treetops. As we slowly gain airspeed, we will soon realize we made a big mistake—our exit route is over the same path I flew earlier when I missed the outpost.

When we reach the canal, we are barely above treetop level (about sixty feet) and around fifty knots airspeed. At the moment we pass over the trees on the far side of the canal, the Viet Cong start firing at us from below. I see a stream of bright green tracers (AK-47) shooting up directly in front of the windshield. Then, with a loud pop, one bullet pierces the underside of the aircraft, careens through the fuselage, and hits the armor plating on the bottom of my seat. An explosion of yellow and red sparks erupts from under my seat, and I feel the impact of shrapnel hitting the backside of my right leg. Instinctively, I flinch, and my thigh hits the right side of the cyclic between my legs. The Huey makes an abrupt tilt to the left and Jim reacts immediately, shifting the cyclic back to center to keep the aircraft straight and level.

It all happens so fast that our door gunners do not have an opportunity to return fire. By the time we realize we are under attack, we are past the area of peril.

As we continue to gain airspeed and altitude, Jim turns to me and says, "Are you hit?" I answer, "I don't know; something hit my legs. Let me check." I run my hands down the backside of both legs and, to my relief, find no blood or injury. I say, "I'm OK. How are you?" Jim says, "You fly and let me check." He does the same and says he is OK and returns to take the aircraft controls. I turn left to check with our crew chief and gunner. They both say they are fine and it appears our passengers are OK.

All of the crew members are unsettled. None of us openly admit it at the time, but we were all scared stiff and emotionally anguished by the life-threatening incident. And, at the same time, we breathe a sigh of relief that we had not been shot down.

Continuing to fly, we realize our aircraft has taken hit(s) from small arms fire, yet the Huey appears to have suffered no serious damage, so we continue our flight to the hospital. Jim banks the Huey to the left and climbs to an altitude of two thousand feet. Taking the map, I calculate a compass heading of 320 degrees. Jim makes a slight heading adjustment, and we begin our flight to My Tho, forty-one kilometers (twenty-five miles) ahead.

Dialing in the hospital radio frequency, I make a radio call advising that we are delivering seven PAX (passengers) with leg and arm wounds. We are instructed to land at the hospital helipad, situated on a pier extending over the Mekong River.

After flying for about fifteen minutes, we see the city lights of My Tho, located on the north bank of the river. A short time later, we recognize the red rotating beacon of the hospital helipad and begin our descent. Closing on the pier, Jim turns on our landing light and brings the Huey to a hover above the big letter H. Lowering the collective, he sets the skids down softly on the wooden planks and rolls the throttle to flight idle.

On the road adjacent to the pier, a Jeep ambulance with open rear panel doors awaits our arrival. Two Vietnamese men carrying a litter approach our helicopter. They load one wounded soldier on the litter and carry him to the ambulance. Returning to our aircraft, they assist the other soldiers as they walk to the ambulance.

Having offloaded our wounded passengers, the crew chief and door gunner inspect our aircraft. Using flashlights, they find a bullet hole beneath the cockpit, but no other damage. Climbing back into the Huey, the crew chief and gunner fasten their safety harnesses and don their flight helmets while Jim rolls the throttle on and brings the rotors to operating rpm. Lifting the collective, Jim brings the Huey to a hover and takes off to the southwest, flying seventy-three kilometers (forty-five miles) to Can Tho Army Airfield. Arriving around midnight, we land, refuel, and shut down in the Green Delta aircraft maintenance area.

ASSESSING THE DAMAGE

The following morning, I walk to the flight line to inspect the damage on Huey 827. Arriving in the hangar area, I am greeted by the maintenance sergeant whose crew are already working on our aircraft. The sergeant takes me to the right side of the Huey, where we get down on our hands and knees to look underneath the helicopter. He points out one bullet hole in the bottom of the fuselage under the cockpit. Then he points to the dog sleeping under the Huey and says with a big grin, "Don't mess with my dog. He's vicious."

Author and Huey 827 on the morning after taking hits

Standing up, the sergeant opens the pilot's door and tells me to look inside. My seat is pivoted backward, and the panel below the seat is removed. He shows me where the AK-47 bullet hit the bottom of my seat, severing the adjusting rod that controls the seat height. Then the sergeant points to a bullet hole in the aluminum wall beneath the radio console and says, "On the other side of that wall is a one-inch diameter bundle of wires. The bullet passed so close to that bundle that it scraped the insulation off the outer wires. The wires in that bundle are critical to the turbine engine operation. Had the bullet severed the wires you would have likely suffered an engine failure." "No kidding," I say. "That was a close call."

After patching the bullet hole and repairing the seat damage on Huey 827, the sergeant presents me with the severed seat adjusting rod as a souvenir. That piece of scrap metal is one of my prize possessions—reminding me of the day I "lost my cherry."

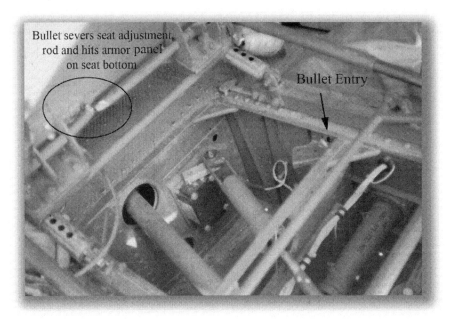

Huey seat tilted back to show severed adjustment rod and bullet entry

Vietnam Veteran Profile: Jim Addington

After Vietnam, Jim Addington served three years at Fort Hood, Texas, and then one year with the 175th Aviation Company in Germany. During his ten years in the Army, Jim was the recipient of the Bronze Star and thirty-nine Air Medals, including one with V device.

When asked about his most memorable combat mission, Jim recounts flying for the 101st Airborne Division during his first Vietnam tour and called upon to rescue five U.S. Marines about to be overrun by the NVA. The Marines were in the tall, dense jungle northwest of Hue in I Corps. With no suitable pickup zone, they used explosives to take out the largest trees, creating a small opening in the jungle canopy. Unable to land in the small clearing, Jim hovered down between the tall trees and lowered a McGuire Rig (rescue rope with personnel loops on the end).

Lifting the Marines up and out of the jungle, Jim struggled to maintain power and dragged the Marines through the treetops. After landing at a firebase, Jim approached the Marines to apologize for taking them into the trees. To Jim's surprise, one of the Marines exclaimed, "Hey, man, no problem! Had you not picked us up we would have been killed within five minutes."

After the Army, Jim flew helicopters offshore for ten years with a commercial helicopter company based in Louisiana. Later, he worked twelve years as a substitute math teacher and nine years as a mental health case manager before he retired in 2009.

Most proud of his family, Jim and his wife have two sons, one granddaughter, and one great-granddaughter.

CHAPTER 22

SKIP RESUPPLIES THE ENEMY

CAPTAIN CARL "SKIP" BELL AND I have both transferred to Green Delta after Lighthorse stood down. Having flown Cobras with the Crusader gunship platoon, Skip has a wealth of experience flying in IV Corps. And, because he served as an armored cavalry platoon leader and also troop commander during his first Vietnam tour, Skip has a unique understanding of combat from the perspective of ground troops. Since the 18th CAC has no gunships, Skip is assigned to fly Hueys with the callsign Green Delta 15.

ASH AND TRASH?

In May 1972, Skip and his crew are flying "ash and trash" missions in Vinh Binh Province, east of Can Tho. Upon landing at the provincial headquarters helipad near Tra Vinh, the senior military advisor (an Army lieutenant colonel) runs out to Skip's aircraft with a troubled look on his face.

The senior advisor describes six small outposts (fortified defensive positions) strategically positioned two klicks (1.25 miles) apart. The outposts are defended by ARVN militia (Regional Force/Popular Force, nicknamed Ruf-Puf) and are aligned in two rows of three forts in each row. Despite being protected by eight-foot-high walls, five of the six outposts have been overrun, and the final outpost is under siege.

Easter Offensive of 1972—On March 30, 1972, the North Vietnamese forces launched the Easter Offensive of 1972 (also known as the Spring Offensive), when two NVA divisions rolled across the Demilitarized Zone to attack I Corps, infiltrating into the five northernmost provinces of South Vietnam. This offensive was not designed to win the war outright but, instead, to gain as much territory and destroy as many units of the ARVN as possible. The NVA's motive was to improve the North's negotiating position as the Paris Peace Accords were drawing to a conclusion.[13] In the Mekong Delta, the NVA rapidly overrun many of the ARVN-fortified outposts, some of which had seen limited enemy advances and were ill-prepared to mount an effective defense or counter-attack.

After explaining that the only remaining ARVN outpost is in desperate need of food and ammunition, the senior advisor asks if Skip and his crew can resupply the isolated fortification. And, the lieutenant colonel adds, "This outpost is surrounded by the Viet Cong." He continues, "You must make only one approach to the outpost; returning for a second pass would be extremely risky." As this message sinks in, Skip thinks, *This is no easy mission.*

The senior advisor closes by saying that this operation will have gunship cover provided by Darkhorse, C/16th Air Cavalry. Headquartered at Can Tho Airfield, Darkhorse is the last

---

[13]   Wikipedia, "Easter Offensive," accessed January 24, 2019, https://en.wikipedia.org/wiki/Easter_Offensive

remaining Air Cavalry unit in the Delta. This piece of information is revealing—the mission is not only dangerous, but the U.S. Command expects trouble. Despite his concern about the risk, Skip is familiar with Darkhorse and is reassured, knowing their Cobra pilots will be covering his Huey from above.

Skip accepts the mission and asks if they need any clearances to fire their weapons. The lieutenant colonel replies, "Both you and the Cobra gunships are cleared 'full suppression.' The area is full of bad guys." This means the helicopter crews can fire upon anything outside the outpost without calling for clearance.

THE STRATEGY

Skip and his crew discuss their mission and develop a plan to minimize their exposure to enemy fire. Flying at altitude (two thousand feet) to the operations area, they will drop to low-level flight after passing over a small village eight klicks (five miles) east of the outposts. After descending to treetop level, Darkhorse Lead will vector (left/right headings) Skip to the outpost under siege in the southern row of three forts, aligned east to west. Arriving at the outpost, Skip will slow the Huey to a high hover over the fort while they will toss the supplies/ammo out the cargo door and exit quickly, minimizing their exposure to the enemy.

THE MISSION

While parked on the helipad, several ARVN soldiers load food and ammunition onto the Green Delta Huey. Once loaded, two ARVNs take a seat in the cargo bay to "kick out" the supplies once they arrive over the fort.

After performing a preflight inspection, Skip and his copilot climb into their seats and begin the startup procedure. Minutes later, with rotor rpm "in the green," they lift off, heading west to the operations area. Climbing to two thousand feet altitude, Skip calls the Darkhorse guns to establish radio contact and coordinate the rendezvous. The gunship pilot replies, "Green Delta 15, this is Darkhorse 34. We will arrive in your area in five mikes (minutes)." Skip immediately recognizes the voice of Captain Tony Snow, a close friend who is flying Cobras for Darkhorse. What a coincidence! Skip's confidence is bolstered, knowing his good friend and very competent gunship pilot will be covering him from above.

Several minutes later, Skip arrives at the predetermined village and makes a sweeping left-hand orbit to scan the terrain. Confident of his course, he descends to ten feet above the ground, flying eighty knots (ninety-two mph) in a westerly direction toward the southern row of forts.

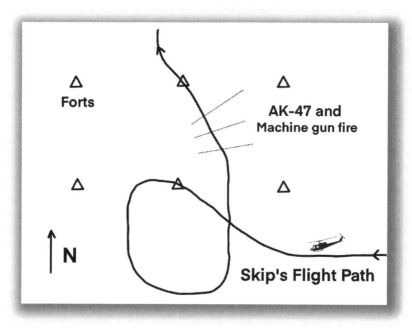

Note: ARVN defensive outposts (sometimes called forts) have a common triangular design. Each of the three walls is constructed of logs, sandbags, corrugated steel, or whatever materials are available and typically covered with dirt, creating a wall of sufficient height to fend off enemy attacks. Around the perimeter, water-filled ditches or concertina wire further deters attackers. A soldier, on lookout, is posted on each apex of the triangle and the central high point to provide 360-degree observation.

As a precaution, Skip sets the cyclic control force trim slightly aft so the Huey will climb upward should he get shot and release the controls. Speaking on the intercom, he tells his copilot to provide backup by placing his hands lightly on the controls. Then, he instructs his crew chief and door gunner to keep a lookout for any enemy activity.

Within a minute or so, the two Darkhorse Cobras arrive overhead. With minor course adjustments from Tony in the lead gunship, Skips flies toward the row of forts. Soon, he sees the first fort in the distance. On the intercom, he tells his crew chief and door gunner to be ready on the M-60 machine guns.

Passing to the left side of the first fort, Skip maintains his course and soon sees the destination middle fort. Pulling back on the cyclic and lowering the collective to reduce power, Skip makes a rapid deceleration. Standing the Huey on its tail, the aircraft shudders and vibrates as it slows from eighty knots to come to hover directly over an open area inside the outpost. So far, so good; no enemy engagement.

Immediately, the ARVNs in the cargo compartment start throwing food and ammo out both cargo doors. Suddenly, one of the ARVNs realizes they are over the wrong outpost and stops tossing the supplies. They are resupplying the enemy!

The crew chief comes on the intercom excitedly saying, "We're over the VC! Let's get out of here!" Skip immediately pulls in power and pushes the cyclic forward to make a fast exit, turning south away from the row of forts. Evidently, the fast-moving Huey surprised the enemy, and once they see supplies falling from the air, they don't shoot but gladly accept the gifts from above.

Flying low across the rice paddies, Skip calls Tony in the lead Cobra. They have a dilemma: a half-loaded Huey and an incomplete mission. They quickly agree that the beleaguered fort is not in the southern row but must be the middle fort in the northern row. To reach that fort, they will have to pass between the forts on the southern row. This is risky since they now have no element of surprise, and the VC will undoubtedly be waiting for them. And, the senior advisor warned against a second pass.

TAKING FIRE—FROM THE RIGHT, FROM THE RIGHT!

Continuing to fly low level, Skip makes a 180-degree turn from south to north and follows Tony's directions to fly through the southern row of outposts. After passing between two forts on the south row, the fast-moving Huey starts receiving heavy small arms fire. Skip pulls the commo trigger on the cyclic and yells, "We're taking fire, taking fire, taking fire!" and releases the radio trigger. Tony comes back with "Which way, which way, which way?" In the meantime, the crew chief and door gunner fire their M-60 machine guns in the direction of the muzzle flashes, making a continuous, loud *Rat-tat-tat-tat-tat-tat-tat-tat-tat*.

Most of the enemy fire is coming from the three o'clock position, but in the heat of battle, Skip cannot remember the clock system. Frustrated by his lack of recall, Skip says, "From the right! From the right!" Within seconds, Tony's rockets are impacting along the right flank of the Huey with loud *kaboom,*

kaboom, kaboom blasts. Bouncing like a car on a bumpy road, the Huey is rocked by shock waves from the nearby explosions. Skip maintains his course and continues flying rapidly toward the fort. As a result of the rockets, the Viet Cong take cover, and the small arms fire subsides. The crew chief and door gunner continue firing their M-60 machine guns to keep the enemies' heads down.

Looking ahead, Skip sees a bright yellow South Vietnamese flag with three horizontal red stripes waving in the breeze above the outpost about 150 meters away. Skips thinks to himself, *Good, it's the friendlies.* Once again, he stands the Huey on its tail to decelerate and comes to a hover over the triangular fort. Skip calls out, "Cease fire! Cease fire!" and the door guns go quiet. After kicking out the remaining supplies and ammo, Skip makes a quick exit to the north and climbs to two thousand feet altitude.

Returning to the provincial headquarters, Skip lands the Huey on the helipad and shuts down to inspect his aircraft. Walking to the helipad, the senior advisor approaches Bell and asks what happened. Skip explains, and the advisor is initially disappointed, but after seeing the bullet holes and minor shrapnel damage on the Huey he expresses his appreciation for their efforts.

After flying back to Can Tho, Bell parks the Huey near the Green Delta maintenance hangar so the damage can be repaired. Later that evening, Skip goes to the officers' club to relax and grab a bite to eat. Walking through the open area of tables and chairs, he hears a familiar squeaky, high-pitched voice coming from the bar: "From the right! From the right!" It is Tony Snow. With a big smile, Skip shakes Tony's hand and offers to buy the first round of beers. The two of them talk and laugh about the day's mission and how they inadvertently "resupplied the enemy."

That's not the end of the story. Two years later, Captain Skip Bell is teaching Armor and Infantry Tactics at the U.S. Army Field Artillery School at Fort Sill, Oklahoma. Walking down the hall one day, Skip hears a loud, squeaky, high-pitched voice yelling, "From the right! From the right!" It is Captain Tony Snow, attending the Field Artillery Officers Advanced Course. Bell is surprised and happy to see Tony again even though he assures Skip that he will never live down his famous radio call in the heat of battle.

Vietnam Veteran Profile: Carl "Skip" Bell

Skip Bell was commissioned an Armor officer through the ROTC program at North Georgia College in 1967. After his first Vietnam tour as an armored cavalry platoon leader/troop commander, he was sent to the Infantry Advanced Course at Fort Benning, Georgia (a few Armor officers were selected to attend the Infantry course). On the first day of class, the attending officers were seated alphabetically, and Skip was among a group of Army aviators. Looking at his classmates he observed, "Most of the officers had recently returned from Vietnam. I noticed that the aviators were not gaunt, hollow-eyed, and underweight the way the rest of us were. They were upbeat, quick-witted, and generally fun to be around. And, they had more money than the rest of us and spent it pretty freely at the officers' club. It was then that I decided I wanted to be an aviator."

After successfully completing the aviation aptitude test and flight physical, Skip received orders for Army Aviation School after completion of the Infantry course. Upon graduation from flight school, he received orders to return to Southeast Asia after attending an AH-1G Cobra transition course. Arriving in

Vietnam in early February 1972, Skip was assigned to Lighthorse Air Cavalry and flew Cobra gunships for the Crusader platoon for almost two months before being transferred to Green Delta when Lighthorse stood down in March.

Following his second tour of duty in Vietnam, Skip Bell served as Armor/Infantry Tactics instructor at the U.S. Army Field Artillery School, Fort Sill, Oklahoma. After obtaining his master's degree in Business Information Systems, he was next assigned to FORSCOM HQ (highly classified repository for war plans and U.S. military unit status) in the Worldwide Military Command and Control System (WWMCCS) at Fort McPherson, Georgia.

Departing the Army after fourteen years, Skip served another seventeen years in the Reserves. During Operation Desert Shield, he deployed to Saudi Arabia with 3rd Army HQ, serving as the WWMCCS Section Chief G6, information officer. Bell retired in 1998 at the rank of colonel after serving as commander of the USAR Garrison Support Unit for Fort Bragg, North Carolina. During his military career, he was the recipient of the Purple Heart, five Bronze Stars (two w/V device), and fifteen Air Medals (one w/V device).

After the military, Skip worked thirteen years for a computer software company that produced tax preparation software. He retired in 2007 as vice president, administration.

When asked what he is most proud of, Skip said, "My most memorable event was graduating from Army Ranger School and surviving two tours in Vietnam, one as a platoon leader/cavalry troop commander on the ground, the second as an aviator. But the thing I'm most proud of are the fine children that my wife and I were able to see grow up to become outstanding, responsible citizens."

Skip and his wife have three children and four grandchildren.

Skip Bell and Crusader Cobra at Chi Lang
Photo courtesy of Skip Bell

CHAPTER 23

CAMBODIAN KIDS

IN MAY 1972, I FLY a highly unusual, covert mission into Cambodia, transporting a Khmer Republic military commander and several dignitaries to a secretive meeting in a small Cambodian city in jeopardy of being overrun by the Khmer Rouge (Communists). This exceptional mission has top-level clearance since it requires our landing in Cambodia, forbidden on most missions across the border.

THE DAY BEFORE

It is late afternoon on May 1, 1972, when I visit the day room to check the 18th CAC mission board to see if I am scheduled to fly the following day. Scanning down the list of ten to twelve Green Delta Huey missions, I see that I am flying copilot on a mission into Cambodia with aircraft commander Sydow. Our scheduled takeoff time is 0615 hours, 20 minutes before sunrise.

TO CHI LANG

In the predawn hours of the following day, I walk to the Green Delta Operations Center to obtain the mission briefing document. There, I meet Captain John Sydow, the aircraft commander for today's mission. John is a tall guy of medium build with dark hair and a big, bushy mustache. He has a pleasant, easygoing demeanor and I soon learn he is a very competent aviator. Having served as a scout pilot with B Troop, 7-1st Cavalry during his first Vietnam tour in 1968-69, he has extensive combat aviation experience.

Reading the mission briefing sheet, we are instructed to fly Huey 836 to Chi Lang on the Vietnam/Cambodia border. There, we will meet with MACV Special Operations Command to receive detailed instructions on today's mission.

Carrying our helmet bags and tactical maps, John and I walk to the flight line where we meet the crew chief and door gunner for Huey 836. After completing our preflight inspection, we board the Huey, crank the turbine engine, and take off to the northwest, flying ninety-six klicks (sixty miles) to Chi Lang. Arriving at the Chi Lang airstrip, we land, refuel, and hover to a PSP (perforated steel planking) helipad adjacent to the runway, where we shut down our aircraft.

Leaving the crew to secure our Huey, John and I walk to the MACV SOCC bunker for the mission briefing. Entering the highly fortified bunker, John and I are greeted by an Army Special Forces lieutenant colonel with MACV-SOG. The colonel tells us we will be flying to Phnom Penh, where we will pick up a senior Khmer Republic military officer and his staff. From there we will fly to Svay Rieng, a Cambodian city located near the Cambodia/Vietnam border.

Toward the end of the colonel's briefing, he tells us our mission is top secret and hands us blood chits for the entire crew. The issuance of blood chits is unusual and indicative of the critical, secretive nature of this mission across the border.

Blood chits are issued to U.S. aviators when they are at risk of being shot down in enemy territory. Made of silk, rayon, or Tyvek, the Vietnam era chits have a message in fourteen languages, the American flag, and a serial number at the bottom. The message states:

I am a citizen of the United States of America. I do not speak your language. Misfortune forces me to seek your assistance in obtaining food, shelter, and protection. Please take me to someone who will provide for my safety and see that I am returned to my people. My government will reward you.[14]

Then, just before we exit the briefing room, the colonel hands John a large roll of masking tape with instructions to tape over the U.S. Army lettering on the tail boom of our Huey. I think to myself, *This is ridiculous! Who else but the U.S. Army would be flying an olive drab green helicopter in Cambodia?* Once again, the Congressional proclamation that no U.S. military forces operate in Cambodia has filtered down to a directive that makes no sense. But who am I to question the intelligence of our senior command? So, we smile and comply.

Lastly, the colonel tells us that a Khmer Republic officer, Major Saroeun, will fly "back seat" as our interpreter and mission coordinator. This is good news since I know Major Saroeun from previous missions. He is a short, stout guy with dark hair and an oval face. Speaking near-perfect English, Saroeun has a fun sense of humor and I enjoy spending time with him. He often speaks of his home, Phnom Penh, telling me of the beauty of the capital city and the wonderful people who live there.

---

[14] Heritage Press International, "Blood chit," accessed January 19, 2019, http://www.usmcpress.com/heritage/blood_chit.htm

Huey tail boom with masking tape
Photo courtesy of Skip Bell

PHNOM PENH

Returning to our Huey, I approach the crew chief and hand him the roll of masking tape, telling him of our mission mandate. With a skeptical look on his face, he turns to mask off the tail boom. The expression on his face tells me that he too thinks the directive is absurd.

After a quick preflight inspection, we climb into the pilot seats and begin the engine start procedure. Soon, the Huey rotor blades are spinning "in the green," and we are ready to launch. About that time, Major Saroeun arrives, boards our Huey, and takes a seat behind the radio console that is mounted between the pilot seats. Plugging his headset into the aircraft's communications cable, Saroeun extends a pleasant greeting and says he's ready to fly.

After calling for radio clearance, I lift the Huey to a hover, taxi to the runway, and take off to the north, setting a course to Phnom Penh Airport 114 klicks (seventy-one miles) in the distance. It is a pleasant flight across the Cambodian countryside, a mixture of green fields, large flooded plains, and small villages interspersed across the flat landscape. In stark contrast to Vietnam, Cambodia is relatively untouched by the war and retains its natural beauty.

Forty-five minutes later, we arrive at Phnom Penh International Airport. After calling for landing clearance, John takes the controls, enters the traffic pattern, and lands adjacent to the refueling area. After topping off our fuel, he lifts the Huey to a hover and taxis across the runway to the vicinity of the airport tower. Setting the Huey down on the concrete, John rolls the throttle to flight idle while waiting for the dignitaries to arrive.

A short time later, a military Jeep arrives and parks near our aircraft. A Khmer Republic General and two staff assistants dismount the Jeep and walk to our Huey. After boarding, we are given map grid coordinates and instructions to proceed southeast to a Buddhist monastery located atop a mountaintop.

THE MONASTERY

John calls the tower for takeoff clearance while I plot our course to the mountain. Taking off, John flies southeast on a compass heading to our destination. Soon, we see a lone mountain in the distance, rising up majestically in contrast to the flat countryside that spreads to the horizon in every direction.

Circling the mountain in a tight left-hand turn, John carefully evaluates the monastery, looking for the best place to land. Then he flies about a klick south and turns 180 degrees, making his approach to land upwind.

Closing on the monastery, John carefully lines up to fly over the rooftops and between two groups of tall trees. From my position in the right-side pilot's seat, watching the decorative rooftops pass beneath the chin bubble and seeing the trees scroll by my window is an impressive sight.

Once past the trees, John continues over a tall wall and gently sets our Huey down in the open courtyard in front of an ornate Buddhist temple. It is then that I realize that John has an excellent control touch, likely acquired while flying the OH-6 as a scout pilot on his first tour. Flying between the trees, with little room past the tips of our rotor blades, requires precise flying skills. With skids on the ground, John rolls the aircraft throttle to flight idle.

Looking around, the architecture is awe-inspiring; richly colored buildings with ornate doorways and decorative rooftops with antler-like finials emerging from gable ends. Arch-covered walkways lead to unknown sanctuaries. Seemingly undisturbed by our presence, shaven-head Buddhist monks in bright orange robes crisscross the courtyard in front of our idling helicopter.

The general exits our Huey and walks to the perimeter of the courtyard, where he meets two Buddhist monks of obvious eminence. After a short conversation, they walk to our aircraft and take a seat inside the cargo bay. Then Major Saroeun comes on the intercom saying we are ready to continue the flight to our destination.

SVAY RIENG

Now, it's my turn to fly. With a heavier load, I monitor the engine torque gauge as I lift upward on the collective and carefully move the cyclic forward. The Huey lifts up and out of the courtyard, passing by the right side of the temple. Taking a compass heading to the southeast, we continue our journey to Svay Rieng.

Arriving near the city, Major Saroeun instructs me to land in the soccer field on the west edge of town. The bright green grass of the soccer stadium is easy to spot and makes an ideal place to land a helicopter. Making my approach on a normal glide path, I slowly descend into the open playing field. I bring the Huey to a hover in the center of the field, and lightly set the skids down on the lush grass.

After shutting down the Huey's turbine engine, the rotor blades are still slowly turning and about to stop when three military Jeeps arrive to transport our passengers. The general turns to John and me and says we are invited to accompany them. John turns to the crew chief and door gunner, who are now tying down the rotor blades, and tells them to stay with the helicopter. The general intercedes, telling us we can leave our helicopter unaccompanied since no one will bother it while we are away. Complying with the general, we gather our belongings and climb into a Jeep for the trip into town. This is a little worrisome since we would never leave our helicopter unattended in Vietnam.

The ride into the city is remarkable. Cambodia is beautiful, especially compared to what we are accustomed to seeing in Vietnam. The boulevards are clean, and the streets are lined with palm trees and blooming bushes. Predominately French, the architecture of the buildings is quite attractive.

Entering the town center, we approach a traffic circle with a fountain in the center of a large circular pool spewing water upward about twenty feet. Driving around the fountain, our Jeeps exit to the north. After traveling about a mile, we arrive at an impressive government building flanked by tall palm trees. Extending upward on the front veranda are six tall granite columns. The beauty of this magnificent structure is astounding, especially in this small city, seemingly in the middle of nowhere.

Coming to a stop in front of the majestic building, we exit the Jeeps and follow the dignitaries up the granite stairs. Passing by the tall columns, we enter through a very tall doorway into an anteroom constructed of marble and granite. Looking down, I cannot help but notice the beautiful polished marble floors.

The dignitaries continue past the anteroom into a large central room and are seated for their meeting. John and I, together with our crew chief and door gunner, are escorted to the right side of the anteroom and take a seat on a sofa behind a short table. Looking around, I am intrigued by the building's grandeur and openness. A cool breeze passes through the large, narrow windows stretching from two feet above the floor to about fifteen feet high. White silken draperies are flowing inward with the breeze. It is here I am reminded of an old movie, titled *Lost Horizon*. It seems as if we have arrived in Shangri-La.

Several minutes later, a servant dressed in white with a towel draped over his left arm enters the anteroom, pushing a serving cart on wheels. He offers us several varieties of oriental beer or cognac. Being on flight duty, we politely decline and ask for sodas instead.

THE CHILDREN

After drinking our refreshments, we decide to go outside and look around. As we walk around the grounds near the building, it is strangely quiet. There are no people. And, unlike Vietnam, no kids are swarming the Americans, seeking handouts.

Minutes later, we realize there is a group of children hiding in the bushes. These kids seem apprehensive and somewhat afraid of us. It is obvious they have never seen Americans. Like most pilots, we carry gum or candy. After some meticulous coaxing with candy, we eventually get the children to come out from hiding. They are adorable kids. The boys are playful, and I cannot help but notice that the little girls have pierced ears and are wearing gold ear pins.

Having a three-month-old daughter back home, I am drawn to the youngest girl who appears to be about two years old. She has long, straight, shoulder-length black hair that encircles her cute little face. Her gold ear pins shine through her hair. I reach down, and she allows me to pick her up. Handing my camera to John, he takes a photo of me holding this precious little girl among the other Cambodian children. This photo captures one of the most pleasant memories of my Southeast Asia tour.

Author and Cambodian children at Svay Rieng

RETURN FLIGHT

When the meeting is over, the dignitaries emerge from the building, ready to return to the soccer field. Giving the children the remaining candy and gum, we wave goodbye and climb aboard the Jeeps to return to our helicopter. Arriving at the soccer field, we find our Huey has not been disturbed as promised.

While our passengers wait near the Jeeps, we start the turbine engine, and within a minute the rotor blades are spinning at flight idle rpm. Motioning to the dignitaries, they load onto our Huey and take a seat. After increasing the throttle to bring the rotor blades to operating rpm, we take off and fly back to the mountaintop, returning the Buddhist monks to the monastery. Then we fly to Phnom Penh, where the general and his staff disembark. After refueling, we lift off and turn south to Chi Lang, where we drop off Major Saroeun and top off our fuel before returning to home base.

Arriving at Can Tho after dark, we have logged seven hours and five minutes of flight time. It has been a long yet rewarding day—a flight I will never forget.

Several days later, I hear a radio news report that reveals the reason for the high-level conference—Svay Rieng is under siege. At the time of the meeting, the Khmer Rouge were closing in, surrounding the city. The general and dignitaries were conferring to plan a resistance strategy.

The radio report continues, saying that Communist rockets exploded in the town square, killing several children. This news saddened me greatly. It is possible that some of the children we met in Svay Rieng may have been killed in the rocket attack. The collateral damage of this war is hell, and this is only a precursor of what is to later transpire in the "killing fields" of Cambodia.

Vietnam Veteran Profile: John Sydow

While serving two tours of duty in Vietnam, John Sydow was the recipient of the Bronze Star and thirty-three Air Medals in addition to the Distinguished Flying Cross with two oak leaf clusters (three awards).

After Vietnam, John was assigned to Fort Knox, Kentucky, as an instructor at the Armor Officer Basic Course and later as commander, D Troop, 10th Armored Cavalry Regiment (ACR). He then served in the Ohio National Guard as commander, N Troop, 107th ACR.

Transferring to Georgia, John served as commander, 1160th Transportation Company (HH) flying CH54A Sikorsky Skycranes at Hunter Army Airfield in Savannah, Georgia. Later, he served as commander of the 151st Military Intelligence Battalion flying OV-1D Mohawk fixed-wing aircraft.

After serving thirty-one years (seven active, nineteen National Guard, and five Reserves), John retired from the military in 1997 with the rank of colonel. During his varied career, he served as an aviation flight instructor, instrument examiner, safety officer, and maintenance officer and was rated in the OH-6, OH-58, UH-1, AH-1G, and CH-54 rotary wing and the OV-1D, U-8F, and C-12A fixed-wing aircraft.

In his second career, John worked for the State of Missouri as a probation/parole officer. His final retirement came in 2009.

When asked about his most memorable life accomplishment, John said, "I am most proud of applying for and receiving a direct commission from warrant officer to 1st lieutenant in the Armor branch after my first Vietnam tour. Then after my second tour, I applied and was approved for a Regular Army commission—not bad for an old WOC (warrant officer candidate)."

John and his wife have four children, two boys, and two girls. Both boys served in the U.S. Navy, with one serving in Iraq. He and his wife have five grandchildren and three great-grandchildren.

CHAPTER 24

ART AND THE ARVNS

ONE OF THE MORE COMMON Green Delta missions is providing aviation support to the fifteen provinces in IV Corp. In this mission, a single Huey helicopter and crew are assigned to support the MACV senior advisor for flight activities in that area. As you might expect, some provinces have more enemy activity and are far more dangerous than others. This story is about one of the *hotter* provinces in the Mekong Delta.

DINH TUONG PROVINCE

In mid-June 1972, Warrant Officer Art Tiller is a relatively new aircraft commander (AC), having received his AC check ride several days earlier. Tiller is of medium height and has a slender build. With his youthful face, he appears to be years younger than his counterpart nineteen-year-old warrant officers, almost as if he's someone's younger brother. But Art is proof that looks can be deceiving. He is a very experienced pilot, having flown for two other aviation units that stood down before being assigned to the 18th CAC.

On this day, Art's mission is flying provincial support for Dinh Tuong province. This assignment gives Tiller reason for concern. Located on the north side of the Mekong River, the

Dinh Tuong province stretches from the west side of Vinh Long to east of My Tho and encompasses the renowned "Plain of Reeds," a hot spot for enemy activity during the entire Vietnam War. In the recently initiated Easter Offensive, North Vietnamese troops, in concert with the Viet Cong, have advanced upon this province, methodically overrunning outposts manned by the ARVNs.

Art's copilot for this mission is a captain who recently arrived for his second Vietnam tour. Like my experiences, Art is outranked in the cockpit and is challenged to tactfully deal with the rank difference and the captain's unfamiliarity with the *new war* situation.

In the predawn hours, Art and his crew complete their preflight inspection and are ready to fly. In less than a minute, the Huey's turbine engine is at flight idle while Art monitors the exhaust temperature. Rolling the throttle on, Tiller brings the rotor blades to operating rpm, calls for clearance, and lifts the Huey to a three-foot hover. Nudging the cyclic slightly forward, he moves the Huey out from between the parallel four-foot revetment walls and continues to the runway apron.

After calling Can Tho tower for takeoff clearance, Art hovers to the center of runway 07, does a pedal turn, and takes off to the east. About thirty minutes later they arrive at Dong Tam, a large military compound on the north side of the Mekong River about five miles west of My Tho, the Dinh Tuong provincial capital.

MISSION BRIEFING

After landing and shutting down their helicopter, a Jeep arrives to transport Art and the captain to a MACV office on the Dong Tam compound. Entering the office, they are greeted by an Army major and an Army captain who give them a briefing on today's mission.

A string of five ARVN outposts are situated along an east/west canal about forty-five klicks (twenty-eight miles) northwest of Dong Tam. Four of the outposts have been overrun and are occupied by the Viet Cong and NVA. The last remaining ARVN outpost is in urgent need of resupply. The NVA occupy the forested area north of the canal, and friendly forces hold the open area south of the canal. If they cannot be resupplied today, the ARVNs will be forced to abandon the outpost this evening under the cover of darkness.

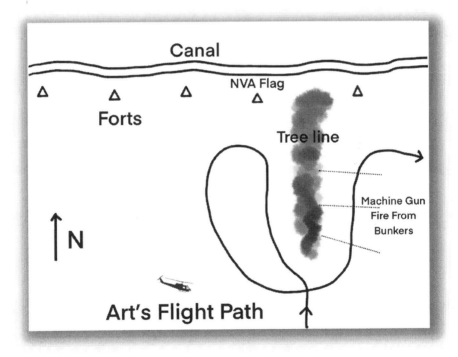

Does this sound familiar? Skip Bell faced a similar situation in the Vinh Binh province a month earlier. Since the Easter Offensive started on March 30, the NVA and VC forces have aggressively overtaken the ARVN outposts. Regardless of the weapons, munitions, and equipment provided by the U.S., the ARVNs are ill-prepared and in some cases reluctant to fight the well-disciplined enemy forces as they advance into the northern regions of the Mekong Delta.

The major tells Art he is to fly a high-altitude reconnaissance of the operations area and then land at a southern location to load munitions before resupplying the outpost. He closes the briefing by saying that he and the captain will ride along on this mission. Art thinks to himself, *This is strange. The MACV advisors typically remain at headquarters and rarely accompany the mission. But who am I to question?*

RESUPPLY MISSION

Returning to the helicopter, the crew chief unties the rotor blades while the copilot captain goes through the Huey startup procedure. Art ponders the mission and evaluates the weather. As usual, it is hot and humid, but today is overcast with a high cloud ceiling. Glancing to the north, he sees dark skies and thinks it may rain later in the day, typical for this time of year.

When the Huey turbine engine is operating at flight idle, Art motions to the two MACV officers who board through the right cargo door and take a seat inside the Huey. After rolling the throttle on and the rotor blades stabilize at operating rpm, the copilot calls for takeoff clearance and lifts off to the northwest, climbing to three thousand feet altitude.

Thirty minutes later, they arrive at the operations area and make a wide circle over the long, straight canal, running east to west with five triangular outposts evenly spaced along the south side of the canal. Art asks the MACV major to identify the friendly outpost and he replies, "We will pick up an ARVN soldier when we load the munitions. He will guide us to the outpost." Art thinks, *This is odd. The major does not know which outpost is friendly?*

> Author's note: This mission is in the same general area where 1st Lieutenant Ace Cozzalio, flying an OH-6 helicopter, knocked out an NVA machine gun bunker, rescuing an Infantry company of ninety soldiers who had been pinned down by enemy fire for over two hours. Since that event in January 1969, this area continues to be a haven for enemy activity.

Swinging southward, the copilot flies about ten minutes to land at a larger outpost with a helipad on the east side. After rolling the throttle to flight idle, six ARVN soldiers load ammo boxes into the Huey's cargo bay until stacked from the floor to ceiling. Once loaded, an ARVN soldier climbs aboard and takes a position behind the center console between the two pilot seats.

WHICH OUTPOST?

Art takes the controls and takes off to the north, climbing to one thousand feet altitude. Minutes later, they arrive about a klick south of the east-west canal. Looking forward, Art sees two outposts, separated by a long line of trees extending southward, perpendicular from the canal. Dropping to fly low-level, about twenty feet above the ground, Tiller flies toward the tree line, intending to target the outpost on the right side of the trees.

Suddenly, the ARVN soldier leans over the console, yelling in Vietnamese and pointing to the outpost on the left side of the trees. Thinking the soldier is identifying the friendly outpost, Art swings left of the tree line. As he approaches the outpost, he sees an alarming sight, a red NVA flag with a bright yellow star in the middle waving in the breeze over the compound. "Sh**, wrong outpost," says Tiller as he banks the Huey in a tight left turn to reverse directions.

Returning to the end of the tree line, Art makes a 180-degree turn, heading to the outpost on the east side of the tree line. Flying just beyond the trees at about twenty-five feet altitude, he flies rapidly toward the outpost. Suddenly, all hell breaks loose as machine gun fire erupts from the tree line. *What the hell,* Art thinks to himself. *They said the south side of the canal was safe.*

Pop-pop-pop-pop-pop-pop-pop-pop can be heard from the trees on the left. On the intercom, the crew chief asks, "Sir, can I shoot back?" Art yells, "Hell yes." Then Art hears the most disappointing sounds ever, a short burst of *Rat-tat-tat-tat* and then nothing. "My gun is jammed," shouts the frantic crew chief. (Note: This is a common occurrence in Green Delta caused by worn-out gas cylinder pistons. Replacement M-60 gun pistons have been on order for over six months).

Looking downward to the left, Art sees muzzle flashes coming from a row of fortified bunkers with machine gun barrels emerging from gun slits. The copilot captain says, "Go lower, you got to be lower," thinking that closer to the ground is safer. At this point, Art is irritated and frustrated, and his adrenaline is high. The MACV major and captain gave him misleading information, and the ARVN pointed to the wrong outpost. Now the captain is second-guessing his flying. Art turns to his copilot and says, "If you think you can do better than me, you can have the aircraft." Art pulls pitch and swings right to climb out of the hot area.

At this point, Art realizes they have lost any element of surprise—the NVA are waiting for him. And, the only approach path to the outpost is heavily covered by machine gun bunkers. Needing fuel and suspecting that his aircraft has taken hits, Tiller turns to the southeast, returning to Dong Tam.

Upon landing and shutting down the Huey, Art and his crew are astonished that there is no damage to their aircraft, not a single hit from enemy fire. How is that possible? Years later, when reading this author's book, *ACE: The Story of Lt. Col. Ace Cozzalio*, Art realizes that the NVA machine guns installed in bunkers have limited elevation. Art and his crew escaped the enemy fire because they were flying above the trajectory of the machine guns. Had they been lower, as the copilot advised, they would have undoubtedly suffered hits from the NVA automatic weapons fire.

RETURN TO THE OUTPOST?

After securing their aircraft, the Green Delta crew heads to the MACV mess hall for lunch. After getting a plate of food from the kitchen serving window, the crew is seated at a rectangular table with seating for twelve and covered with a red and white checkered tablecloth.

During their meal, the copilot captain turns to Art and says, "Tiller, I think I know what is going on here. These guys (the MACV major and captain) are running out of war. They need some combat experience to get their 'ticket punched' and advance their careers after peace is declared." The captain continues, "They are going to ask you to attempt the resupply mission again, and neither you nor I think that is wise. You cannot say no. You can, however, give a qualified yes. Just tell them you will gladly try it again, but this time you need air support from a couple of gunships."

Art thinks, *That is an excellent idea. The captain has redeemed himself after earlier urging me to make a serious mistake by flying lower.* Tiller responds, "Thanks, Captain. Sounds good to me."

About the time they finish eating, the major and captain approach the crew and pull up a couple of chairs. The major says, "Now that you guys have had something to eat, we would like to try the resupply again." Art responds with, "Roger that, sir, only this time we will need air cover from a couple of Cobra gunships. That area is too hot for a single aircraft without gun cover."

The expression on the major's face turns quickly from a smile to dismay as he says, "Are you kidding? Are you trying to start a war or something?" Then the two officers abruptly stand up and leave the mess hall.

Returning to their Huey, the Green Delta crew unloads the ammo boxes, refuels, and returns to Can Tho, glad that this mission is over.

LESSONS LEARNED

Years later, Tiller says this mission taught him many lessons, but the most important was to respectfully use the "qualified yes" response when faced with similar high-risk situations.

Vietnam Veteran Profile: Art Tiller

After Vietnam, Art Tiller served one year at Fort Lewis, Washington, with B Troop, 3rd Squadron, 5th Cavalry until his military commitment was completed in 1973. In Vietnam, he flew 750 hours and was the recipient of fifteen air medals.

After the Army, Art began a forty-year career flying both rotary and fixed-wing aircraft for air medical ambulance companies. In his last ten years of commercial flying, Art was training captain and check airman flying EC135, AS350, and A109 helicopters.

Art recalls one very memorable rescue in 1998 while flying a Bell 222U helicopter. A solo hiker had fallen into a hole and broken his leg at 10,500 feet in Wyoming's Big Horn Mountains. Facing treacherous, mountainous conditions, Art landed his aircraft on a small, uneven ledge. Hooking his right skid behind a rock, Art set his helicopter down in a risky, nose-high, left-roll position with the rock keeping the aircraft from sliding down the mountainside. After shutting down, Art, the paramedic, and nurse retrieved the injured hiker and carried him on a stretcher to the helicopter. The hiker, a NASA research pilot and former Navy pilot, later wrote, "I have observed many examples of superb airmanship, but Mr. Tiller's maneuvering of his...helicopter...to a landing in rough terrain on a rugged, small, non-level landing zone was as fine an example as I have ever seen."

Art Tiller and Airbus EC135
Photo courtesy of Art Tiller

Upon retiring in 2017, Art had accumulated over 17,000 hours in both rotary and fixed-wing aircraft. When asked about his aviation career, Art said, "I am most proud of flying emergency medical helicopters for thirty years." He continues to fly a Van's RV-12 airplane in his leisure time.

Art and his wife have a blended family of one son, two daughters, and a grandson. As a proud grandfather, Art commented, "The feeling I get when holding a grandchild is better than any high I got from aviation—truly incredible!"

CHAPTER 25

AMERICAN ADVISOR KILLED

ONE MISSION I FLEW WITH Green Delta was especially disturbing. We were called to pick up an American advisor who had been killed in a battle with the Viet Cong. Over time, I had seen many deceased ARVN and Viet Cong soldiers, and I was at a point where seeing the bodies became routine. However, this experience involving a dead American was very upsetting. It felt personal, as if one of my fellow crew members had died.

EASTER OFFENSIVE OF 1972

As mentioned in earlier chapters, the 1972 Easter Offensive resulted in the NVA and Viet Cong attacking and seizing as much territory as possible. Ultimately, the offensive spread to areas of South Vietnam previously untouched by the war. One of these areas was the Go Cong Province in IV Corps, forty-five klicks (twenty-eight miles) south of Saigon. Go Cong was considered one of the most secure of South Vietnam's forty-four provinces and, before the offensive, had been classified as one hundred percent pacified by the Saigon government.

THE BATTLE

Rudolph Kaiser is the senior American advisor to Go Cong Province. Working with the South Vietnamese, Kaiser established defensive positions throughout the province and trained the local militia forces (also called regional forces) to fight and defend their homeland.

Note: The South Vietnamese Regional Forces were Army of the Republic of Vietnam (ARVN) militia. Recruited locally, they fell into two broad groups— Regional Forces and the more local-level Popular Forces (the RFPFs, called Ruff-Puffs by American forces).[15] Following Vietnamization, these units once again came back to prominence as they became better trained and tasked with carrying out wider area operations despite lacking artillery and air support. They would serve as front-line provincial defense units while Regular Forces were typically deployed against conventional People's Army of Vietnam (NVA) units.[16]

In late July 1972, Kaiser received intelligence reports that a Viet Cong battalion had entered Go Cong Province from the north. Choosing to act offensively, Kaiser assembled the militia and rallied the forces to attack the VC as they advanced southward. Meeting the enemy in the open rice paddies, the two sides fought a fierce battle, and Kaiser was killed.

As later reported in several news sources, "They ran into a 'hornet's nest' of Viet Cong firing B40 rocket launchers and hand grenades. Survivors of the ambush reported that Kaiser was

---

[15]Andrew Wiest. *Vietnam's Forgotten Army: Heroism and Betrayal in the ARVN* (NYU Press, 2009), pp. 75-85

[16] Ngo Quang Truong, "Territorial Forces," 1978, https://www.vietnam.ttu.edu/star/images/1127/11270103001a.pdf: U.S. ARMY CENTER OF MILITARY HISTORY

wounded by one explosion and killed by another as he was being treated. Kaiser's body was left at the ambush site and was recovered the following morning."[17]

THE MISSION: RETRIEVE KAISER'S BODY

On the morning of July 27, 1972, Captain John Knoch and I are alerted to fly the mission to retrieve Kaiser's body. This is my first time to fly with John, who is a second tour aviator, having served his first Vietnam tour in 1968, flying Hueys with an assault helicopter company.

Arriving at the TOC, John and I pick up the mission briefing sheet that includes map grid coordinates of the pickup location and the radio frequency of the regional militia. We ask about the circumstances of his death and are told a story somewhat different than the one later reported by official sources. We are told that Kaiser rallied the militia to advance against the Viet Cong, but once the fighting began, the South Vietnamese militia retreated. While attempting to regroup the regional forces, Kaiser was shot and killed. His body was left lying in the rice paddies until the following day.

Walking to the flight line, John and I locate our aircraft, Huey 829, and greet our crew chief and door gunner, telling them about today's mission. After a preflight inspection, I climb into the right seat with John in the left. After starting the turbine engine and once the rotor blades are "in the green," I lift the Huey to a three-foot hover, move forward out of the revetments, and taxi to the runway. Upon receiving clearance from the tower, I take off to the east and climb to two thousand feet. Banking left to a compass heading based on the map grid

---

[17] George Epser, "Rudolph Kaiser Is Killed In Cong Ambush," *Colorado Springs Gazette Telegraph,* July 28, 1972, page 1

coordinates, I fly toward our destination: an open rice paddy about fourteen klicks (nine miles) northwest of the town of Go Cong.

Arriving in the area thirty minutes later, I descend to one thousand feet while John calls the militia, telling them we are inbound to their location, and asking that they pop a smoke grenade. Seconds later, we see red smoke spiraling upward in the distance. John calls to identify the smoke color, and the militia confirms it is red. I swing the nose of the Huey to the left and lower the collective to begin my descent to the red smoke spiraling upward from the open rice paddy. Passing through one hundred feet altitude, a regional militia soldier walks toward us, waving his arms, and motioning for me to land. I continue downward and come to a hover in front of the soldier, who is standing in ankle-deep muddy water.

Glancing right, I see the ground beneath the Huey is a muddy rice paddy with pools of water on the surface. Lowering the collective, I set the skids down atop the soft mud, holding just enough pitch in the rotor blades to keep the skids from sinking.

Since I flew the inbound segment, it is now John's turn to fly our outbound leg. Turning to look at him, I say, "Hey, John, it's all yours now," and John replies, "I have the controls." John places both hands on the controls, holding the aircraft lightly atop the mud. I release my hands from the cyclic and collective and turn my attention to what is happening outside our helicopter.

Looking out the windshield, I see a group of South Vietnamese militia gathered about 150 feet in front of our aircraft. Soon, four soldiers reach down and pick up Kaiser's body. Plodding through the wet mud, they carry him toward our aircraft. When they get closer, I can see that Kaiser's face is an ashen gray color and his body is limp.

Once they are directly in front of the Huey, one of the soldiers stumbles, and they drop Kaiser's upper torso in the mud. To me, this is the ultimate insult. I am shocked and disturbed by the lack of respectful handling of the body.

Breaking the silence, our crew chief, who was watching the event, comes on the intercom saying, "I'm going to help." I turn left to see the crew chief disconnect his commo cord, jump out the left side of the Huey, and trudge through the mud to assist the militia. They lift and carry Kaiser's body to the right-side cargo door where they gently place Kaiser on the cargo bay floor. Then the crew chief uses a towel to wipe the mud from his body and prepare him for the flight. As I watch, I think, *What a solemn and reverent act of respect.*

Once Kaiser's body is in place, John brings the Huey to a three-foot hover and does a pedal turn to the left, and we take off to the northwest. The crew is silent as we climb to two thousand feet altitude and fly to Saigon. We are saddened by the death of a fellow American who was killed while serving his country and disturbed by the way the South Vietnamese militia handled his body.

Landing at Hotel 3, a large helipad near Tan Son Nhut Airbase, John hovers toward a waiting military ambulance truck and sets the Huey down on the concrete parking area. After the rotor blades slow to flight idle, four Army personnel carrying a folding stretcher approach our aircraft. Placing Kaiser's body on the stretcher, they solemnly walk to the ambulance and slowly position his body inside the open doors. After closing the doors, they drive away in the ambulance.

John calls the tower for takeoff clearance, and they clear us to take off to the south. Lifting off, we climb to two thousand feet altitude. It is a sad and solemn flight back to Can Tho.

JOHN PAUL VANN

Rudolph Kaiser was a protégé of John Paul Vann, the senior American advisor in the Central Highlands who died in a helicopter crash the previous month. Vann was instrumental in developing the combat strategy for the latter part of the Vietnam War. Foretelling the problems of the war, Vann was highly critical of South Vietnamese tactics, notably their tendency to use excessive airstrikes and artillery without putting ground units into VC territory.[18]

He was also one of the few to identify the absence of commitment and determination on the part of the South Vietnamese forces. By accompanying ARVN units to the field, Vann quickly observed, to his dismay, that the South Vietnamese Army lacked the will to fight. In the face of enemy fire, far too many ARVN officers and soldiers chose not to engage the enemy and took flight. Vann once said, "ARVN troops would not risk conducting search-and-destroy missions but instead assumed defensive positions whenever possible."[19] He believed the American advisors could provide the necessary training and tactics to give the South Vietnamese forces the confidence and resolve to achieve success in battle.

Rudolph Kaiser was dutifully leading by example and performing the role that his friend, John Paul Vann, envisioned,

---

[18] Peter Kross, "John Paul Vann: Man and Legend," *Vietnam Magazine*, April 2007, http://www.historynet.com/john-paul-vann-man-and-legend.htm

[19] Peter Kross, "John Paul Vann: Man and Legend," *Vietnam Magazine*, April 2007, http://www.historynet.com/john-paul-vann-man-and-legend.htm

and, in doing so, led to his demise. The published account of the battle stated, "Like Vann, he [Kaiser] had a predilection for 'getting into the action.'"

METAPHOR OF THE WAR

I realize that the dropping of the colonel's body by the ARVN soldiers was unintentional. But, to me, at that particular time in my Vietnam service, this event served as a metaphor for the South Vietnamese Army's role in the war. My belief was that we, the United States of America, were there to promote democracy and assist the South Vietnamese government in protecting their country from a Communist takeover. Yet, what I saw were too many of the ARVN soldiers who exhibited indifference and a decided lack of interest in fighting for their country. It seemed they would prefer not to make the effort and, instead, "drop the U.S. in the mud."

I witnessed this firsthand when flying with Lighthorse. On several occasions, we were tasked with inserting an ARVN infantry company into an LZ with the expectation that the ARVNs would sweep a two- to three-kilometer area to engage and eliminate the Viet Cong forces. Late in the day, we were called to retrieve the ARVNs at the exact place where they were inserted that morning—they never moved, just sat in place all day, waiting to be retrieved.

Years later, when the South Vietnamese government fell to the Communists, a vast number of ARVN soldiers were placed in reeducation camps (essentially prisons) for as many as ten years. I often wondered if these same soldiers longed to have the United States return and rescue them, or perhaps they wished they had fought harder for their freedom.

However, in my honest evaluation of the South Vietnamese people's plight, I recognize that the Vietnamese people have known nothing but war since 1945 when the French occupied the country as their colony and fought the Viet Minh. With the defeat of the French at Dien Bien Phu in 1954, the United States stepped in to support the South Vietnamese against North Vietnam and the Viet Cong. This evolved into the Vietnam War. The South Vietnamese people have never known peace and have little reason to believe it will ever be achieved. And, the South Vietnamese have experienced the extremes of political corruption, in both the government and the military. Promise after promise has been made and broken. It is not very surprising that their spirits are broken, and they have little faith in the positive outcome of the war.

Ultimately, the United States is also guilty of breaking its promise. President Nixon promised South Vietnam the U.S. would deliver "severe retaliation" against North Vietnam should they break the ceasefire. But, "on June 19, 1973, Congress passed the Case-Church Amendment, which called for a halt to all military activities in Southeast Asia by August 15, thereby ending twelve years of direct U.S. military involvement in the region.

"In the fall of 1974, Nixon resigned under the pressure of the Watergate scandal and was succeeded by Gerald Ford. Congress cut funding to South Vietnam for the upcoming fiscal year from a proposed 1.26 billion to 700 million dollars. These two events prompted Hanoi to make an all-out effort to conquer the South."[20] Owing to South Vietnam's weakened state and lack of support from the U.S., this would only take fifty-five days.

---

[20] Lauren Zanolli, "What happened When Democrats in Congress Cut Off Funding for the Vietnam War," History News Network, Columbian College of Arts & Sciences, https://historynewsnetwork.org/article/31400

Vietnam Veteran Profile: John Knoch

John Knoch enlisted in the Army in 1966. After basic training, he attended Army Airborne School, earning his "jump wings." Later, after completing a minimum of thirty jumps, he earned his senior parachutist badge. Then, John was selected to attend Officer Candidate School, where he graduated as a 2nd lieutenant in the Field Artillery Branch. After OCS, John applied for and was approved to attend Army Flight School.

John Knoch in U.S. Army Flight School, 1968
Photo courtesy of Susan Oblad

After earning his silver flight wings in 1968, John received orders for Vietnam and flew Hueys with the 68th Assault Helicopter Company, flying out of Bien Hoa in III Corps. During this tour, he received the Army Commendation Medal for locating four severely injured crew members whose helicopter crashed in dense jungle. While his crew tended to the injuries, John flew his Huey high above, calling for and coordinating the medevac rescue.

After returning stateside in 1969, John attended the Rotary Wing Flight Instructor Course and, after that, the Field Artillery Advanced Course.

In 1972, Knoch returned to Vietnam, serving his second tour flying with Green Delta. John retired in 1986 at the rank of major after serving twenty years in the Army. During his service, he was the recipient of twenty-eight Air Medals, the Bronze Star Medal with oak leaf cluster, and the Distinguished Flying Cross.

John Knoch died in 1998 at age fifty-one.

CHAPTER 26

THE SCROUNGE MISSION

BACKGROUND

COMMISSIONED OFFICERS IN THE ARMY have both a primary assignment and a secondary assignment. In Vietnam, my primary duty was helicopter pilot while I had four secondary assignments during my one-year tour: material and supply officer, POL (petroleum, oil, and lubricants) officer, and airfield security officer (twice). Like most pilots, I would rather be flying but recognized my obligation to perform a secondary job. The multiple duties create stressful situations at times, especially when learning a new job that I am unfamiliar with, and, at the same time, being scheduled to fly.

POL OFFICER

One afternoon, after returning from a flying mission, I am told to report to the company executive officer (XO). Walking to headquarters, I enter the XO's office, salute, and say, "You wanted to see me, sir?" The captain replies, "Yes, Lieutenant, you are the new airfield POL officer." Frankly, I have no idea what a POL officer does, but I try to feign interest when I just want to fly helicopters.

I inquire about the job, and the captain mentions that the previous POL officer (another lieutenant) was relieved because the Vietnamese locals were caught stealing fuel. I am thinking, *That explains why the Japanese motorcycles spew smoke and smell like JP-4 aviation fuel when the local citizens go careening through the streets of downtown Can Tho.* The captain challenges me to develop a fuel accountability system to prevent fuel theft. I salute, do an about-face, and exit the office thinking, *What a challenge—how to stop fuel theft, and I know nothing about POL.*

The following day, I walk to the POL shack where I meet my staff, five enlisted men and two Vietnamese workers. Fortunately for me, one of the enlisted men, Sergeant Rogers, has received Army POL training. The others know a little about maintenance, but mostly just follow Sergeant Rogers's directions.

Taking me behind the POL shack, Rogers shows me a bright yellow fuel truck with SHELL printed in large red letters on the side of the large tank. Climbing on top, he opens the tank and points inside. The crafty Vietnamese had installed a partition inside the 12,000-liter tank. When the Vietnamese drivers offloaded aviation fuel, the airfield received eight thousand liters, with four thousand liters behind the partition being sold on the local market. This reportedly happened for an extended period of time until one day when Sergeant Rogers thought to look inside the supposedly empty truck. Discovering the partition, Rogers looked up to see the Vietnamese driver in a dead run, disappearing in the distance.

Next, Sergeant Rogers and I climb into the POL Jeep and drive to the airfield fuel storage area. Driving south across the east/west runway, we pass by a long, narrow lagoon of water, about forty feet wide, that borders the south side of the runway. Aligned next to the lagoon are a row of eight large rubber fuel bladders holding ten thousand gallons each. Measuring approximately thirty feet long and fifteen feet wide, the bladders expand to four feet high when filled with fuel. Lying flat on the ground, the bladders are surrounded by five-feet-high sandbag revetments. Interconnecting the bladders is a system of three-inch pipe running to the helicopter refueling pads nearby. Two electrical pumps pressurize the system.

Sergeant Rogers explains that there are no fuel meters to measure either input or output from the bladders. The only input measure is each truck being offloaded, and the only output measure is each pilot's notation of fuel pounds dispensed in the fuel record forms. Both measures are highly inaccurate.

FLOW METERS

As the weeks pass, I try to determine a way to measure fuel deliveries and usage. It is blatantly obvious what is needed—flow meters in the input and output distribution lines, and I have no idea where to obtain them. Sergeant Rogers has attempted to requisition flow meters through normal channels without success.

After giving this predicament some thought, I contact a friend, Captain Rick Coplen, who is assigned to U.S. Army Headquarters at Long Binh, near Saigon. Coplen tells me he has connections with people in Army HQ who might help me locate POL parts. He suggests I travel to Long Binh.

My hooch mate, Donny O'Connor, has similar supply problems. As motor pool officer, Donny needs truck and Jeep parts, especially engines and spark plugs.

Several days later, I visit our commanding officer, Major Douglas Thorp, and explain that without flow meters, I have no means to develop an accountability system to stop fuel theft. And, after mentioning that Donny needs motor pool parts, I propose he allow Donny and me to make a trip to Long Binh seeking the required materials and supplies. Major Thorp agrees and suggests we ask others in our unit to see what they too might need.

After meeting with several officers and NCOs in the company, I develop a list of needed items. The most critical parts topping our want list are gas cylinder pistons for the M-60 machine guns mounted on the Hueys. Most of the gas cylinder pistons are badly worn, causing the machine guns to jam after firing five or six rounds—a critical shortcoming when the enemy is shooting at us. The gun pistons have been on requisition for over six months, and every inquiry is answered with, "Wait your turn. The gas cylinder pistons are on backorder." Meanwhile, our crew chiefs and door gunners are constrained to firing short bursts when protecting our Hueys from enemy fire.

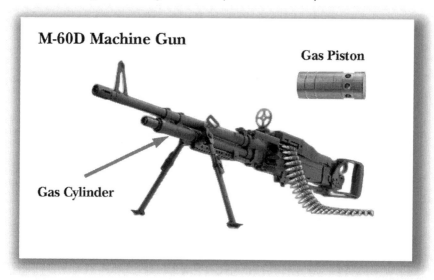

M-60 machine gun and gas piston
Courtesy of Numrich Gun Parts Corporation

SCROUNGE MISSION

It is mid-August 1972 when Donny and I prepare for our mission to scrounge parts and supplies. Being a motor pool officer has its advantages. Donny arranges to take a three-quarter-ton truck on our journey. After loading the truck with excess inventory for bartering, we drive the truck to the flight line and enter the loading ramp of a Chinook heavy-lift helicopter for our flight to Long Binh.

Flying to the Saigon area, the Chinook drops us off at Bien Hoa Army Airfield, twenty-four klicks (fifteen miles) northeast of Saigon, where we start our search. Our first stop is the local motor pool where Donny makes arrangements to swap parts and supplies for spark plugs and several excess deuce-and-a-half (M-35 2½-ton cargo truck) engines. From there, we work our way southeast to Long Binh.

Upon our arrival at Army Headquarters, I meet with Captain Coplen, who puts me in touch with a materials and supply person who knows where I might locate POL parts. He, in turn, refers me to a third person who takes me to the Long Binh Airfield and shows me two Conex containers full of new flow meters, valves, and pipe connections. This is everything I need, and best of all, it is surplus and free for the taking.

Donny and I use our remaining days searching for available parts and supplies. While Donny is trading for motor pool parts, I am seeking a variety of parts and supplies on our want list. With each transaction, we sharpen our bartering skills by trading for items we need and other things we don't need but recognize as valuable commodities for trading. In some instances, we are given excess parts and supplies just to get rid of them. We take everything we are offered and assemble the numerous items in Conex containers at the Long Binh airfield staging area. We soon realize that we are pretty adept at this process, getting almost anything we desire by asking questions, following up on leads, and being relentless in our search.

GAS CYLINDER PISTONS

About midway through our materials hunt, Donny and I go to the supply depot in Long Binh hoping to acquire M-60 gas cylinder pistons. Entering the long white building with a corrugated tin roof, we give the six-month-old requisition form to a civilian employee standing behind the three-foot-tall supply counter and ask that he fill our order. He goes in the back room and returns with a long, narrow box that he sets on the counter in front of us. It is filled with new gas cylinder pistons, each one gleaming through individually wrapped clear plastic. I am thinking, *Outstanding! We found the pistons!*

With our requisition form in hand, the U.S. government employee says, "You don't have priority and will have to wait until your order is filled through normal distribution channels." I blurt out, "Priority my ass! Our guys' lives are at risk because we don't have gas cylinder pistons." Then he says, "Well, there are things that might speed up the process." It is blatantly obvious; he wants a bribe.

I turn to look at Donny. From the expression on his face, I can tell he is as mad as hell, just like I am. I glance at Donny's hand atop his Browning 9mm holstered pistol (NVA officer's weapon—a war trophy that Donny carried daily), and my mind visualizes another rendition of the OK Corral about to be played out in the supply room.

The tension is extreme, but I realize an escalating confrontation may jeopardize our ability to get the gas cylinder pistons. Turning back to the civilian employee I ask, "What will it take to change our priority?" He answers without hesitation, "A case of Jack Daniel's and a case of beef steaks might improve the process."

I motion to Donny, and we leave the supply room. We are upset, yet we know we can make the deal. After making several trades, we return the following day with a case of Jack Daniel's and a case of frozen steaks. We leave with a box of new gas cylinder pistons, enough to replace the gas pistons in all the machine guns in our unit with some to spare.

FREE STUFF

On another day, while scrounging for parts in Long Binh, we happen upon a large supply tent filled with uniforms and other military equipment. Inside, we find a 2nd lieutenant who recently arrived in-country and was given the assignment to move everything to Tan Son Nhut Airbase in Saigon, about ten miles away. He admits he has no idea how he is going to accomplish this task and tells us we can take anything we want.

This is like winning the lottery. Grabbing jungle boots, boonie (jungle uniform) hats, first aid kits, fire extinguishers, emergency radios, and camouflage jungle fatigues, we load everything we can carry into our truck. Much of the equipment will be used to trade for other things we need. We keep the first aid kits because most of the kits on our helicopters have been depleted and lack essential medical supplies.

Being pilots, we wear Nomex flight uniforms and are not issued jungle fatigues. So, Donny and I pick out a set of camouflage fatigues and take them to a Vietnamese alteration shop to have our name and rank sewn on and tailored to fit. Our new image in jungle fatigues and boonie hats seems more appropriate for scroungers.

RETURN TO CAN THO

After obtaining all the items on our want list, we call Green Delta Operations, requesting they send three Chinook helicopters to pick up our loot. When the Chinooks set down at Long Binh Airfield, we have forklifts ready to load three large crates of deuce-and-a-half engines, two Conex containers of POL parts, another Conex container of miscellaneous parts/supplies, and our loaded three-quarter-ton truck.

On the return trip to Can Tho, Donny and I talk about our accomplishments. We succeeded in obtaining everything we had hoped to acquire, including all the Motor Pool and POL parts and even the highly desired gas cylinder pistons. In addition, we are returning with first aid kits, fire extinguishers, and other items. We are pleased with our material acquisition exploits, and we anticipate our fellow pilots and crew members in Green Delta will be delighted as well.

Landing at Can Tho Airfield in the late afternoon, the Chinook helicopters hover to the runway apron and slowly settle to the ground. Inside the lead Chinook, Donny and I, wearing our new jungle fatigues and boonie hats, are seated in the three-quarter-ton truck waiting for the loading ramp to deploy. Once the platform touches the ground, we proceed down the ramp and drive off the airfield.

After parking the truck near our hooch, we walk through the Green Delta company area, expecting to be greeted with congratulatory remarks like, "Wow, you guys got gas cylinder pistons!" Or, "You guys filled three Chinooks—that's awesome!" Instead, we find a solemn mood. An announcement made that afternoon told of the ongoing Easter Offensive in the north.

Vietnam Veteran Profile: Donny O'Connor

Donny's younger brother, Gerry, an Army helicopter pilot flying a Charlie Model Huey gunship, died in a crash in the Mekong Delta in 1970. Donny called the loss "a life changer for me. I'm the oldest of seven boys and his death hit me hard." At the time, Donny was a 2nd lieutenant "on orders" to Fort Monmouth, New Jersey. To honor his brother's memory, Donny requested and was approved for Army Flight School. Following graduation, Donny flew Hueys in the very same area where his brother had flown two years earlier: the Mekong Delta based out of Can Tho.

After serving a year in Vietnam, Donny was assigned to Fort Carson, Colorado, as a staff officer and later as commander of a supply and service company. Departing the military in 1975, O'Connor had six and a half years' service, and was the recipient of sixteen Air Medals, two with V device, and the Bronze Star Medal.

Donny O'Connor and Colorado National Guard Huey
Photo courtesy of Donny O'Connor

Missing the thrilling challenges and excitement of aviation, Donny joined the Colorado National Guard in 1986 and returned to flying. He served as company commander, safety officer, and test pilot of UH-1, OH-6, and OH-58 helicopters. After attending the Fixed Wing Qualification Course, he flew the C-26 Metroliner. Upon retirement in 2007, Donny had twenty-two years military service.

In civilian life, Donny was general manager for a glass company and an award-winning salesman for a steel buildings company flying a Cessna 182 for sales appointments, primarily in Nebraska. Later, he owned a highly successful insurance company in Denver.

Donny's passion is riding motorcycles on extended trips, having crossed the United States four times on two-lane highways and once to Alaska. Some of his happiest times are on the open road, riding his two-wheeled adventure machine.

Donny and his wife have a combined family of two sons and six grandchildren.

CHAPTER 27

HOW I "LOST" MY FANCY PILOT'S WATCH

1972 EASTER OFFENSIVE—PILOT VOLUNTEERS

RETURNING FROM OUR SCROUNGE MISSION, Donny and I are walking through the company area toward our hooch when our hooch mate, Tim Halstrom, greets us. Tim is quick to tell us about a pilot meeting held earlier in the afternoon in which they were provided an update on the Easter Offensive. The pilots are told the ground battle against the NVA forces that infiltrated across the Demilitarized Zone in March is raging on and aviators are in demand. The Army needs additional pilots to reinforce the aviation units in the two northernmost Corp areas of South Vietnam and is soliciting volunteers. Applications for this reassignment will be accepted for the next twenty-four hours.

After a short discussion, Donny, Tim, and I agree that this could be an opportunity to get more flight time in another aviation unit. All three lieutenants in the HOG hooch (Halstrom, O'Connor, and Gooch) volunteer. Tim Halstrom and I are approved. Green Delta Command denies Donny O'Connor's request, saying his motor pool duties are essential to the unit. We feel bad about Donny, having hoped that the three HOGs could be reassigned together.

Many of the lieutenants and none of the captains in Green Delta volunteer to transfer. Since captains outnumber lieutenants by over two to one (twenty-eight captains vs. twelve lieutenants), the captains are satisfied to remain in place, while the lieutenants, who are on the receiving end of details and other unsavory assignments, prefer to take their chances with another unit. And, just like Tim and me, the other volunteering lieutenants have high hopes of getting more flight time in a different aviation unit.

After receiving our reassignment orders, 1st Lieutenants Tim Halstrom, Bill Fesler, Don Miles, and I board a helicopter for Saigon. Our final destination: Pleiku in II Corp (also called the Central Highlands). I am a little apprehensive about leaving the familiar, flat terrain of the Mekong Delta area where I have been flying for the past ten months. Familiarizing myself with the mountainous terrain of II Corps and the challenges that come with high-altitude flying are a real concern. Nonetheless, I am looking forward to flying for a different unit, hopefully an Air Cavalry unit.

RIPPED OFF BY KIDS

After landing at Tan Son Nhut Air Base, we find we have an extra day before our flight to Pleiku. This is great news; we can enjoy some R&R time before our journey north. We four lieutenants decide to go to downtown Saigon to see the sights. Departing the air base, we check into a hotel and change into our khaki uniforms. Wearing our uniforms is an Army requirement that, frankly, makes the U.S. soldiers easy targets for pickpockets and thieves. Realizing this, Don Miles empties his wallet and puts his folded bills (around $100) in the breast pocket of his shirt. The others put their money in their shoes while I put my wallet in my front pants pocket. Off we go to explore downtown Saigon.

Bill Fesler, who was stationed in Saigon during his first Vietnam tour, is familiar with the city, so he becomes our tour guide. As we discuss our options, one of the guys suggests we find something to eat. Bill tells us about a Chinese restaurant. We all agree that Chinese food sounds great, especially compared to the meals served in the mess hall.

Note: Bill Fesler was an infantry enlisted soldier stationed in Cholon as a parachute rigger during his first Vietnam tour. Cholon, a Saigon suburb, is predominantly Chinese.

We hail a couple of two-person cyclos (three-wheeled bicycle rickshaw with the driver in the rear), and Bill gives directions to our drivers. Soon, we are off, meandering through narrow streets bustling with activity. As our journey progresses, we see fewer and fewer Americans until most everyone is Chinese. We have traveled deep into the Cholon district of Saigon.

Arriving at the restaurant, Bill recognizes one of the wait staff and asks for a table. Once seated, we are all given menus in Chinese. After taking one look at the menu, we are clueless, but Bill comes to the rescue. He takes charge and orders all our meals. Soon, the wait staff brings plate after plate of amazing Chinese dishes. We have a magnificent lunch. I will always remember the huge fried crab claws—delicious.

After lunch, we walk outside the restaurant and hail another pair of cyclos. Seated in the clamshell enclosure of the pedaled taxis, I am awestruck by the intense colors of the sidewalk vendors, restaurants, and storefronts as we pass down the narrow streets on our ride back to central Saigon. We ask to be dropped off on Tu Do Street, where we are caught up in the throngs of people moving along the crowded sidewalk. It is exciting to be in the capital city and to be immersed in the noises, the spicy aromas, and the Vietnamese language being spoken all around us. The French-inspired architecture is impressive, and so is the enormous War Memorial depicting two larger-than-life South Vietnamese Marines in combat.

After walking about a mile, someone in our group suggests we get a drink, so we turn down a side street and enter a bar. Once we are seated, we order a round of Ba Moi Ba beers from the Vietnamese bar girls. After telling tall tales and drinking a couple of beers, we decide to continue our sightseeing. Taking money from the breast pocket of his khaki shirt, Don graciously pays the bar girls for our drinks.

Departing the bar, we walk down the sidewalk, returning to Tu Do Street. Before reaching the intersection, a group of Vietnamese kids swarms us, begging for handouts. They tap Don on his backside. Instinctively, he grabs for his empty wallet. At the same time, one of the kids slits his breast pocket with a razor blade and steals all his money. Before we realize what has happened, the kids run off, disappearing into the crowd of people. As I recall, Don lost about $75. Evidently, the bar girls were in cahoots with the kids and told them of Don's hidden stash.

"LOST" MY WATCH

We continue walking down Tu Do Street, discussing Don's misfortune with the juvenile pickpockets. Several blocks later, we come upon an ice cream parlor decorated with alternating black and white floor tiles and the typical small tables with bent wire chairs.

While standing on the sidewalk outside the ice cream parlor, a group of three Vietnamese men approaches us, asking to purchase our wristwatches. I am wearing my big Seiko Chronograph, purchased shortly after arriving in Vietnam. Every pilot worth his salt wears a fancy chronograph watch. I never figured out how to use all its features, but it sure looks cool. They offer me $100 for the watch that cost me $60 at the PX (Post Exchange). I say, "No way." I have no intention of selling my fancy wristwatch.

Bill Fesler has a similar watch and is intrigued by the offer. He turns to our group and says, "Hey, I can sell this watch for a profit and buy another one at the PX." Then he follows the men into the ice cream parlor. Several minutes later he returns to the sidewalk waving a roll of bills. Bill approaches me and says, "Gooch, go sell your watch; you can always buy another one." It sounds too good to be true, but I tell myself, *What the heck; I can always buy another watch.*

I follow the men inside the ice cream parlor and am seated across from the primary barterer at a linoleum-topped table with four chairs. The man counts out $100 in U.S. currency in ones, fives, and tens. Then he rolls the bills tightly and puts a rubber band around the roll. As we start to make the exchange, another Vietnamese man standing behind me starts yelling, "Warranty, you give warranty." I turn to him and say, "I don't have a warranty." While my attention is diverted, the first man swaps the roll of bills with another roll. I turn back to complete the trade, being careful not to let go of my watch before I have the roll of money in my hand.

After the exchange, I get up from the table and walk out the door. About the time I reach the sidewalk I have a terrible, sinking feeling about the deal. "Bill," I say, "did you count your money?" Bill raises his hand, showing me his roll of bills still tightly wrapped with a rubber band, and says, "Yeah, I counted it in there." I quickly pull the rubber band off my roll of currency and count my money. The outer bill is a U.S. five-dollar bill and inside is a wad of Vietnamese Piaster. I sold my fancy watch for less than $10. Bill opens his money roll and finds the same. We turn to look for the Vietnamese men, and they are nowhere to be seen.

At this point, we stop to survey our situation. We have been in Saigon less than four hours and have lost $75 and two expensive watches. Then one of our group says, "I've had enough of Saigon; let's get the hell out of here." We all agree. Waving down four motorcycle taxis, we return to our hotel near the Tan San Nhut Air Base. The next morning, we board a C-130 Air Force cargo plane bound for Pleiku.

Yes, I still miss my fancy watch.

Author in Nomex flight uniform and "lost" watch

Vietnam Veteran Profile: Bill Fesler

After Vietnam, Bill Fesler served in Germany, Fort Rucker, and Fort Hood in assignments that included director of logistics for an Area Support Group, instructor pilot, and branch commander for the Crusader "Combat Skills Branch." Having served two tours in Vietnam (his first tour was enlisted) he was the recipient of the Bronze Star and eleven Air Medals. Fesler retired from the Army in 1991 as a lieutenant colonel after serving twenty-nine years.

After the military, Bill worked as a Department of Army civilian for twenty-one years, serving as a test officer for Command, Control, and Communications and for the Aviation Test Directorate at West Fort Hood, Texas, and finally as the G4. His second retirement was in 2013.

When asked what he is most proud of, Bill said, "Coming home from Vietnam was a biggie; however, serving on a Joint Staff for three years, managing Logistics for multi-service Naval Operations in the Caribbean (Operation Ocean Venture) was quite an accomplishment: housing, food, ammunition, travel."

Bill and his wife have four children, thirteen grandchildren, and two great-grandchildren.

**Bill Fesler and Green Delta Commanding Officer's
Guardian 6 Huey**
Photo courtesy of Bill Fesler

P A R T   4

CAMP HOLLOWAY—PLEIKU

17TH AVIATION GROUP

CHAPTER 28

AIRFIELD SECURITY

SEATED IN THE JUMP SEATS that line each side of the C-130 cargo plane, we four lieutenants have no notion of where we are headed. Occasionally, we look out the aircraft windows and view a landscape much different from the flat rice paddies of the Mekong Delta. Instead, we see densely treed, mountainous terrain intermixed with bright green valleys—a beautiful, yet dissimilar terrain.

About an hour and a half later, the large cargo plane begins its descent into Pleiku. We take turns looking out the small side window to get a glimpse of our new home. After landing and taxiing to the apron where other aircraft are parked, the cargo ramp lowers and we walk out, carrying our duffle bags and flight helmets.

Bill Fesler and I have orders for the 17ᵗʰ Aviation Group (Combat) based at Camp Holloway in Pleiku. Halstrom and Miles have orders for other aviation units. After stopping to ask for directions, Bill and I grab our belongings and walk to the 17ᵗʰ Aviation Headquarters office.

Entering the CO's office, I salute and say, "Lieutenant Gooch reporting, sir." I hand my orders to Lieutenant Colonel Frederick MacManus, who already has my personnel file. After perusing my records, MacManus looks up at me and says, "Lieutenant, you have more flight hours than most pilots assigned here. Your new job will be a non-flying duty assignment so other pilots can accumulate flight time."

Surely, he sees the disappointment on my face as he explains that I am being assigned to Headquarters Company, 17th Aviation Group and will assume the duties of security officer for Camp Holloway, responsible for both the airfield and the surrounding facilities. Bill Fesler is told the same thing, so we alternate duty, one night on and one night off.

It is disheartening not to have a flying assignment, but once I become accustomed to the security officer role, I realize it is a decent job and a good way to complete the last two months of my Vietnam tour of duty. And, this duty assignment comes with its advantages. Working nights, Bill and I have command and control of the entire Camp Holloway facility, and, best of all, no higher-ranking officers are awake to unnecessarily interfere with our duties.

AIRFIELD SECURITY

Located in the central highlands 378 klicks (235 miles) north of Saigon, Camp Holloway is one of the larger Army bases in II Corp.

The airfield security system consists of defensive bunkers spaced about forty-five meters (147 feet) apart that wrap around the perimeter of the large airfield and Army facility. Some bunkers are elevated in towers twelve to fifteen feet above the ground, while others are fortified structures at ground level. Beyond the bunkers are concentric rows of concertina razor wire and beyond that are buried electronic sensors. A two-mile-long dirt road lies just inside the perimeter of bunkers, circling the Camp Holloway facility.

Every evening, just before sundown, a deuce-and-a-half truck carries Chinese mercenaries and their weapons to the security perimeter, dropping the paid soldiers at every other bunker. US soldiers are assigned to man bunkers between the mercenaries. Residing on Camp Holloway with their families, the Chinese are good soldiers, and I find them very dependable.

Landlines connect every bunker to the tactical operations center (TOC). Housed in a fortified facility, the TOC serves as the command and control center for the Camp Holloway security system. It is staffed by an NCO security specialist, a Vietnamese radio operator, and a Chinese interpreter who translates the communications with the mercenaries in the bunkers.

MORTARS

Located near the northern end of the airfield runway is an Infantry mortar section whose duty is to monitor the electronic sensors outside the perimeter and defend the airfield with mortar fire should the sensors be activated. The mortar section is a crucial component of the overall airfield security, yet the U.S. soldiers assigned to this facility have been neglected. Their living quarters are shoddy, and they have little or no training on the operation of the mortar.

Bill Fesler and I realize we have a problem that must be promptly addressed. We develop a plan to improve not only the Mortar crew's training but also their living conditions. We start by having their living area cleaned up and arrange to have a shower built. In the late evenings, after the officers' club is closed, we take the movie and projector from the O-club and show the film in the mortar section area. Once the mortar crew realize we care about their welfare, their morale improves, and they make a concerted effort to function as an effective team.

Being an Armor officer, I am not familiar with the mortar. Bill, on the other hand, is an Infantry officer and well versed in mortar operation. During the day, Bill and I train the mortar crew on the care, cleaning, and firing of the 81mm mortar. Rotating each soldier through the functions of ammo bearer, gunner (aiming), and assistant gunner (firing), they learn every aspect of mortar operation.

To facilitate rapid reaction firing, we develop a firing grid of predetermined coordinates (azimuth and elevation) for every sensor buried outside the perimeter. This firing grid is posted on the wall inside the mortar bunker near the sensor light panel. When a particular sensor is activated, a colored and numbered light illuminates on the sensor panel (example: red 9). Referring to the firing grid, the operator instantly knows the firing coordinates of that sensor's location.

Springing into action, the mortar crew scrambles to the 81mm mortar located next to the bunker, enclosed by a three-foot wall of sandbags. The ammo bearer gathers the mortar round while the gunner quickly dials in the predetermined azimuth and elevation. Then, on command, the assistant gunner drops the mortar round in the tube, firing into the illuminated sensor's area. After several days of practice, the mortar crew becomes so proficient that they can fire a mortar round on target within twenty seconds of receiving fire instructions.

SECURITY PATROL

When it is my duty night, I first check in with the TOC to see if there are any imminent threats or other issues I need to be concerned with. Then, after climbing into the airfield security Jeep equipped with a VRC-12 radio and long whip antennae, I drive around the entire airfield perimeter, stopping at the mortar section and several bunkers along the way. Bill and I make this security patrol at random intervals throughout the night.

Most nights are uneventful and quiet along the perimeter. Occasionally, I receive a call from an American soldier in a bunker who thinks he sees something outside the perimeter. Responding immediately, I drive to the bunker and let the soldier use my starlight night vision scope to scan the area. Once the soldier sees the bright green illuminated landscape and realizes there are no enemy threats, he is relieved and satisfied that no one is encroaching upon the perimeter. This happens fairly often once the word gets out that I have a night vision scope. I don't mind because it gives me an opportunity to interact with the soldiers and breaks the boredom of a long night.

TANKS!

One evening around midnight, I am standing outside a bunker near the far end of the runway when I feel the ground vibrate and hear a familiar and unmistakable sound—Tanks! Calling the TOC on the Jeep radio, I ask if there is any reported armor activity in the area and am told no.

Jumping into my Jeep, I race back to the TOC, where I instruct the Vietnamese radio operator to call the local ARVN installations to see if there are any reports of friendly armor units operating in the area. Meanwhile, the ground continues to rumble, and the clatter of tank tracks becomes louder. The landlines are ringing with soldiers in the bunkers reporting tanks headed in our direction. After placing radio calls to several ARVN units, the Vietnamese radio operator has found no armor units in the local area. My mind is racing; do I sound the alert? I highly doubt it is enemy tanks, especially since the sound is coming from the east, where Highway 19 approaches and runs past Camp Holloway's southern perimeter.

Then, when the noise is so loud that it seems the tanks are inside our compound, the Vietnamese radio operator turns to me with a big smile and says, "Friendly tanks." In less than a minute, an ARVN armored cavalry troop of M-48 tanks and M-113 armored personnel carriers goes rolling past Camp Holloway, shaking the ground and emitting a loud *clack-clack-clack* sound of tank treads. With a sigh I think, *What a relief—it's friendlies!*

Later, I learn this troop is part of the ARVN 3rd Armored Cavalry Squadron, headquartered in Pleiku. The ARVN units are required to obtain clearance before passing Camp Holloway but, like other interactions with the South Vietnamese, it didn't happen, and no one seems to be concerned—except me and the soldiers manning the bunkers.

CHAPTER 29

FLYING IN THE CENTRAL HIGHLANDS

SINCE I WORK ALTERNATING NIGHTS on airfield security, I arrange to fly with local aviation units on my off-duty days. Most flights are "ash and trash" or other noncombat missions from Pleiku to Army bases at Kontum, Dac To, An Khe, Qui Nhon, Ninh Hoa, and Nha Trang, to name a few.

One day in late September, I am flying copilot for the 57th Assault Helicopter Company (The Gladiators) on a group courier mission to Nha Trang. The aircraft commander for this flight is 1st Lieutenant Paul Carmichael. Paul is an accomplished pilot in the final months of his tour. A typical day for Paul and other Gladiator pilots is to fly a combat assault in the highly contested areas north of Kontum or to support the 1st Air Cavalry Division flying out of An Khe. It was during these missions that Paul took "hits" on his aircraft on three separate occasions; the most serious was a .51-caliber round in the tail rotor.

Today's mission is a welcome break for Paul. The weekly group courier mission to Nha Trang is a "piece of cake" compared to the danger and stress associated with combat assaults. Typically, this flight delivers mail or other supplies and transports new pilots and crew members from Nha Trang to

Pleiku. For me, I am looking forward to this flight because it will be my first opportunity to fly over a large portion of the Central Highlands.

THE MANG YANG PASS

It is on the first leg of this flight that I witness a highly unusual sight. Flying our Huey at 3,800 feet altitude (nosebleed altitude for a pilot accustomed to flying in the Mekong Delta), we are following Highway 19 from Pleiku to the east. Midway on our flight, Paul mentions that we are approaching the Mang Yang Pass. Being new to the Central Highlands, his comment means little to me.

Flying between two rows of mountains running southeast, with Highway 19 switch-backing through the valley below, Paul turns slightly left toward a long, sloping ridge that stretches southward from the highest peak. The gently curved top of the ridge is covered with emerald-green grass. This treeless ridgeline is beautiful, yet mysterious, and I soon learn it has a sad and gruesome history.

When we get closer to the rounded knoll, I see long, evenly spaced rows of what appear to be depressions in the grass. The perfectly spaced rows crisscross the green hillside going up and over the top and stretch far left and right, encompassing a massive area. Paul tells me the depressions are the graves of 1,600 French soldiers killed in the final battle of the French Indochina War in 1954. He continues, saying the Mang Yang Pass remains an enemy-occupied area to this day, and we should not fly any lower, or risk being exposed to enemy anti-aircraft gunfire.

Mang Yang Pass

THE LAST BATTLE OF THE INDOCHINA WAR

Later, I learn the story of Mang Yang Pass. The French had been fighting the Viet Minh since 1945, but in 1954, the tide of war turned. By June, almost all of the Central Highlands belonged to the Communists. To save the French Groupement Mobile 100 (G.M. 100), the High Command ordered this large military unit to evacuate An Khe and relocate to Pleiku by vehicle convoy on Highway 19.

All along the route, the long line of G.M. 100 vehicles were slowed by enemy assaults. Then a fierce battle erupted as they neared the Mang Yang Pass, located midway between the two cities. At noon, swarms of Viet Minh encircled the lead elements of the convoy. Attacked from all sides, it suffered hundreds of killed and wounded. Futilely, the convoy continued to struggle forward.

Miles back, the rear of the convoy was also attacked. In hours of hand-to-hand combat, G.M. 100 suffered hundreds more casualties. Burning trucks and vehicles were strewn for miles along the road. Dead soldiers littered the ditches, and wounded men suffered alone, afraid to scream for fear of capture or worse.

By nightfall, only a few companies remained. At dawn, these soldiers loaded their weapons one last time. Then, led by their commanders, they fixed bayonets, and in the ghostly light of parachute flares, they advanced to their death.

Afterward, the French were permitted to bury their dead on the high ridge above Highway 19 but were forbidden to place any gravestones or markers on the burial sites. The soldiers were buried in deep graves, standing upright and facing Paris. The graves were filled with lime, over which the grass has never grown. This was the last battle. Six weeks later, the French Indochina War was over.[21]

ON TO NHA TRANG

As we continue flying over the massive cemetery, I look down at row after row of graves running in every direction. A cold chill runs up my spine as I think of the magnitude of the deaths in this final and, arguably, useless battle. And, it is another reminder of the death and destruction in this beautiful, yet troubled country—war has raged here since 1945.

---

[21] James Martin Davis, "Midlands Voices: Graveyard in the clouds," *Omaha World-Herald*, May 26, 2018

After landing at An Khe to load a package and refuel, Paul and I continue our flight to Ninh Hoa and Nha Trang. After landing, refueling again, and shutting down our aircraft, we deliver our cargo and take a break to eat lunch at the mess hall. Later, we load the mail, pick up two passengers, and reverse our route, returning to Pleiku.

On this day we logged six hours and twenty minutes of flight time. For Paul, this was an uneventful and somewhat relaxing mission. But, for me, it was my introduction to the beautiful mountains and lush green valleys of the Central Highlands. And, a haunting glimpse into the savage brutality of Vietnam's war-plagued history.

Paul befriended many of the Vietnamese children. He enjoyed joking with the kids and making them smile whenever possible. In this photo, a Vietnamese boy is posing as the Huey's crew chief while wearing flight gloves, a survival vest, and a flight helmet.

Paul Carmichael and Vietnamese boy
Photo courtesy of Paul Carmichael

Vietnam Veteran Profile: Paul Carmichael

Following his tour of duty in Vietnam, Paul served as a company commander in Germany. Later, while serving as an aviation company commander at Fort Bragg, North Carolina, his unit deployed with the 1983 Invasion of Grenada. After a special operations assignment at Key West, Florida, and serving as a battalion commander at Fort Bragg again, he served in Operation Desert Shield in Saudi Arabia. His last assignment was with Air Force Special Operations at Hurlburt Field, Florida.

After serving twenty-four years in the Army, Paul retired in 1994 with the rank of lieutenant colonel. During his military career, he flew over three thousand hours and was dual rated in both rotary and fixed-wing aircraft. Paul was the recipient of the Bronze Star Medal, twenty Air Medals, and the Legion of Merit.

Following his retirement from the Army, Paul started his second career as a financial planner and continued in this role for thirteen years.

In 2007, Paul followed his passion for nature photography, and his art is displayed in two galleries in Key West, Florida.

When asked about his military service, Paul said, "I am most proud to have served with my fellow pilots and crew members in Vietnam and that I lived to tell about my experiences. Additionally, I am proud to have earned master aviator wings, a distinction my son recently attained as well."

Paul and his wife have a blended family of five children and seven grandchildren.

CHAPTER 30

SHORT-TIMER

THE SECURITY OFFICER JOB KEEPS me busy, and my time in Pleiku seems to pass by at a regular tempo. After a month on the job, I join the coveted ranks of the short-timer, those having less than thirty days remaining in-country. Like most soldiers, I keep a short-timer calendar, marking off the remaining days and eagerly anticipating the date I will depart Vietnam.

In October, the enemy activity near Pleiku intensifies. At night, the NVA fire rockets at Camp Holloway. Initially, the rockets strike far from the airfield boundaries, but with each subsequent night, the NVA's accuracy improves. The explosions come closer and closer until they are hitting inside our security perimeter.

As a short-timer, I have a heightened level of anxiety because of the uptick in enemy activity. Having heard stories about the guy who got shot or severely injured in his last days in-country gives me cause to be cautious, not wanting to be the next fateful story. As the days go by, the nightly NVA bombardment gets closer, and eventually a couple of rockets impact within two hundred feet of our hooch. The attacks are extremely unsettling, and my DEROS date (Date of Estimated Return from Overseas) cannot come soon enough.

SEVEN DAYS EARLY

I am now down to the last week in-country, with seven days remaining on my short-timer calendar. It is early morning, and I am exiting the mess hall when someone tells me to report to the commanding officer. This is strange since I have never been summoned to see the CO.

Entering the commanding officer's office, I walk to the front of his desk, come to attention, give a hand salute, and say, "Sir, you wanted to see me." Lieutenant Colonel MacManus says, "Yes, Lieutenant, I am flying to Saigon this afternoon. You are welcome to accompany me, and I will sign your orders to leave early if you like." Gleefully, I answer, "Yes, sir, that would be fantastic!" The colonel says, "Get your things together and be here at 1300 hours."

Having less than four hours to prepare before the scheduled departure time, I rush to my hooch and start packing. Once I have my gear together, I go around the facility, saying my goodbyes to everyone I know.

While visiting the TOC, the guys from the mortar section find me and present me with a yellow baseball cap that is embroidered with "You Ask! We Blast!" on the front and "Gooch—The Best LT" on the back. They also give me a bottle of Seagram's Crown Royal in a fancy purple velvet bag (I still have the Crown Royal bag and the bright yellow baseball cap). I am overwhelmed that the mortar guys thought enough of me to acquire these going-away gifts ahead of my departure, and then scramble to find me when they heard I was leaving early. I thank them and as I walk away, I'm flooded with emotions. I'm overjoyed to be leaving, but humbled by the gratitude of these young men, and all too aware that I'll probably never see them again. My last thought is that I hope they all make it home safely.

That afternoon I join the CO and board a U-21 Beechcraft King Air bound for Saigon. As we roll down the runway, gaining airspeed for takeoff, two rockets explode near the runway. I breathe a sigh of relief, thankful to get out of this area and delighted to depart seven days early.

NAM DEPARTURE

Upon arriving in Saigon, my out-processing goes smoothly, and I am scheduled to fly stateside the following day. A couple of officers who are scheduled on the same flight invite me to join them for a last-time dining experience in Saigon. Recalling my previous visit to Saigon, I decline, deciding it is wise to stay on the Tan Son Nhut Air Base.

The following day, wearing my khaki uniform and carrying my duffle bag, much like the day I arrived, I walk out of the airfield terminal onto the concrete apron and see a most beautiful sight: the "Freedom Bird," an American Airlines jetliner with boarding stairs leading to an open door on the large plane.

As I walk toward the stairway, I reflect on that moment a year ago when I arrived in Vietnam. Much like then, the day is hot, and the air is filled with a mixture of distinct smells, but it is much different now. I am accustomed to the heat, and the odors are unremarkable, my senses dulled by the ever-present smell of the Vietnamese lifestyle and jet fuel.

Placing my duffle bag on the luggage cart, I walk up the stairway and experience a sense of reality—it is happening, the moment I have looked forward to for the past year. I am leaving Vietnam! Entering the aircraft, the cool air conditioning hits me in the face, and I feel another step closer to civilization. Walking down the aisle, I take a window seat and get settled in for the long ride home.

As I wait for the plane to load, I reminisce about the past year. I have had incredible experiences; mostly good, and the bad I hope to soon forget. But above all are the memories of the men I served with, flew with, and discovered to be extraordinary, talented, and dedicated people. These aviators would risk their own lives to come to your rescue should you be in jeopardy. Many have become good friends and, although I don't realize it at the time, those friendships, formed and bonded during war, will remain strong and last a lifetime.

Soon, everyone is onboard and settled in their seats. The doors close, and the plane taxies to the end of the runway, where it makes a slow turn to line up for takeoff. I will always remember the mixed sense of excitement and relief as the pilot advances the throttles and the jetliner travels faster and faster down the runway. When the wheels lift off the ground, everyone on the plane gives a loud cheer of elation.

Climbing upward, I look out my window to see Vietnam pass beneath the airplane. As we penetrate the white, puffy clouds, music starts playing in the cabin. I will never forget the song, and how it touches my emotions and lifts my spirits. It is the Mamas and Papas singing "California Dreaming."

The End

Or wait, this is just the beginning of life after Vietnam.

Read On

CHAPTER 31

LIFE AFTER NAM

UPON OUR LANDING AT TRAVIS Air Force Base after the long flight from Vietnam, we were given the directive to change into civilian clothes before going off base or continuing our travel to our homes. I complied but was disturbed by what it implied. I was proud to have served in Vietnam and was proud to wear my uniform. While in Vietnam, we had heard about American servicemen walking through airports and being confronted by war protesters who yelled at, spit on, and were verbally offensive to them. Yet, it seemed a distant and unreal event in the country I loved so much. I felt that, inevitably, someone back home must appreciate my having served in Vietnam. I was soon to find out how wrong I was.

In my year's absence, many in America were upset about the Vietnam War and openly expressed their discontent. There were demonstrations on college campuses, marches on Washington, D.C., protests at the 1972 Republican National Convention, and the ultimate insult to those serving in the military: Jane Fonda's visit to North Vietnam, sitting on a North Vietnamese anti-aircraft gun, and speaking on Hanoi Radio, imploring U.S. pilots to stop the bombings.

Upon my return to the States, I attempted to assimilate into the early 1970s society that seemed to have grown increasingly bitter in the year of our absence. In a very short time, I learned not to mention my Vietnam service and, in most cases, not to disclose that I served in the Army.

In one instance, while searching for off-base housing near an Army post where I was stationed, the reverend of a small church who owned the rental property asked me about my service. I proudly replied that I was an Army helicopter pilot returning from Vietnam. He asked, "Did you fly that Cobra?" I proudly replied, "Yes, I did." Then he asked, "Did you kill any babies?" I was dumbfounded and offended. I was so shocked by his question that I had no reply, realizing it would do no good to get upset and attempt to reason with this opinionated, ill-informed individual. I promptly left.

After departing the Army in 1974, I was hired by a Fortune 500 Corporation primarily because of my military leadership experience. Within the first two weeks on the job, I learned not to mention I was in the Army and, under no circumstances, divulge I served in Vietnam. If I did mention my service, I suffered looks of disgust or words of condemnation from the other employees. Strangely, the corporation's hiring motives were misaligned with the management and workforce of the same company.

As a result of the way we Vietnam Veterans were treated, we set aside our pride, never spoke about the war, and tried our best to push the memories of the war into the depths of our subconsciousness. For some veterans, this worked, at least temporarily, but for others, they suffered PTSD as a consequence, and the VA was ill-prepared to either identify or treat this serious condition.

The other outcome of the tragic treatment of our Vietnam Veterans is that many stories, much like the stories told in this book, have never been shared. Stories of extraordinary heroism and courage are lost forever. For that, I am truly sad because it is through the telling of these stories that the veteran experiences a cathartic effect and the person hearing the stories develops an understanding of what we experienced and why we are proud of our Vietnam service.

THE TIDE TURNS FOR VIETNAM VETERANS

This attitude of maligning the Vietnam Veterans continued for twenty-plus years until the first Gulf War in 1992. The turnabout of American ideals was quick and dramatic. American flags were proudly flown from the back of pickup trucks. Bumper stickers with yellow ribbons proclaimed "Support Our Troops." Patriotism returned, and the public was, once again, proud of those who served in the military.

It was then, twenty years after returning from Vietnam, that I received my first "Thank you" when an eighteen-year-old store clerk making a delivery to my car saw the Vietnam Helicopter Pilots Association decal on the rear window. He asked, "Did you serve in Vietnam?" I paused for a moment, suspect of the response I might receive from my reply. Then, I answered, "Yes, I flew helicopters." Without a moment's hesitation, the young man said, "Thank you for your service," and shook my hand. Wow! I was so awestruck by this young man's words of gratitude that it brought tears to my eyes.

Today, I receive many thank yous when I wear my ballcap with the image of a Huey helicopter on the front and the Vietnam service ribbon on the side. I sincerely appreciate each and every thank you, especially those from the kids and young adults whose parents, grandparents, or other elders have taught them to respect those who serve in our military, protecting our valuable freedoms.

WELCOME HOME

When other Vietnam Veterans notice my Huey hat, they approach me with an outstretched hand and say "Welcome home" or "Hey, where did you serve?" Seeing the easily recognizable Huey image ignites a spark inside them, and they eagerly tell me their "Huey stories."

Many of the veterans I meet were Infantry soldiers who tell me the familiar *wop-wop-wop* sound of a Huey's rotor blades was music to their ears, signifying their ride out of harm's way. For others, they tell me the Huey saved their life when they were wounded in battle, with the Huey swooping in to carry them to medical care. Interestingly, no one says they had a dislike of the Huey because it carried them into battle; instead, there is common affection for this incredible helicopter and the aviators who flew it.

THE AVIATORS

The aviators whose stories are told in this book served proudly in Vietnam. Upon returning to the States, they experienced the indignation and insults of an ungrateful American public for many years, yet they stood tall, persevered, and didn't let that deter their life's goals or their ambitions. Many aviators continued flying or otherwise served in the military. Others took a career path outside the military. Each and every one of them is successful in their careers and their families. And, each and every one of them will tell you they are proud to have served in Vietnam and would gladly serve beside their fellow aviators again were they younger and had the opportunity. I am honored to have served with these outstanding men and privileged to be able to share their stories. And, I am extremely blessed to have them as my lifelong friends.

**Anderson, Tolar, Kelly, and Author
at 2017 Lighthorse Reunion**

Vietnam Veteran Profile: Rex Gooch

Upon returning from Vietnam in November 1972, Rex Gooch was stationed at Fort Leonard Wood, Missouri. In 1973, Gooch suffered life-threatening injuries in an OH-58 helicopter crash while on a training mission in Oklahoma. He stated, "I believe it was the grace of God that saved my life that day. He has a plan for everyone and wasn't finished with me. Later on, I committed to placing God first in my life and strive daily to live a life that pleases Him." Rex departed the Army in 1974 after serving four years active duty. During his military service, Gooch was the recipient of nine Air Medals and the Bronze Star Medal.

After the Army, Rex worked for four major corporations in areas of increasing responsibility in Industrial Engineering and Human Resources. In 1994, Gooch was awarded the "Employee Benefits Professional of the Year" by *Employee Benefit News* in recognition of a 401(k) plan promotion for a national company with 21,000 employees that increased employee participation over one hundred percent in six months.

Rex worked twenty-seven years in the private sector and retired in 2001 as vice president of Compensation and Benefits. Now, he and his wife live and travel full-time in a motor home, enjoying America.

In 2009, Rex had the unique opportunity to fly a Huey again, and, remarkably, the same Huey he flew in Vietnam, thirty-eight years earlier. Huey 217, mentioned in chapters six, seven, eight, and eleven was returned stateside and rebuilt into a Bell 210 with 400 more horsepower, larger rotor blades, and a larger tail rotor.

This impressive aircraft is owned and operated by WorldWind Helicopters in Arlington, Washington. Thanks to Rick Dominy, WorldWind general manager and Vietnam combat helicopter pilot, Rex was invited to fly the newly designated N610WW once again. With Rick in the left seat and Rex in the right seat, Gooch flew Huey 217 for one hour and thirty minutes to include a confined area landing in the Cascade Mountains east of Seattle. His reaction? "Wow, what an awesome aircraft and what a thrill to fly Huey 217 again!"

Huey 217, now a Bell 210 - N610WW
Photo courtesy of Heath Moffatt

In 2015, Rex wrote and published his first book, titled *ACE: The Story of Lt. Col. Ace Cozzalio*. The book was awarded a Bronze Medal in the 2016 Independent Publisher Book Awards (IPPY). The annual IPPY Awards, with over 5,000 entrants, is the "World's Largest Book Awards Contest," honoring independent authors and publishers worldwide.

Rex and his wife have two children and two grandchildren.

When asked about his most memorable experience, Rex said, "Flying with the incredible aviators in Vietnam, especially the pilots and crewmembers of Lighthorse Air Cavalry."

The End

Author after flying Huey 217 in 2011

ACKNOWLEDGMENTS

I WOULD LIKE TO THANK all the people who graciously helped with this project by providing their stories and information. Without their assistance, this book could never have been written.

Lighthorse Troopers

George Anderson
Wes Bartley
Don Callison
Larry Coates
John Doherty
John Elliott
Keith Harris
Jack Hosmer
Johnny Hutcherson
Gary Larrow
Dudley Oatman
Chris Rash
George Schmitz
Tom Tolar
Gary Winsett

David Antrim
Carl "Skip" Bell
Loran "Bear" Bryant
Ralph Chapman
Tim Dahlen
Tom Egleston
Walt Gale
Ken Hibl
Wade Huddleston
Dale Johnson
Ray Murphy
Andy McJohnston
Mike Rokey
Led Symmes
Bill Wiscombe

Green Delta Pilots

Jim Addington
John Harris
Donny O'Connor
Art Tiller
Dan Toothman

Bill Fesler
Tim Halstrom
Don Miles
John Sydow

Friends of the Project

David Axley
Paul Carmichael, 57ᵗʰ AHC
Pat Kelly
Phil Marshall, 237th Med Det
Sean O'Connor
Tony Snow, C/16ᵗʰ Cavalry
Ray Wilhite
Rick Dominy, WorldWind
  Helicopters

Don Axley
Kit Lavell, Navy Black Ponies
Tom Norton, 44th Med Bde
Bob Peetz, Navy Black Ponies
Matt Weston
Lenny Young
Tim Grey

MILITARY MEDALS

Air Medal—Meritorious achievement while serving with the Armed Forces in aerial flight. During the Vietnam War, one Air Medal was awarded for every twenty-five hours of combat assault flights, fifty hours of combat support flights, or one hundred hours of noncombat service flights (administrative or VIP flights).

Meritorious Service Medal—The Meritorious Service Medal may be awarded to members of the Armed Forces who distinguish themselves by outstanding noncombat achievement or by meritorious service to the United States, but not of a degree that would warrant the award of the Legion of Merit.

Purple Heart—The Purple Heart Medal is awarded to members of the armed forces of the U.S. who are wounded by an instrument of war in the hands of the enemy and posthumously to the next of kin in the name of those who are killed in action or die of wounds received in action.

Bronze Star—Awarded for heroic achievement, heroic service, meritorious achievement, or meritorious service in a combat zone.

Soldier's Medal—The Army Soldier's Medal is awarded to any member of the Armed Forces who while serving with the Army distinguishes themselves by heroism not involving actual conflict with an enemy.

Distinguished Flying Cross—Heroism or extraordinary achievement while participating in an aerial flight.

Legion of Merit—The Legion of Merit is awarded to any member of the Armed Forces of the United States who has distinguished himself or herself by exceptionally meritorious conduct in the performance of outstanding services and achievements.

Silver Star—The third-highest personal decoration for valor in combat. The Silver Star Medal is awarded primarily to members of the United States Armed Forces for gallantry in action against an enemy of the United States. The required gallantry, while of a lesser degree than that required for award of the Distinguished Service Cross, must nevertheless have been performed with marked distinction.

Medal Devices:

V device—Distinguishes an award for heroism or valor in combat

Oak Leaf Cluster—Miniature bronze or silver twig of four oak leaves with three acorns on the stem that denote subsequent decorations and awards. Bronze oak leaf clusters denote an additional award, and silver oak leaf clusters denote five additional awards.

GLOSSARY

AC—Aircraft commander, the pilot designated by aviation unit authority as being in command of an aircraft and responsible for its safe operation and accomplishment of the assigned mission.

AGL—Above ground level

AK-47—Soviet 7.62-caliber assault rifle with thirty-round curved magazine

AMC—Air mission commander

AO—Area of operations; i.e., mission area

ARVN—Army of the Republic of Vietnam; i.e., South Vietnamese Army

Ash & trash—Noncombat mission carrying ammo, supplies, or personnel

Autorotation—Descending maneuver where the helicopter engine is disengaged from the main rotor system and the rotor blades are driven solely by the upward flow of air through the rotors. Nearing the ground, the pilot lifts the collective, increasing the pitch (angle) in the rotor blades, slowing the descent and enabling the pilot to make a controlled landing.

BA-MOI-BA—Vietnamese beer. Vietnamese for "33" on label. Ba Moi being 30 and Ba being three. Moi counts 10s.

Backseat—U.S. advisor and ARVN counterpart riding in the passenger compartment of the Command & Control Huey helicopter

Blood chit—A notice carried by military personnel and addressed to any civilians who may come across an armed-services member—such as a shot-down pilot.

Boonie hat—Wide-brimmed camouflage hat worn with jungle fatigues in Vietnam

Bubble—Curved Plexiglas windshield

Bunker—Fortified fighting position, typically dug into the ground with gun ports for shooting

C-rations—An individual canned, pre-cooked, and prepared wet ration. It was intended to be issued to U.S. military land forces when fresh food or food prepared in mess halls or field kitchens was not possible or not available.

C&C—Command & Control helicopter; typically a Huey carrying the air mission commander who controls the air mission

Cav—Cavalry

Cav Pack—For Lighthorse VR and search and destroy missions; two OH-6 scouts and two AH-1G Cobra gunships accompanied by a C&C Huey

CO—Commanding officer

Cobra—Bell AH-1G helicopter gunship. This dedicated helicopter gunship replaced the Charlie Model Huey gunship.

Collective—Control stick on the left side of the pilot. Lifting the collective increases pitch (angle) in the rotor blades for lift. On the end of the collective is a motorcycle-like grip that controls power to the engine. The collective controls the vertical movement of the helicopter.

Chalk—Flight position during a mission. Chalk 1 is the lead, Chalk 2 is the middle position, Chalk 3 is trail.

Charlie—Nickname for Viet Cong, derived from phonetic alphabet: Victor Charlie

Chicken plate—Heavy chest protector body armor made of aluminum oxide ceramic covered with cloth

Chin bubble—Plexiglas window near the pilot's feet allowing visibility of the ground in front of the helicopter

Chinook—Twin-engine, tandem rotor heavy-lift helicopter. The Chinook's primary roles are troop movement, artillery placement, and battlefield resupply.

Commo—Communications

CONEX—A large standardized shipping container, designed and built for intermodal freight transport, meaning these containers can be used across different modes of transport—from ship to rail to truck—without unloading and reloading their cargo

Cyclic—Stick between pilot's legs that controls left-right and forward-backward movement of the helicopter. Essentially, the cyclic tilts the rotor disk in the direction of desired movement.

Cyclo—Three-wheeled bicycle taxi. It is similar to a rickshaw with bicycle propulsion instead of human.

DEROS—Date of expected return from overseas. A soldier's expected day of departure from Vietnam.

DMZ—Demilitarized zone established as a dividing line between North and South Vietnam as a result of the First Indochina War. During the Vietnam War, it became important as the battleground demarcation separating North from South Vietnamese territories.

FAC—Forward air controller. Air Force propeller-driven aircraft used for tactical air support and fire direction.

Flechette—One-inch-long, fin-stabilized nails that look like small metal darts. Flechettes are housed within 2.75-inch Hydra-70 rockets. Fired from Cobra gunships, each rocket disburses approximately 2,200 flechettes with a red puff of smoke to mark the release point.

Free-fire zone—Area where any person is deemed hostile and a legitimate target by U.S. forces

GIs—American soldiers. This term originated during World War II and was derived from "Government Issue."

Grunts—An affectionate name given to infantry soldiers

Guard—Emergency radio frequency monitored by aircraft in Vietnam; 243 MHz UHF or 121.5 MHz VHF

Guidon—Swallow-tailed troop flag and mast denoting troop, squadron, and regiment letters and numbers. Cavalry guidons are composed of a field of red in the upper half above white in the lower half.

Gunship—Helicopter with heavy armament, such as rockets, minigun, and/or grenade launcher

Hooch—Slang term for a place to live, either a soldier's living quarters or a Vietnamese hut. The typical Vietnamese hooch was a thatched-roof dwelling.

Huey—Bell UH-1H utility helicopter carrying six to eight soldiers and gear; manned by a crew of four—two pilots, a crew chief, and a door gunner

Intel—Intelligence reports

IV Corps—Southernmost military quadrant in Vietnam, the Mekong Delta

Jinking—To make a quick, evasive turn. When flying a helicopter, the pilot jinks left and right to avoid becoming a target.

KIA—Killed in action

Khmer Republic—The pro-United States, military-led, republican government of Cambodia that was formally declared on October 9, 1970

Khmer Rouge—The name popularly given to the followers of the Communist Party of Kampuchea (CPK). The Khmer Rouge army was slowly built up in the jungles of Eastern Cambodia during the late 1960s, supported by the North Vietnamese Army, the Viet Cong, and the Pathet Lao.

Klick—Military slang for kilometer (.62 miles)

Loach—Hughes OH-6A Light Observation helicopter, also called a scout

LOH—Light observation helicopter; *see* Loach

LZ—Landing zone

MACV—Military Assistance Command, Vietnam

MACV SOCC—MACV Special Operation Command Center

MACV SOG—Studies and Observations Group. SOG was a highly classified, multi-service United States special operations unit that conducted covert unconventional warfare operations prior to and during the Vietnam War.

McGuire Rig—Long nylon rope suspended from a helicopter to extract soldiers from the jungles of Vietnam

M-16—Colt 5.56-millimeter assault rifle carried by U.S. troops

Medevac—Medical evacuation by helicopter

Mic—Microphone

Mikes—Radio-speak for minutes

N_1 speed—Speed of the first compressor fan in the Lycoming turbine engine

Nails—*See* Flechettes

Nam—Slang for Vietnam

Nomex—Flame-resistant material used in flight uniforms and gloves

NVA—North Vietnamese Army

OCS—Officer Candidate School

O-club—Officers' club

PAX—Aviation terminology for passengers

Pedal turn—While at a hover, the pilot, using the anti-torque foot pedals, turns the helicopter's nose left or right, rotating the helicopter on its vertical axis

PIC—Pilot in Command, the pilot who is ultimately responsible for the aircraft's operation and safety during flight. In Army Aviation, pilots log the PIC designation if they are responsible for the aircraft and have yet to be qualified as aircraft commander.

PSP—Perforated steel planking used for runways and aircraft parking areas

PX—Post Exchange

PZ—Pickup zone

Revetment—A barricade protecting aircraft against mortar or rocket attack. Commonly, a four-foot-high wall protecting helicopters on the flight line.

RPG—Chinese Communist rocket-propelled grenade fired from a shoulder-held launcher

Ruf Puf—Regional Force/Popular Force (Regional South Vietnamese Militia)

Search and destroy mission—To seek out and destroy the enemy.

Sortie—A group of helicopters assembled for a single attack or insertion of troops

Slick—UH-1 Huey helicopter without rockets or heavy armament

Snake—Cobra gunship

Squadron—Unit containing four troops, such as an air cavalry squadron

TOC—Tactical Operations Center

Tour—Tour of duty; one year in duration, unless extended

Trail formation—Each helicopter following one behind the other

Translational lift—Mode of flight where the helicopter transitions from hovering "ground effect" to forward flight. Additional lift is created by horizontal flow of air across the rotor blades.

Troop—Cavalry unit with approximately two hundred troopers

VC—Viet Cong, also known as the National Liberation Front, was a mass political organization in South Vietnam and Cambodia with its own army.

VR—Visual reconnaissance

Vector—To direct an aircraft in flight to a desired point by providing left and right course corrections

Wingman—A pilot whose aircraft is positioned behind and outside the leading aircraft in a formation. Responsible for covering the lead aircraft

WO—Warrant officer; a military rank above the highest enlisted rank and below the lowest officer rank; addressed as "Mister"

WOC—Warrant Officer Candidate. Candidates are students in the Warrant Officer Rotary Wing Aviator Course (WORWAC), designed to train helicopter pilots with no previous military flying experience. Upon graduation candidates become warrant officers.

Wobbly one—Warrant officer 1, entry level of five possible warrant officer ranks

XO—Executive officer

Rex Gooch

INDEX

Made in the USA
Columbia, SC
15 November 2019